APOSTLES AND BISHOPS
IN EARLY CHRISTIANITY

The Collected Works of Hugh Nibley
Volumes published to date:

Old Testament and Related Studies

Enoch the Prophet

The World and the Prophets

Mormonism and Early Christianity

Lehi in the Desert/The World of the Jaredites/There Were Jaredites

An Approach to the Book of Mormon

Since Cumorah

The Prophetic Book of Mormon

Approaching Zion

The Ancient State

Tinkling Cymbals and Sounding Brass

Temple and Cosmos

Brother Brigham Challenges the Saints

Abraham in Egypt

The Collected Works of Hugh Nibley: Volume 15

APOSTLES AND BISHOPS IN EARLY CHRISTIANITY

Hugh Nibley

Edited by
John F. Hall
John W. Welch

Deseret Book Company
Salt Lake City, Utah
and
Foundation for Ancient Research and Mormon Studies
at Brigham Young University
Provo, Utah

© 2005 The Foundation for Ancient Research and Mormon Studies and
    Hugh Nibley and Associates, LC

All rights reserved. No part of this book may be reproduced in any form or by any means without permission in writing from the publisher, Deseret Book Company, P O. Box 30178, Salt Lake City, Utah 84130. This work is not an official publication of The Church of Jesus Christ of Latter-day Saints. The views expressed herein are the responsibility of the author and do not necessarily represent the position of the Church, of Deseret Book Company, of the Foundation for Ancient Research and Mormon Studies, or of the editors.

DESERET BOOK is a registered trademark of Deseret Book Company.

Visit us at deseretbook.com

Library of Congress Cataloging-in-Publication Data

Nibley, Hugh, 1910–
  Apostles and bishops in early Christianity / Hugh Nibley ; edited by John F. Hall and John W. Welch.
    p. cm. — (The collected works of Hugh Nibley ; v. 15)
  Includes bibliographical references and index.
  ISBN 1-59038-389-3 (hardbound : alk. paper)
  1. Episcopacy—History of doctrines—Early church, ca. 30–600.
2. Bishops—History—To 1500. 3. Apostolate (Christian theology)—History of doctrines—Early church, ca. 30–600. 4. Apostles. I. Hall, John F. II. Welch, John W. (John Woodland) III. Title.
  BV670.3.N53 2004
  262'.12'09015—dc22
                                                                    2004023387

Printed in the United States of America   70582
Phoenix Color Corporation, Hagerstown, MD

10   9   8   7   6   5   4   3   2   1

Contents

Editors' Preface	vii
Overview	xiii

1. The Office of Bishop in the Early Christian Church as a Whole — 1

The Waxing and Waning of the "Consensus"	1
An Apostle Is Not the Same as a Bishop	7
When Bishops Became the Highest Officers in the Church	23
Seeing James as the Presiding Bishop of the Church	31
The Bishop as an Office in the Lower Priesthood	36
Dependence on Jewish Sources for Church Practices Relevant to the Bishop	42
The Jewish and Worldly Origins of the Office and Title of Bishop	56
Changes in the Office of Bishop	61
Roman Origin of a Divine Office?	74
The Importance of Each Bishop Becomes Tied to the Prominence of His City	83
The Fight for Power	99
In Search of a General Authority	102
The Glories (and Duties?) of a Bishop	111
Are the Council and the Synod the Apostolic Voice?	133
The Gospel of Bigness and Power	144

2. **The Office of Bishop in the Church in Rome**   147
    In Search of a Missing Link   147
    Questions about the Account of the
        Ordination of Clement as a Bishop   152
    Finding (or Not Finding) the Bishop
        (or Bishops) of Rome   157
    Strife over the Elections of the Bishop
        of Rome   164
    The Establishment of an Episcopal Hierarchy
        and College of Cardinals   173
    The Roman Role and the Big Four   176
    The Double Apostolate: Peter and Paul   185
    Clement to the Corinthians—Proof of
        Roman Supremacy?   189
    The Leading Role the Roman Church
        Did Not Play   194
    Establishing a Connection with Peter—
        A Return to Matthew 16:18   222
    Emperors, Popes, Synods, and Rome   228
    Claims of Apostolic Succession   232
    The Argument of Diffusion   234

Editors' Postscript   239
Index   247

Editors' Preface

In 1954 Professor Hugh W. Nibley taught a class at Brigham Young University about the office of bishop in early Christianity. It is hard to imagine anyone better than Hugh Nibley to shed light on this challenging and intriguing topic. Fortunately, as he prepared for class he typed his lectures virtually word-for-word on his manual typewriter and then read them out loud to his students in the old-school tradition of truly delivering a "lecture" (in Latin, *lectura* means "words about to be read"). After these lectures were delivered, Nibley set these "notes" aside and went on to address other pressing demands on his time. This publication now makes his 155 pages of typescript available for the first time.

Bishops were as important in early Christianity as they are in the church today. In the New Testament, the duties and desired attributes of the bishop are listed twice, once in Paul's first letter to Timothy and again in his epistle to Titus. Bishops served during the first Christian century in several areas of the eastern Mediterranean—Jerusalem, Corinth, Philippi, Smyrna, Ephesus, and Hieropolis. Catholics claim that Peter was the first bishop of Rome, and Eastern Orthodox Christians assert that he was the first bishop of Antioch.

Most likely, Peter ordained the first bishops in both of these major centers.

The importance of this subject is exceeded, however, by its complexity and obscurity. One grapples to understand how those bishops functioned, what authority they possessed, how they related to the apostles or other priesthood offices, and what changes occurred in the course of the first few centuries of the Christian era with respect to these episcopal overseers. Answers to these puzzles are buried deep within the lines of many early Christian writers, whose texts are often inaccessible to the general reader. While Nibley draws attention to many revealing details in the early patristic literature, his forays into these materials are adventuresome and exploratory and thus were not intended to be definitive or conclusive.

Although Professor Nibley never returned to this research to see it through to publication, the arguments he presented in these lectures relate closely to other materials he published around that same time. In particular, *The World and the Prophets*, volume 3 in the *Collected Works of Hugh Nibley*, contains a series of weekly broadcasts entitled "Time Vindicates the Prophets." The broadcasts were delivered on KSL Radio from 7 March to 17 October 1954, the same year in which this class on the early Christian bishop was taught at BYU. The broad historical and theological developments charted in those radio talks provide the background against which to understand Nibley's arguments concerning the loss of prophetic gifts and apostolic ministrations in the early church. Even more to the point, *Mormonism and Early Christianity*, volume 4 of the *Collected Works of Hugh Nibley*, compiles his writings on early Christian historiography, notably his series from the *Improvement Era* called "The Way of the Church" (1955) and his article published in the prestigious journal *Church History* entitled "The Passing of the Primitive Church: Forty Variations on an Unpopular Theme" (1961). His discussions on those pages concerning church history, record keeping, censorship, forgery, authority, change, and apostasy comprise the wider context in which he had approached the more specific topic of the bishop in these lectures.

The style and tone of this typescript will undoubtedly strike most readers as dated and coming from a previous era of academic discourse, as we (and he) readily acknowledge. Still, we believe that this material is useful and interesting to academicians for several reasons. These pages display Nibley's gifts as a lecturer during his seventh year of instruction at Brigham Young University. The sheer tenacity and clarity required to type out one's lecture notes in this degree of detail is amazing. Few professors make such preparations for class. This material also reflects a great deal of research into the enduring primary sources, the results of which are presented here in a logical, sustained, flowing form of demonstration and argumentation. Of course, Nibley also drew on and interacted with the secondary works of Protestant scholars, and he often joined with them in their attack on Catholic history and Catholic historians. But at the same time, he pushed the arguments far beyond the positions that had been staked out by others, and he raised significant questions for future explorations concerning the history of early Christianity.

In 1997, John W. Welch first noticed these pages among various other papers in Nibley's files, and they were examined and deemed worthy to edit and publish. That process has proceeded gradually over several years. Several individuals have contributed to the production of this edition, and we acknowledge and appreciate their valuable contributions. Margaret Robertson, an editorial assistant for *BYU Studies*, checked and standardized each typed manuscript page against an electronic version and, in the process, expanded abbreviations, regularized spelling, and created new paragraphs, sections, and subsections. Joseph Ponczoch worked on the monumental task of determining the source of each quotation in the text and confirming the consistency of the manuscript's arguments. This proved truly formidable because fewer than one of every twenty quotations in the typescript included even minimal citation information, and twenty-five to thirty breaks or textual gaps of varying proportions existed in these lecture notes. Because of the condition of the original manuscript and the considerable interval of time since its composition, we and our assistants (even with Nibley's suggestions) have been unable to locate the sources of all references and have found it impossible to reconcile each instance of missing text. Footnotes indicate those quotations that stem from still unidentified sources. To the extent possible and appropriate, this rough text has been edited to ensure fluid argumentation, smooth reading, and source documentation. Some subheadings and clarifying translations have been added. The translations we have provided appear in brackets.

In bringing this book through the publication process, many others have rendered extraordinary service. Shirley S. Ricks and Sandra A. Thorne have been sensitive and persistent in their editorial and managerial roles, insuring consistency, clarity, and accuracy. Emily Ellsworth and Paula W. Hicken have attended to the difficult task of proofreading. Jeremy R. Bird and Jacob D. Rawlins have met a number of challenges in typesetting these pages with footnotes in Latin and Greek. We also appreciate Phyllis Nibley's keen eye in reviewing the page proofs.

Today, much of the research reflected in these 1954 lectures would need to be brought up to date, as the positions of all these schools of thought and the ecumenical relations between the churches have migrated considerably during the intervening half century between the 1950s and now.[1]

---

1. Suggested studies include Peter Brown, *The Rise of Western Christendom*, 2nd ed. (Malden, MA: Blackwell, 2003); W. H. C. Frend, *The Rise of Christianity* (Philadelphia: Fortress, 1984); Adrian Hastings, ed., *A World History of Christianity* (Grand Rapids, MI: Eerdmans, 1999); Philip Jenkins, *The Next Christendom: The Coming of Global Christianity* (New York: Oxford University Press, 2002); Francis E. Peters, *The Harvest of Hellenism* (London: Allen and Unwin, 1972); and Rodney Stark, *The Rise of Christianity* (San Francisco: HarperCollins, 1997).

The reader should be mindful that these writings are essentially lecture notes and do not constitute a finished product. Indeed, further research and many new lines of investigation remain to be pursued regarding the ecclesiastical structure of the early church. By publishing this provocative and significant Latter-day Saint scholarship from the mid-twentieth century, we do not wish to provoke sectarian disputes; instead, we hope to facilitate and stimulate those further discussions about the authority and functions of the early Christian bishop, while at the same time advancing a fuller understanding of the progression of Latter-day Saint intellectual history. Readers will find these lecture notes just as informative and engaging as the popular recordings and published transcripts of Nibley's later lectures on the Book of Mormon and Pearl of Great Price. For these and many other reasons, including this material in the *Collected Works of Hugh Nibley* seems more than justified, if not inescapable.

John F. Hall
John W. Welch

Overview

Professor Nibley divided these 1954 lectures into two parts: in the first half of the course, he offered a broad investigation of the duties and significance of apostolic and episcopal officers throughout the early Christian church; in the second part he focused on the same issues and their particular manifestations in the church at Rome. Overall, Nibley argues that the office of the apostle was one of general jurisdiction, whereas the office of the bishop was local in nature; accordingly, bishops could not be the automatic successors of the apostles when that office was lost from the church. All attempts to ascribe supremacy to the bishop of the Roman Church surface many centuries later than the era of Peter in Rome and arise concurrently with what Nibley calls the "gospel of bigness and power" that ultimately overshadowed the councils and synods.

Part 1: The Office of Bishop in the Early Christian Church as a Whole

Part 1 begins by summarizing pertinent perspectives of Catholic and Protestant scholars who have wrestled with basic issues in early Christian ecclesiastical history. Two theories of how church organization developed coexisted in the late nineteenth century. The prevailing consensus proclaimed that the early Christian church had developed its hierarchical organization through imitating and *adopting* broad elements of contemporary Jewish and pagan society. The minority view propounded the "presidential hypothesis," which suggested that the church developed its hierarchical organization through accommodation by *adapting* the Jewish college of presbyters to create an organization, of which the bishop was the presiding member in early Christian communities. Though all parties agreed that Christ had established an *ecclesia*—a society or church of some kind—most disagreed regarding its actual organization. Many, in fact, posited an absence of any formal church organization. This lack of consensus undermines the strength of prevailing scholarly opinions and opens the way for a reexamination of the two main offices in question, the apostle and the bishop.

The discussion then focuses on the relationship between apostolic and episcopal officers in the years immediately following the resurrection of Jesus and investigates how each office derived from Jewish and pagan religious and administrative traditions. Nibley adduces numerous sources supporting his contention that apostles traveled, were sent out into all the world, and were special delegates who supervised the work of local church officers. Moreover, he emphasizes that local churches were not individual corporate societies but constituent branches of the kingdom of God on earth, functioning under the direction of the apostles. The Twelve Apostles were not mere general messengers or missionaries, but specially commissioned delegates of Jesus Christ. "All concede that the apostles were men of unique station and endowment—special witnesses possessing prophetic gifts" (p. 13, below). Early Christian apostles concerned themselves more with the spiritual organization of the church than with its physical structure and local administration.

Nibley then shows that the early Christians understood two kinds of priesthood, one general and the other local, one higher and the other lower, one apostolic and the other episcopal. Bishops and bishoprics in the early Christian church served a purpose very different from that of the apostles. After the deaths of the apostles, the men who eventually came to function as the highest officers in the church had initially exercised only local administrative authority in accord with their ordination under the hands of various apostles. As the Latin title *episcopus* (Greek ἐπίσκοπος, meaning "overseer") implies, bishops' duties were supervisory and protective; they kept watch over the flock of saints and gave warning and counsel when trouble arose. Deacons and priests were ordained and made responsible to assist the bishops, just as Christ and the apostles were to assist the Father. It was Adolf von Harnack who defined this distinction when he recognized the presence of two levels of authority, or priesthoods, within the early church. Apostles, prophets, and teachers, he noted, were traveling, general, spiritual authorities; bishops, priests, and deacons, on the other hand, were local, administrative, judicial authorities. Thus the respective natures of the apostolic and episcopal offices were initially quite different: the former itinerant, the latter localized; the one spiritual, the other temporal.

From this it follows that the office of the bishop was different in kind, not just in degree or assignment, from that of the apostle. Consequently, the death or disappearance of all the apostles caused a serious stir in church organization. Each remaining church officer did not simply ascend one metaphorical rung on the hierarchical ladder of ecclesiastical responsibility and authority to fill the void; rather, they all retained their customary measure of responsibility and authority, at least for a time. The era of the apostolic fathers ensued, characterized by a noticeable absence of any general ecclesiastical authority. Ignatius, Clement, Polycarp, and other bishops originally ordained by one or another apostle continued to plead with churches in other locales to repent and to be obedient. However, they made such appeals only as concerned friends and observers, never presuming to issue orders "as an apostle."[1] Not one of these early apostolic church fathers ever appealed to his episcopal office to lend authority to his instructions to churches outside his local jurisdiction. Indeed, they demur from such action, specifically noting their lack of authority to so function. As Nibley demonstrates, these men who received authority directly from apostles recognize that they do not possess apostolic authority, but only that of local officers.

Nibley sees James, the bishop of Jerusalem, as an interesting exception to the normal rule, suggesting that James served simultaneously as a local bishop and also in a general church capacity. According to numerous early sources, James, brother of the Lord, was chosen and ordained bishop of Jerusalem by Peter, James, and John and was thereafter shown particular respect and honor, for James not only was given episcopal authority—that is, temporal and administrative authority—over Jerusalem, but he also was given charge over the temporal affairs of *all* cities with Christian churches. Thus, Peter ordered Clement to send to James word of Clement's ordination under Peter's hands. Under James's supervision, general church councils may have been held. Although not a traveling authority, he was a general authority. Nibley explains the position of James by comparison with the office of the presiding bishop in the restored Church of Jesus Christ of Latter-day Saints.[2]

---

1. Ignatius, *Epistola ad Philadelphenses*, in *Patrologiae Cursus Completus . . . Series Graeca*, ed. J.-P. Migne, 161 vols. (Paris: Migne, 1857–66), 5:828 (hereafter *PG*).

2. Nibley's view that James may have held a general church office similar to that of the current Latter-day Saint presiding bishop is conjectural. His argument rests on the evidence of a spurious document that makes mention of Peter's reporting to James the ordination of Clement as a bishop at Rome. A more reliable source, Eusebius (*Ecclesiastical History*, 2.1.2–5), identifies James as the first bishop at Jerusalem and cites Clement of Alexandria as providing information that James was ordained un-

The lectures next explore the origins of the office of bishop in terms of Jewish roots and pagan connections. Indeed, many early Christian church offices were adapted primarily from Judaism and secondarily from Hellenic and Mesopotamian institutions. The nature of the episcopal office in its earliest Christian manifestations bears out its Jewish origins. Nibley proposes that since Old Testament times, the title of bishop was applied to a limited, commissioned overseer who examines and reports local conditions to a higher authority. In the early Christian church, this office differed greatly from the spiritual stewardship of apostles, prophets, and teachers. Bishops were ordained and commissioned by the apostles in order to relieve them of temporal concerns and to permit them to focus on spiritual cares. Thus Peter was said to have ordained Linus, Cletus, and Clement to perform episcopal functions in his stead in Rome.

It was such temporal status that led to an overall secularization and despiritualization of the role and behavior of bishops, especially as civic prominence and civil borrowings engendered competing claims, struggles, and pride. From the earliest days of the church, a bishop was associated with a city for which he had responsibility or stewardship. As a result, each city associated itself ever increasingly with its bishop, and the public nature of the episcopal office encouraged each bishop, particularly in Rome and in important provincial cities, to perform his duties with magisterial

---

der the hands of Peter, James, and John. While James certainly at some time occupied episcopal office, one should note that "Paul attributed to James General Authority status as an Apostle. He reported that on the occasion of a visit to Jerusalem when he abode with Peter for fifteen days, 'others of the Apostles saw I none, save James the Lord's brother' (Gal. 1:19). . . . James, the brother of the Lord, whether he served as bishop of Jerusalem, or Presiding Bishop of the Church, obviously came to receive a calling to join the Twelve." John F. Hall, *New Testament Witnesses of Christ: Peter, John, James, and Paul* (American Fork, UT: Covenant Communications, 2002), 180–81.

dignity and to become a model of behavior, as if he were a political magistrate. The fact that ecclesiastical boundaries usually corresponded with political boundaries surely encouraged the association of ecclesiastical offices with political magistracies. The correlation between ecclesiastical and political office grew even more apparent when the public election of bishops, and the riotous throng that accompanied each election, became routine. Nevertheless, the primacy of any one bishop over all others remained unheard of for many centuries.

Part 1 thus concludes with an exposition of the gradual changes that occurred in the qualifications, selection, functions, and duties of bishops, along with the accompanying accumulation of honors heaped upon each bishop and the development of episcopal councils and synods as the primary means of governing the entire Christian church in the absence of any acknowledged general authorities. By the fourth century, the principle that a bishop was more important if he came from an important city had become a guiding, though unwritten, principle of the general church. One catalyst of this process was the increased convening of local councils and synods, beginning in the latter half of the second century. For such councils, the bishops of cities within a particular province generally gathered to the capital city of that province. Under these circumstances, the bishop of the provincial capital presided. By the middle of the third century, general councils were being held annually. During this era measures of supremacy in council shifted from the age of a city's church to such factors as the fame of its origin, its proximity to other churches, and its political significance. However, there existed no standing rule of hierarchy within these councils.

Nibley portrays Constantine as virtually a self-proclaimed bishop, who came to assure resolution of doctrinal disputes that in a succession of previous councils and synods had failed to be mediated. This view of Nicaea was prevalent in the 1950s. While current scholarly hypothesis continues to accept Eusebius's depiction of the emperor as divinely appointed, a sort of earthly vice-regent of heaven, a variety of issues including the reliability of Eusebius's account, complicate reconstructing the events of the Nicene council or their implication for the actual or theoretical authority of bishops. That Constantine's temporal power was the essential determinant of episcopal compromise is undisputed. Moreover, the emperor's invitation for attendance to bishops from throughout the Roman Empire clearly established the precedent for future churchwide councils.

Ecumenical councils met regularly after the Council of Nicaea and continued to bestow ever greater power on the church and some of its officials. In the absence of apostolic authority, councils and synods became the means of governing the entire church. The increasing authority that accompanied the resolutions of these meetings strengthened in the minds of many the belief that "whatever [was] done in the holy synods of the bishops [had] the force of the divine will itself."[3] Hence the arguments for authenticity began to emphasize numbers: "Whatever such a large number of bishops agrees on must be taken as arrived at not automatically, but by God's suggestion."[4] In this guise surfaced the "gospel of bigness and power."

Part 2: The Office of Bishop in the Church in Rome

In part 2, Nibley discusses the same problems and developments in ecclesiastical authority and jurisdiction as in part 1 by analyzing specifically the controversial emergence of episcopal authority at Rome, which was ultimately manifested in the papacy. He points out difficulties in the Roman Catholic search for the "missing link" between Peter and the

---

3. Eusebius, *Vita Constantini* 3.20, in *PG* 20:1080.
4. Socrates Scholasticus, *Historia Ecclesiastica* 4.12, in *PG* 67:492.

first bishops of Rome, raises questions about the account of the purported ordination of Clement by Peter as his successor, and compares the primacy of the Roman Church with that of three other major Christian churches (at Constantinople, Alexandria, and Antioch).

The bishopric of Rome demands particular attention for its increasingly insistent claims of ecclesiastical supremacy. Roman Catholics have long claimed Peter as the source of their authority and have supported this claim by quoting certain words of the Lord to Peter indicating his future presidency in the church. Of course, Roman Catholic scholars acknowledge that the issue lies not in Peter's relation to the Lord but in Peter's relation to Clement and to the church at Rome. At issue are the details of that fateful moment of transmission, not from Christ to Peter, but from Peter to his successor. Missing is evidence indicating whether Peter ever was bishop of Rome and, if so, whether Clement immediately succeeded Peter in that office. That link should also clarify the offices and duties of Linus, Cletus, Clement, and Peter—all four of whom allegedly held office in Rome simultaneously—and provide further information why Peter ordained Clement to the office of bishop rather than apostle, if he had intended for Clement to replace him as the leader of the entire Christian church.

A spurious letter from Clement to James attempts to clarify many of these issues but, according to several scholars, is a contrived document that lacks evidentiary standing. There are several versions of this letter of Clement to James the Just, bishop in Jerusalem, in which Clement describes his ordination at Peter's hand and reports the instructions received from Peter's mouth shortly before the great apostle's death. In each version, Peter directs Clement to write James as soon as he (Peter) is dead, explaining his qualifications for the episcopal office and the experiences he has had with Peter in Rome. Clement assures James that he has been a close, personal friend and apprentice to the apostle—"Tell James not to worry," advises Peter, "because a well-trained man has taken my place."[5] Nibley observes that arguments attributed to Clement emphasize his own temporal preparation and overlook the more important requirement of spiritual selection and confirmation. Moreover, he asserts that these letters stand as evidence that a transition took place between the end of the first century and the beginning of the third century, particularly in Rome, whereby bishops replaced the apostles as people of paramount influence in the Christian church.

Indeed, the episcopal lists for the early Roman Church differ significantly. Peter, Linus, Cletus, and Clement generally begin each list, but their order often varies (on some, Linus follows Cletus), their names often vary (some texts read Anacletus instead of Cletus), and the dates marking the beginnings of their respective ministries always vary (no dates, in fact, are certain until the early third century). Each version of the spurious letter of Clement to James identifies its writer as the *third* bishop to follow Peter in Rome, identifying him as a successor to Linus and Cletus as well as to Peter. And beyond all this, the nature and duration of Peter's presence in Rome is historically unclear.

According to Nibley, the complete absence of any clear principle of episcopal succession in Rome is attested by the immense strife and confusion that attended the election of bishops in that city. As occurred elsewhere throughout the empire, elections were often accompanied by bribery, rioting, senatorial and imperial intervention, and competition among elective bodies. For a millennium, the papal succession rested variously in the hands of European monarchs, Italian noblemen, affluent families, city mobs, successful generals, and scheming churchmen. The twelfth century saw the establishment of a college of cardinals composed of the most influential bishops, in whose hands the selection of the successor to

---

5. Clement, *Epistola ad Jacobum* 19, in *PG* 2:56.

a deceased pope eventually came to rest. In theory these men formed a council comparable to the Twelve Apostles, though they themselves never presumed apostolic origins.

Episcopal hierarchy was established from the bottom up rather than from the top down, and the case of Rome was no exception. Nibley emphasizes that the bishop *de facto*, if not *de jure*, succeeded the apostle as the highest office in the church merely by default. For centuries, Roman Church officials possessed only nominal prominence in councils and synods. It was not until late in the fourth century that bishops of Rome successfully advanced the doctrine of Petrine succession even in the West. The independence of Hilary and Augustine, two western bishops, is clear evidence of the equal authority of various episcopacies. Antioch, Constantinople, and Alexandria all enjoyed prestige and prominence equal to or greater than that of Rome. These four cities stood together—never alone—as the largest and greatest churches. Each church independently claimed primacy and constantly harped on the theme of their individual priority and precedence, but no church ever attained such official acclaim because of opposition from the others. Every attempt by Rome to assert its supremacy was matched at one time or another by the churches in Antioch, Constantinople, and Alexandria.

In time, the arguments of eminence and preeminence were no longer based on city size but rather on whether a church had been founded by an apostle or subsequently by someone else. And when cities started appealing to their apostolic foundations as proof of superior merit, the principle of equality was quashed by the useful fiction of the "double apostolate." Constantinople took fourth place by this criterion, because Peter had lived in each of the other three but never in the new imperial capital, the New Rome. Although Peter exercised his authority at Antioch years before taking residence at Rome, nevertheless Antioch was, on grounds of size and power, accorded the stature of the third city of Christendom, while, because of Mark's legendary role in founding its Christian community under Peter's direction, Alexandria, larger and more important than Antioch, was considered the second most important see. In this contest, Rome came in first because that city could claim the simultaneous missionary service of both Peter and Paul.

In spite of this and other claims, no solid case can be made for the early primacy of Rome. Nibley points out that if there had been a general church authority to succeed the apostles, the apostolic fathers would certainly have made mention of that authority and confronted him with their concerns. In the first generation after the apostles, individual bishops like Clement write to offer advice to churches in locales over which they do not preside, giving that advice as brothers in Christ rather than as those in authority. Nibley argues that this stands as proof of the absence of church-wide authority. Clearly Clement's letters to the Corinthians in no way compare in authority to Paul's letters to the same body. The letters of Clement to the church at Corinth echo the distressed, yet unauthoritative, petitions of Ignatius, Polycarp, Irenaeus, and others. No one claimed apostolic or other general ecclesiastical authority, but each bishop justified himself by feelings of love and urgency.

If ever there was an opportunity for Rome to assert her claim, the Council of Nicaea was it, Nibley claims. Had the primacy of Rome been a fact, she would have resolved all the most burning controversies of the first four centuries by appeal to her own priority. She could not claim that authority, however, and as tensions increased, church fathers began proposing different criteria for authority, such as size of the church or city, antiquity of the church, origin of the church, or location of the church. Moreover, if Rome were the seat of general authority within the church, it is odd that, time and again, Rome did not play the leading role one would have expected.

Although Roman Catholic scholars of the past have attempted to prove that popes convened all synods, it is clear that emperors summoned at least the first eight. And in fact, all six reasons for calling a universal synod (general heresy, papal disagreement, crusade, papal heresy, cardinals stalling elections, or reform) would have been obviated if the Roman Church had been acknowledged from the beginning as the divinely established head. The clearest and boldest Roman claims of papal supremacy appeared in the fourteenth century, beginning with the bull *Unam Sanctam* of 1302. The tardiness of such a bold proclamation bespeaks the authoritative uncertainty that reigned in the church left behind by the apostles.

Supporters of the Roman position have never failed to return to Matthew 16:18 to substantiate their claim of preeminence. Roman Catholics and their opponents both agree that the all-important phrase in that verse is not "thou art Peter" but "the gates of hell shall not prevail." The rock, Nibley mentions, is always identified with revelation, never with Peter himself. But regardless of these details, Protestant scholars have clearly demonstrated that no argument for spiritual supremacy grounded itself on this verse during the first three centuries.

Finally, the ecclesiastical histories clearly manifest that disharmony was prevalent in the early centuries of Christianity. So also, according to Nibley, the writings of the apostolic and early church fathers abound with uncertainty and confusion regarding any source of central authority or leadership. Fourth-century claims of apostolic succession are unconvincing, as much with respect to Rome as anywhere else in the early Christian world. Arguments used anciently to assert catholic orthodoxy, for example, by virtue of the diffusion of uniform gospel teachings throughout the church, actually provide evidence against the presence of some churchwide authority within the system, which had it existed should have been mentioned in such a context. Countless bishops composed letters of warning, instruction, and chastisement, both to single churches specifically and to all churches universally, but they never presume to speak with, or recognize in another, apostolic authority. These bishops appealed to the members of the church solely in the name of love, concern, or fear, and, by the fourth century, the best counsel any one of them could offer was to follow tradition and obey the voice of the council and the synod.

John F. Hall
John W. Welch
Joseph Ponczoch

1
The Office of Bishop in the Early Christian Church as a Whole

It is astonishing how little is known about the nature and organization of the early church. So little is known, in fact, that a large and influential number of Protestant churchmen were able to maintain for many years that there never was a church in the time of Christ and the apostles. By the same reasoning some of them also concluded that Jesus had never lived. But there is a great difference between a little information and none at all, and today [1954] it is not only generally agreed that there was a church, but also that the church organization was all-important in the ministry of the Lord and the apostles.

The Waxing and Waning of the "Consensus"

Ernest Renan, in the spirit of nineteenth-century liberalism, claimed that the early Christians "knew little else than the law of love."[1] J. B. Lightfoot had suggested the theory that "the episcopate was formed not out of the apostolic order by localisation, but out of the presbyterial by elevation."[2] That is,

---

1. "Jusqu'ici, elle n'a guère su qu'aimer." Ernest Renan, *L'Antechrist* (Paris: Michel Lévy Frères, 1873), i.
2. J. B. Lightfoot, *Dissertations on the Apostolic Age* (London: Macmillan, 1892), 155.

the bishop was not an office bestowed from above by general authority, but one that grew up locally. This was the "presidential hypothesis"—that each church had its own college of elders governing it, of which the bishop was merely the president.³ The church was thus a local community, a human society, and nothing more; everything was interpreted in purely political terms. This theory proposed that churches existed because they were found by experience to be a practical expedient and for no other reason: "The church can exist without any organization, but the church cannot persist without organization."⁴ The prevailing doctrine of the 1880s, designated by Olof Linton as the "Consensus," went even further. The high church theory of that time was that the foundation of the early church was the necessary and indispensable office of preacher. The Consensus abolished both that and the apostolate and, says Linton, thereby abolished the religious nature of the church! "The church organization is a purely secular [profane] structure."⁵ Edwin Hatch, in *The Organization of the Early Christian Churches* (1881), claimed that the church developed by a gradual evolution and did so by absorbing elements which were already present in the society, following pagan and especially Jewish patterns.⁶

Rudolf Sohm went to the opposite extreme while still denying the church any real organization. *Ekklesia* means public assembly, "the ruling popular assembly of the Greek city state,"⁷ and its equivalent is the Hebrew *qāhāl*, "the solemn

---

3. Olof Linton, *Das Problem der Urkirche in der neueren Forschung: Eine kritische Darstellung* (Uppsala: Almquist and Wiksells, 1932), 4–5.

4. "Die Kirche kann ohne Organisation sein, kann aber ohne Organisation nicht *bestehen.*" Linton, *Das Problem der Urkirche*, 8, emphasis in original.

5. "Die Gemeindeverfassung ist ein rein profanes Gebilde." Linton, *Das Problem der Urkirche*, 29.

6. Edwin Hatch, *The Organization of the Early Christian Churches: Eight Lectures Delivered before the University of Oxford, in the Year 1880* (London: Rivingtons, 1881), 26–32, 57–81.

7. Rudolf Sohm, *Kirchenrecht*, 2 vols., Systematisches Handbuch der deutschen Rechtswissenschaft 8 (Munich: Duncker and Humblot, 1923), 1:6.

assembly in the presence of God of the people of Israel."[8] This is the sense of *ekklesia* in the New Testament. Sohm states that "the word has no social content but is purely dogmatic."[9] Any idea of a local community can have nothing to do with this idea of the church: "Only the church is organized, . . . but it cannot be put into any legal organizational structure."[10] Karl Holl argued that the Twelve were historical but that they had no office. Holl agreed with Sohm's theory of absolute opposition between *Amt* [office] and *Geist* [spirit][11]—a theory which Gunkel easily disproved.[12] On the other hand, Roland Schütz said "the Twelve" was all office and therefore could not be historical.[13] So there were two schools: the apostolate was genuine but not hierarchic, or it was hierarchic but not genuine.

A standard statement of the case was that of Otto Scheel in 1912: "The churches," he said, "were corporations, that is, societies. They arose independently [*autonom*] and spontaneously side by side. There was no common bond between them. Every church chose its own officers."[14] Against this

---

8. "Das feierlich vor Gott versammelte Volk Israel (hebräisch Kahal)." Sohm, *Kirchenrecht*, 1:17.

9. "Das Wort Ekklesia [drückt] keinen socialen Begriff [aus] . . . sondern lediglich ein dogmatisches Werturteil." Sohm, *Kirchenrecht*, 1:19.

10. "Nur die Ekklesia ist organisiert. . . . Die Ekklesia ist der rechtlichen Organisation unfähig." Sohm, *Kirchenrecht*, 1:22.

11. Karl Holl, "Der Kirchenbegriff des Paulus in seinem Verhältnis zu dem der Urgemeinde," *Sitzungsberichte der preussischen Akademie der Wissenschaften, Berlin* (1921): 928, in *Gesammelte Aufsätze zur Kirchengeschichte* (Tübingen: Mohr, 1928), 2:50–51; Sohm, *Kirchenrecht*, 1:4.

12. Source unidentified.

13. Roland Schütz, *Apostel und Jünger: Eine quellenkritische und geschichtliche Untersuchung über die Entstehung des Christentums* (Giessen: Töpelmann, 1921), 71–78.

14. "Die 'Kirchen' waren örtliche Vereinigungen, Korporationen, also 'Gemeinden,' Sie bestanden 'autonom,' selbständig neben einander. Ein Gemeindeverband existierte nicht. Jede Gemeinde wählte ihre Vorsteher." Otto Scheel, *Die Kirche im Urchristentum mit Durchblicken auf die Gegenwart*, Religionsgeschichtliche Volksbücher für die deutsche christliche Gegenwart 4.20 (Tübingen: Mohr, 1912), 5, quoted in Linton, *Das Problem der Urkirche*, 119.

Johannes Weiss "discovered" that for Jesus the kingdom of God was no mere community of pious people but a divine institution. That meant that the kingdom and the church must be very different things—the one spiritual, the other official.[15] Adolf von Harnack objected: what is wrong with having *Amt* and *Geist* together in the same institution—even dependent on each other?[16] The scholars simply could not see it: it had to be one or the other.

Those involved in the great controversy granted that there was a church, but disagreed over whether that posited an organization. The church by its very nature is an organization. The phenomena of primitive Christianity cannot be explained on any but a corporational basis: there are motions passed, elections, etc. This is the "spirit" controversy: the *charisma* as a free, formless principle versus the idea that the Spirit can and does bring about order, law, and discipline.

Today the tendency is no longer to regard the church as a late emergence but to seek its origin even in the time of Jesus. In all camps, the dependence of the individual is now being emphasized. It was Harnack who started this: "The development goes from the whole to the part."[17] "*Ekklesia*," says Sohm, means "*Gesamtkirche*, of which the local churches are only copies."[18] Harnack, Pierre Batiffol, Henri Leclercq, and Wilhelm Koester oppose Sohm and believe that *ekklesia* in Matthew 18:17 refers to a single local church but that the idea of the general church was derived from it—and that it

---

15. Johannes Weiss, *Die Predigt Jesu vom Reiche Gottes*, 2nd ed. (Göttingen: Vandendoeck and Ruprecht, 1900), quoted in Linton, *Das Problem der Urkirche*, 120–21.

16. Quoted in Linton, *Das Problem der Urkirche*, 123.

17. "Die Entwickelung geht zunächst vom Ganzen zum Teil." Adolf von Harnack, *Entstehung und Entwickelung der Kirchenverfassung und des Kirchenrechts in den zwei ersten Jahrhunderten* (Leipzig: Hinrichs, 1910), 38.

18. "'Ekklesia' [bedeutet] immer 'Gesamtkirche' und die Enzelgemeinde [ist] nur 'Darstellung' derselben." Rudolf Sohm, quoted in Linton, *Das Problem der Urkirche*, 136.

THE OFFICE OF BISHOP IN THE EARLY CHRISTIAN CHURCH

happened very soon, in time to be used by Paul.[19] Opposing the Consensus, Sohm said that *Gemeindebeschlüsse* [local community decisions] were merely local *Anerkennungshandlungen* [confirmatory procedures], accepting central decrees. He points to the basic primitive Christian belief that the church must act as a totality, a unit: a majority vote is not enough—the minority always joins the majority so that all things are done in perfect unanimity.[20] The Consensus had identified authority with the force of personality (the personality of Jesus, of Paul, etc.), but it is now recognized that this is not the early Christian view, which always traces the authority to a gift from God and insists that it rests on God's approval. The Consensus has modernized, or humanized, the idea of "charisma."[21] "The local branch is a reproduction of the heavenly *ekklesia*. Therefore, it must be organized just like the *Gesamtekklesia*: The local society [ward] is a scale model of the church."[22] This is the present state of things.

To support this, Theodor Schermann observes that without an organization there would be no rites, no ordinances, no liturgy.[23] Hans Lietzmann notes that the earliest records speak of the process by which one joins the church, an *Aufnahmeritus* that meets us fully developed in the Acts and in

---

19. Pierre Batiffol, *L'Église naissante et le Catholicisme* (Paris: Lecoffre, 1909), 90; Henri Leclercq, "Église," in *Dictionaire d'Archéologie Chrétienne et de Liturgie*, ed. Fernand Carol and Henri Leclercq (Paris: Librairie Letouzey et Ané, 1925), 4.2.2220–38; Wilhelm Koester, *Die Idee der Kirche beim Apostel Paulus*, Neutestamentliche Abhandlungen 19.1 (Münster: Aschendorff, 1928), 1–15; see also Linton, *Das Problem der Urkirche*, 138–42.
20. Rudolf Sohm, quoted in Linton, *Das Problem der Urkirche*, 188–95.
21. Linton, *Das Problem der Urkirche*, 195.
22. "Die Gemeinde ist im Kultus Darstellung der himmlischen Ekklesia. Als solche muss sie wie die Gesamtekklesia organisiert sein. . . . Die Gemeinde [ist] ein Abbild der Kirche." Linton, *Das Problem der Urkirche*, 196.
23. Theodor Schermann, *Die allgemeine Kirchenordnung, frühchristliche Liturgien und kirchliche Überlieferung*, Studien zur Geschichte und Kulture des Altertums, 3 vols. in one (Paderborn: Schöningh, 1914–16), 2:5–7.

the Epistles and that without a definite and even strict organization would be impossible. This is not, however, apparent in the Gospels, says Lietzmann;[24] yet T. W. Manson notes in 1950 that it is precisely in the Gospels that "we begin with the fact that Jesus did gather a community around himself *during the course of his ministry;* and we may well ask what it was, if it was not the church.... It will not do to regard this group merely as the more or less regular disciples of a somewhat unorthodox travelling Rabbi.... The more the Synoptic evidence is studied, the more clearly the fact emerges that what Jesus created was something more than a new theological school. It was a religious community, of which he was the leader."[25]

"It is plain," Kirsopp Lake wrote in 1911, "that a community which is momentarily expecting a complete and catastrophic change in the character of society is unlikely to possess more than the necessary minimum of organization; it is not less plain that as soon as this expectation passes into the background the need of organization will be increasingly felt."[26] This is typical of the orthodox theological seminary type of thought: of course it is plain, other things being equal (but the mission of the Lord means nothing if it does not mean that other things are not equal). The Lord prescribed a special organization, however illogical that might seem to the man in the seminary. When the *parousia* [second coming] failed to transpire, according to Lake, then it was plain that an organization was indicated—yet precisely at this time the organization disappeared, leaving the church in a vacuum until the fourth century.

---

24. Hans Lietzmann, *Geschichte der Alten Kirche*, 3 vols. (Berlin: de Gruyter, 1932), 1:55.

25. T. W. Manson, "The New Testament Basis of the Doctrine of the Church," *Journal of Ecclesiastical History* 1 (1950): 3–4, emphasis added.

26. Kirsopp Lake, "The Shepherd of Hermas and Christian Life in Rome in the Second Century," *Harvard Theological Review* 4 (1911): 37.

An Apostle Is Not the Same as a Bishop

To all the world. Holl, pointing to the well-known fact that the earliest Christian church was a missionary organization, drew the obvious conclusion that "no missionary church begins with autonomous branches."[27] Missionary work spreads from a center and is concerned with bringing others into a well-defined group.[28] Apostle means missionary, and the whole activity of the apostles is conditioned by this fact, which of course posits the existence of a church. They succeeded in converting the world, according to present Catholic doctrine, "not gradually and by successive instruction," according to Giovanni Battista Pighi, "but by the interior instruction of God in an instant. Suddenly ... all nations which are under heaven heard and believed in the Son of God."[29] He quotes John Chrysostom to prove this, forgetting the worried conclusion that Chrysostom draws from this interesting premise: "If that is so, then the end should have come long ago, since it was explicitly stated that when the apostles had once preached to all nations, then would the end come."[30] Chrysostom's only possible conclusion, which he swallows with a wry face, is that the apostles cannot have accomplished their mission after all, since the church is still on the earth.

But all agree that the apostles did spend their time preaching to the nations and then passed away, almost all at once and suddenly, leaving no apostles in their place. The

---

27. "Keine Missionskirche beginnt mit autonomen Gemeinden." Karl Holl, quoted in Linton, *Das Problem der Urkirche,* 198.

28. Linton, *Das Problem der Urkirche,* 198.

29. Source unidentified.

30. εἶπεν ὅτι ὅταν κηρυχθῇ τὸ εὐαγγέλιον ἐν πᾶσι τοῖς ἔθνεσι, τότε ἥξει τὸ τέλος· καὶ ἰδοὺ πρὸς τὸ τέλος λοιπὸν ἐφθάσαμεν. τὸ γὰρ πλέον τῆς οἰκουμένης κατηγγέλη· λοιπὸν οὖν τὸ τέλος ἐνέστηκε. John Chrysostom, *In Epistolam ad Hebraeos* 21.3, in J.-P. Migne, ed., *Patrologiae Cursus Completus . . . Series Graeca,* 161 vols. (Paris: Migne, 1857–66), 63:152 (hereafter *PG*).

apostles must have been special officers of some sort, it is assumed. Their work was closely centralized in Jerusalem—the main office to which we may assume they would repair for yearly conferences to make reports on their missions in the presence of the whole church and to which at other times they would steadily send written reports on their work. The gathering of Israel and Judah was the missionary work of the apostles, says Eusebius (confusing the first with the second coming of Christ and forgetting, as all do, that the specific nature of their mission is very clearly stated in the scriptures many times). Eusebius goes on to describe how later they came together and worked at uniting the church, "no longer going forth as they had done originally."[31]

Special delegates. Many studies have shown the name *apostle*, when specifically applied to the Twelve, to mean more than a messenger or missionary—it means a "special delegate." "Our Lord was not introducing a new term but adopting one which from its current usage would suggest to His hearers the idea of a highly responsible mission," wrote Lightfoot.[32] Further investigators have come to almost general agreement that the genius of the apostolic office was that the holder of it was a special witness. There were many "apostles," as we read in the *Didache;* but the Twelve, "the perfect year of the Lord," were something very special. "At the present time," says Peter in the *Clementine Recognitions,* "do not look for any other prophet or apostle except us. There is one true prophet and twelve apostles."[33] He explains that no one is to be accepted as a true missionary who does not have a duly signed certificate from the main office at Jerusalem.[34]

---

31. Source unidentified.
32. J. B. Lightfoot, *Saint Paul's Epistle to the Galatians,* rev. ed. (London: Macmillan, 1921), 94, quoted in Linton, *Das Problem der Urkirche,* 74.
33. *Sed neque propheta, neque apostolus in hoc tempore speretur a vobis aliquis alius praeter nos. Unus enim est verus propheta, cuius nos duodecim apostoli verba praedicamus. Recognitiones Clementinae* 4.35, in *PG* 1:1330.
34. *Recognitiones Clementinae* 4.35, in *PG* 1:1330.

THE OFFICE OF BISHOP IN THE EARLY CHRISTIAN CHURCH 9

The discovery of the *Didache* led Holl to conclude, and most Protestant scholars now concur, that the apostolic authority did not come (as was once thought) purely as a charismatic gift, but that it was an ordained office along with all its spirituality.[35] From the beginning, wrote Lietzmann, "the Twelve appear as a compact group in which only three men stand out as individuals. These were," he says, "Peter, James, and John, the pillars of the primitive church."[36] The importance of these three is significant. It puzzled the experts from the first that while the office of apostle had to be accompanied by the gift of prophecy, it did not come spontaneously in a spiritual way nor was there among the apostles a perfect equality; in fact, the Twelve removed any validity to the claim that all believers must have been of equal spiritual authority. There was a definite hierarchy in the earliest church (Acts 5:22). The church is a totality and acts not as a majority but as a unit, Harnack noticed; but at the same time, "the church was an *abgestufte Totalität* [hierarchical entity]."[37] While we see in the church a definite local organization, wrote Eduard Meyer, "the highest authority was held by the Twelve, and at their head was Peter."[38] Harnack's thorough study of non-Christian sources regarding Peter showed that he was far and away the most important man in the church. After he and James were dead for at least twenty-four years, Eusebius specifically states that "John the beloved returned from Patmos and continued to govern the

---

35. Source unidentified.
36. "Die Zwölf erscheinen als kompakte Gruppe von der sich als Individuen nur Petrus und der Zebedaïde Johannes ablösen. Diese beiden bilden mit Jakobus zusammen die 'Saülen' der Urgemeinde." Lietzmann, *Geschichte der Alten Kirche*, 1:59.
37. Linton, *Das Problem der Urkirche*, 194.
38. "Die höchste Autorität aber bilden die Zwölf, und an ihrer Spitze Petrus." Eduard Meyer, *Ursprung und Anfänge des Christentums* (Darmstadt: Wissenshaftliche Buchgesellschaft, 1962), 3:263–64.

churches."³⁹ He cites a very old source telling how, as long as an apostle remained alive, the spoilers and dissenters had to content themselves with lurking in dark corners, only to throw off all disguise and come out boldly into the open the moment the last apostle was dead.⁴⁰ Plainly the apostles had a kind of authority that none of their successors had. They were conceived of as the twelve judges of Israel and so were limited to that number.

The persistence of Jewish ideas in the church is now more recognized. Harnack and Sohm both recognized that the missionary pattern of the church was that of the Jews and not that of the Hellenistic local missions of traveling wise men and reformers. On the other hand, Holl noted that while the Jewish system might also have produced "apostles of the churches," it could not possibly have produced "apostles of Jesus Christ," which was something absolutely unique.⁴¹ A Jewish scholar, Hermann Vogelstein, has shown that the general idea of an apostle as "an authorized representative" was familiar to the Jews, that it was not a "mystical" concept, and that an apostle could only be one actually sent out by Christ himself.⁴² Vogelstein, being unmindful

---

39. ἐπειδὴ γὰρ τοῦ τυράννου τελευτήσαντος ἀπὸ τῆς Πάτμου τῆς νήσου μετῆλθεν ἐπὶ τὴν Ἔφεσον, ἀπῄει παρακαλούμενος καὶ ἐπὶ τὰ πλησιόχωρα τῶν ἐθνῶν, ὅπου μὲν ἐπισκόπους καταστήσων, ὅπου δὲ ὅλας ἐκκλησίας ἁρμόσων, ὅπου δὲ κλῆρον ἕνα γέ τινα κληρώσων τῶν ὑπὸ τοῦ πνεύματος σημαινομένων. Eusebius, *Historia Ecclesiastica* 3.23.6, in *PG* 20:257.

40. ὡς δ' ὁ ἱερὸς τῶν ἀποστόλων χορὸς διάφορον εἰλήφει τοῦ βίου τέλος, παρεληλύθει τε ἡ γενεὰ ἐκείνη τῶν αὐταῖς ἀκοαῖς τῆς ἐνθέου σοφίας ἐπακοῦσαι κατηξιωμένην, τηνικαῦτα τῆς ἀθέου πλάνης τὴν ἀρχὴν ἐλάμβανεν ἡ σύστασις, διὰ τῆς τῶν ἑτεροδιδασκάλων ἀπάτης· οἳ καὶ ἅτε μηδενὸς ἔτι τῶν ἀποστόλων λειπομένου, γυμνῇ λοιπὸν ἤδη τῇ κεφαλῇ, τῷ τῆς ἀληθείας κηρύγματι τὴν ψευδώνυμον γνῶσιν ἀντικηρύττειν ἐπεχείρουν. Eusebius, *Historia Ecclesiastica* 3.32.8, in *PG* 20:284.

41. Holl, "Der Kirchenbegriff des Paulus," 930 n. 1.

42. See Hermann Vogelstein, "The Development of the Apostolate in Judaism and Its Transformation in Christianity," *Hebrew Union College*

of the direct nature of Paul's calling as a missionary, says that Paul changed all that.[43] However, among the Jews, according to Vogelstein, "the name of apostle does not confer an absolute position, but it merely determines his relationship to one who assigned him his commission."[44] This, he concludes, makes the Christian apostle an office entirely dependent on Christ and not a Jewish institution at all. Mark 3:14, Vogelstein notes, shows that the apostolic office "is as original as Jesus himself."[45]

General officers. From the fact that "the apostles went from place to place without remaining long anywhere," Harnack says there are three possibilities to be deduced: (1) they went forth without any care for the future, (2) they committed the direction of the church to local men (this would explain James the Just), or (3) they kept the direction of things in their own hands. Harnack thinks the first of these is the most likely, though "the second possibility was at a very early date accepted as normal procedure."[46] The third possibility appears in Paul's writings and in the general directorate at Jerusalem under James. Jerusalem was always very important. But on one thing all are agreed: the apostles were traveling general authorities, "essentially itinerant," "a nomadic apostolate," "a fraternity officiating in the establishment of a worldwide institution, forming itself everywhere

---

Annual 2 (1925): 112, 114; Vogelstein, "Die Entstehung und Entwicklung des Apostolats im Judentum," *Monatschrift für Geschichte und Wissenschaft des Judentums* 49 (1905): 428; and Linton, *Das Problem der Urkirche*, 91.

43. Vogelstein, "Development of the Apostolate," 118; and "Die Entstehung und Entwicklung des Apostolats," 447–48.
44. Vogelstein, "Development of the Apostolate," 119.
45. "... so original wie Jesus selbst." Vogelstein, quoted in Linton, *Das Problem der Urkirche*, 93–94.
46. "Die Apostel gingen von Ort zu Ort, ohne irgendwo lange Zeit zu bleiben. . . . Die zweite Möglichkeit wurde aber recht früh als die normale angesehen (Apg. [Acts] 14:23)." Adolf von Harnack, quoted in Linton, *Das Problem der Urkirche*, 198.

into identical Christianities, cooperating among themselves, having the same faith, the same cult, the same authorities."[47] This is a surprising thing, says Batiffol: "Christianity was born catholic."[48] But if the system was so strong and so workable, why did it suddenly disappear? "In the earliest times," writes Louis Duchesne, "there was a perpetual circulation of apostles, of missionaries, of prophets, of teachers."[49] This work was within the church, please note, not merely to the Gentiles. "But when the first age of the church passed away, this itinerant, ubiquitous [i.e., general] personnel disappeared entirely, and nothing was left but the local ecclesiastical organizations."[50] What had happened? Didn't the church need general officers anymore? Could they be trusted independently to follow the right path? As we know, this led to frightful results. And there was to be no more general authority until such authority emerged in the fifth century in "the great Babylon of the West, so accursed to the Jewish prophets."[51]

The cold comfort to the church with the passing of the apostles was that if the apostolate was gone, other offices remained, and that these offices were not invented to fill the apostolic vacuum but had existed alongside the apostolic

---

47. ". . . une fraternité, essaimant sur toute la terre sans se détendre, se formant partout en petites chretientés pareilles, coopérantes, ayant même foi, même culte, même autorités." Batiffol, *L'Église naissante et le Catholicisme*, x.

48. "La chrétienté est née catholique." Batiffol, *L'Église naissante et le Catholicisme*, xi.

49. "Avait aux premiers temps une perpétuelle circulation d'apôtres, de missionnaires, de prophètes, de docteurs." Louis Duchesne, *Origines du Culte Chrétien: Étude sur la Liturgie Latine avant Charlemagne*, 5th ed. (Paris: de Boccard, 1925), 14.

50. "Les premiers temps passes, une fois disparu tout ce personnel itinerant, ubiquiste, il ne resta plus que les organizations ecclésiastiques locales." Duchesne, *Origines du Culte Chrétien*, 14.

51. "La grande Babylone de l'Occident, tant maudite des prophètes juifs." Duchesne, *Origines du Culte Chrétien*, 14.

office from the very beginning. Yet the antiquity and authenticity of these ancient offices was a very strong argument against their possibly representing a succession to the apostles. Bishops, priests, teachers, and deacons had functioned for many years during the lifetimes of the apostles. In no way did they compete with or duplicate the work of apostles—they had their own work to do, and it was a full-time job. To expect them over and above that to take over the totally different business of governing the general church was out of the question. Duchesne comments on the perplexing fact that the great bishopric of Rome, while equipped with all the offices and machinery necessary for the administration of a city bishopric, had not the slightest trace of the equipment, offices, assistants, and traditions necessary for running a church.[52] What makes this disturbing is that Jerusalem from the beginning did have such an administrative setup. But no one expected the bishop of any city to take over the work of an apostle. This is amusingly shown in the famous forged letters of Clement to James, in which Peter is represented as assuming the bishopric of Rome only to leave the city immediately after having appointed no less than three bishops to act in his place since he had to be about the business of an apostle and could not possibly spend his days in the city.[53]

No established pattern for replacement. All concede that the apostles were men of unique station and endowment—special witnesses possessing prophetic gifts. When men thus endowed were removed, who could take their place? An *Ersatz* [substitute] was necessary, Sohm observed, and "from this necessity arose the episcopate." The bishop is therefore "a highly spiritual substitute, the direct predecessor of our present-day pastors."[54] But how can one be a

---

52. Duchesne, *Origines du Culte Chrétien*, 15–16.
53. Clement, *Epistola ad Jacobum*, in *PG* 2:32–56.
54. Source unidentified.

spiritual substitute? Only by a spiritual calling and ordination, Sohm decided: The bishop must have been a presbyter, but his office does not belong to the presbyters (as the "presidential school" maintained). The presbyters are only a social class enjoying an honorable position in the society.[55] Thus Sohm amended Harnack: there were two priesthoods, but they were both spiritual. This is Sohm's usual incapacity to see any possibility of reconciliation between *Amt* and *Geist*, now seen as a quaint myopia: no necessary conflict exists between the two which, far from being mutually exclusive, may well be mutually dependent. Many have insisted that the episcopate and the presbyterian offices were identical. Certainly in very early sources the "successors" of the apostles are consistently depicted as the "presbyters." In the *agape* [church], says the *Apostolic Constitutions*, the presbyters represent the apostles "as counselors of the bishop and the crown of the church, for they are the sanhedrin and council of the church."[56]

But this sort of equivalence has nothing at all to do with actual succession. Harnack had noted that the local church is but a scale model of the main church if it has officers whose relationships to each other correspond to the relationships of higher functionaries.[57] They certainly do not share the power of those functionaries, which they only reflect or resemble. The fact that all share the same spirit does not mean, as is so commonly maintained, that all share the same office, authority, and function. Thus the reader takes his portion at the *agape* "in honor of the prophets,"[58] the pastor or bishop

---

55. Sohm, *Kirchenrecht*, 101–2.
56. τοῖς δὲ πρεσβυτέροις . . . διπλῆ καὶ αὐτοῖς ἀφοριζέσθω ἡ μοῖπα εἰς χάπιν τῶν τοῦ κυρίου ἀποστόλων, ὧν καὶ τόν τόπον φυλάσσουσιν ὡς σύμβουλοι τοῦ ἐπισκόπου καὶ τῆς ἐκκλησίας στέφανος· εἰσὶν γὰρ συνέδριον καὶ βουλὴ τῆς ἐκκλησίας. *Constitutiones Apostolicae* 2.28.4, in *PG* 1:673.
57. Quoted in Linton, *Das Problem der Urkirche*, 51, 136, 196.
58. εἰ δὲ καὶ ἀναγνώστης ἔστιν, λαμβανέτω καὶ αὐτὸς μοῖραν μίαν εἰς τιμὴν τῶν προφητῶν. *Constitutiones Apostolicae* 2.28.5, in *PG* 1:673.

receives his share "as a priest,"[59] the deacons receive double shares "as the reward of Christ,"[60] and the laymen must make any appeals to authority to the deacons only, since God can only be approached through his Son, Christ.[61] All kings, princes, etc., must be obeyed in religious matters "as the deacons of God."[62] "Let a virgin be pure as the temple of God, as the house of Christ, as the lodging place of the Holy Ghost."[63] "Let the widows and orphans be the equivalent of the altar and the virgins of the censers."[64] If God made Moses a god to Pharaoh with Aaron as his prophet, says the *Apostolic Constitutions* in speaking of the higher offices of the church, "why should not you think of the mediators of your doctrine as prophets, and reverence them as gods? As the bishop represents Moses, so the deacon does Aaron ... as Christ does nothing without the Father, so the deacon does nothing without the bishop ... as the Son is the messenger and prophet of the Father, even so the deacon is also the messenger and prophet of the bishop."[65] The deacon

---

59. ἀφοριζέσθω δὲ ἐν τῇ δοχῇ τῷ ποιμένι ἔθιμον . . . ὡς ἱερεῖ. *Constitutiones Apostolicae* 2.28.2, in *PG* 1:673.
60. διπλοῦν διδόσθω τοῖς διακόνοις εἰς γέρας Χριστοῦ. *Constitutiones Apostolicae* 2.28.3, in *PG* 1:673.
61. οὐδὲ γὰρ τῷ παντοκράτορι θεῷ προσελθεῖν ἔστιν, ἐὰν μὴ διὰ τοῦ Χριστοῦ. οὕτως οὖν καὶ οἱ λαϊκοὶ πάντα ὅσα βούλονται διὰ τοῦ διακόνου φανερὰ τῷ ἐπισκόπῳ ποιείτωσαν. *Constitutiones Apostolicae* 2.28.6, in *PG* 1:674.
62. ὡς θεοῦ διακόνοις. *Constitutiones Apostolicae* 4.13.1, in *PG* 1:825.
63. ἡ παρθένος οὖν αὕτη ἔστω ἁγία σώματι καὶ ψυχῇ, ὡς ναὸς θεοῦ, ὡς οἶκος Χριστοῦ, ὡς πνεύματος ἁγίου καταγώγιον. *Constitutiones Apostolicae* 4.14.2, in *PG* 1:825.
64. αἵ τε χῆραι καὶ οἱ ὀρφανοὶ εἰς τύπον τοῦ θυσιαστηρίου λελογίσθωσαν ὑμῖν· αἵ τε παρθένοι εἰς τύπον τοῦ θυμιατηρίου τετιμήσθωσαν καὶ τοῦ θυμιάματος. *Constitutiones Apostolicae* 2.26.8, in *PG* 1:668–69.
65. εἰ γὰρ Ἀαρών, ἐπειδὴ ἤγγελλεν τῷ Φαραὼ παρὰ Μωσέως τοὺς λόγους, προφήτης εἴρηται . . . διότι μὴ καὶ ὑμεῖς τοὺς μεσίτας ὑμῶν τοῦ λόγου προφήτας εἶναι νομίσητε καὶ ὡς θεοὺς σεβασθήσεσθε; Νῦν γὰρ ὑμῖν μὲν ὁ Ἀαρών ἐστιν ὁ διάκονος, Μωϋσῆς δὲ ὁ ἐπίσκοπος . . . ὡς γὰρ ὁ Χριστὸς ἄνευ τοῦ πατρὸς οὐδὲν ποιεῖ, οὕτως οὐδὲ ὁ διάκονος ἄνευ τοῦ

must not even give to the poor without first asking permission of the bishop, for were not Aaron and Miriam rebuked for acting without consulting Moses? "Let the good bishop be honored, loved, and feared as a Lord, as a master, as a high priest of God, as a teacher of piety. For who hearkens to him, hearkens to Christ."[66] "Follow ye all the bishop as Jesus Christ," says Ignatius, "and follow the presbyterium as the apostles."[67] "We must look upon the bishop as upon the Lord himself."[68] "As our Lord never did anything without the Father, neither by his own authority nor through the apostles, so may you do nothing without the bishop nor try to be justified of yourselves."[69] Quoting Psalm 81:6: "Ye are Gods, and all sons of the Most High," the *Apostolic Constitutions* explains: "the bishop presides over you as being honored by the esteem [judgment] of God, by which he rules the clergy and leads all the people. And the deacon stands by and supports him as Christ does the Father. . . . For the deaconess is to be honored by you as the type of the Holy Ghost. . . . And as no one can believe in Christ without the Holy Ghost, so no woman may approach a deacon of a bishop except through a deaconess. And the presbyters [priests] are to you the type of the apostles" whom Christ

---

ἐπισκόπου . . . καὶ ὥσπερ ὁ υἱὸς ἄγγελός ἐστιν καὶ προφήτης τοῦ πατρός, οὕτως καὶ ὁ διάκονος ἄγγελος καὶ προφήτης ἐστὶν τοῦ ἐπισκόπου. *Constitutiones Apostolicae* 2.29.1–2.30.2, in *PG* 1:676–77.

66. τὸν μέντοι ποιμένα τὸν ἀγαθὸν ὁ λαϊκὸς τιμάτω, ἀγαπάτω, φοβείσθω, ὡς κύριον, ὡς δεσπότην, ὡς ἀρχιερέα θεοῦ, ὡς διδάσκαλον εὐσεβείας. ὁ γὰρ αὐτοῦ ἀκούων, Χριστοῦ ἀκούει. *Constitutiones Apostolicae* 2.20, in *PG* 1:633.

67. πάντες τῷ ἐπισκόπῳ ἀκολουθεῖτε, ὡς Ἰησοῦς Χριστὸς τῷ πατρί, καὶ τῷ πρεσβυτερίῳ ὡς τοῖς ἀποστόλοις. Ignatius, *Epistola ad Smyrneos* 8.1, 9.1, in *PG* 5:949–52.

68. Source unidentified.

69. ὥσπερ οὖν ὁ κύριος ἄνευ τοῦ πατρὸς οὐδὲν ἐποίησεν, ἠνωμένος ὤν, οὔτε δι' ἑαυτοῦ, οὔτε διὰ τῶν ἀποστόλων· οὕτως μηδὲ ὑμεῖς ἄνευ τοῦ ἐπισκόπου καὶ τῶν πρεσβυτέρων μηδὲν πράσσετε. Ignatius, *Epistola ad Magnesios* 7.1, in *PG* 5:668.

THE OFFICE OF BISHOP IN THE EARLY CHRISTIAN CHURCH

sent through the world to teach the gospel.[70] "I am one with the bishop, the presbytery, and the deacons," says Ignatius. "With them I shall have my share in God."[71] "The presbyters are the true successors of the apostles," he explains.[72] "Give heed to the bishop that God may give heed to you."[73]

Here we have equivalents—but not in absolute kind or degree, but only in relative authority to each other. Would anyone maintain that the deacon is Christ on earth? He is merely like Christ for the sake of illustration in one respect. The presbyters are not apostles or successors to apostles; they are compared to a sanhedrin, a body assisting the Lord in his work. Deacons are compared, for example, to Christ, Aaron, the Holy Ghost, the apostles, and bishops. All are engaged in the same sacred calling, all hold offices of varying degree; but the fact that the work is all for the same purpose, that all priesthood functions at certain clearly marked levels, and that these levels resemble each other does not mean that these offices are all the same. It is necessary to insist upon this, since the claim that the bishop continues the apostolic office rests precisely on this argument of equivalence. Thus Batiffol notes that the church "is not a society in which all are equal, but one in which a divinely instituted power is perpetuated, some being invested with it to sanctify, teach, govern the other. The

---

70. ἐγὼ εἶπα· θεοί ἐστε καὶ υἱοὶ ὑψίστου πάντες . . . ὁ γὰρ ἐπίσκοπος προκαθεζέσθαι ὑμῶν ὡς θεοῦ ἀξίᾳ τετιμημένος, ἢ κρατεῖ τοῦ κλήρου καὶ τοῦ λαοῦ παντὸς ἄρχει. ὁ δὲ διάκονος τούτῳ παριστάσθω ὡς ὁ Χριστὸς τῷ πατρί. . . . ἡ δὲ διάκονος εἰς τύπον τοῦ ἁγίου πνεύματος τετιμήσθω ὑμῖν. . . . καὶ ὡς οὐκ ἔστιν εἰς τὸν Χριστὸν πιστεῦσαι ἄνευ τῆς τοῦ πνεύματος διδασκαλίας, οὕτως ἄνευ τῆς διακόνου μηδεμία προσίτω γυνὴ τῷ διακόνῳ ἢ τῷ ἐπισκόπῳ. οἵ τε πρεσβύτεροι εἰς τύπον ἡμῶν τῶν ἀποστόλων ὑμῖν νενομίσθωσαν. *Constitutiones Apostolicae* 2.26.4–7, in PG 1:668.

71. ἀντίψυχον ἐγὼ τῶν ὑποτασσομένων τῷ ἐπισκόπῳ, πρεσβυτέροις, διακόνοις· καὶ μετ' αὐτῶν μοι τὸ μέρος γένοιτο σχεῖν ἐν θεῷ. Ignatius, *Epistola ad Polycarpem* 6.1, in PG 5:724.

72. Source unidentified.

73. τῷ ἐπισκόπῳ προσέχετε, ἵνα καὶ ὁ θεὸς ὑμῖν. Ignatius, *Epistola ad Polycarpem* 6.1, in PG 5:724.

bishops, successors of the apostles, are thus not an office of ministry bestowed upon them by the faithful, but a *potestas* of divine right. Such is the principle of the hierarchy."[74] But aside from the fact that the perpetuation of the offices without the *potestas* is just what Tertullian objected to in the church of the third century,[75] Batiffol assumes that the mere statement of the proposition proves it: there was a hierarchy, and so it happens that bishops succeed apostles.

Higher priesthood of apostles. According to a letter attributed to Anacletus, there are two types of priesthood: (1) the Lord sent the apostles into the various provinces, but when their converts became too numerous to handle, (2) he then sent out the seventy-two disciples. "Now the bishops occupy the place of the Lord's apostles, while the presbyters occupy that of the seventy-two disciples."[76] They "hold the places [*locum tenent*]" once held by these, but it does not follow that their priesthood or authority is identical, but only that those earlier officers had been replaced by another kind. Note that Anacletus is here trying to explain how presbyter and bishop should have identical functions—the seventy-two simply took over the work of the apostles. But if the seventy-two were the true successors of the apostles, then the bishops must have succeeded them, and the presbyters, the followers of the seventy-two, must thereby be also the successors of the apostles. It is a very confusing attempt to explain something. After all, Ignatius did say just that. It was long maintained by many that *episcopus* and *presbyterus* held one and the same office, and the theory was that the president of the college of presbyters gradually became the bishop of the entire local

---

74. Source unidentified.

75. Tertullian, *De Pudicita* 21, in J.-P. Migne, ed., *Patrologiae Cursus Completus . . . Series Latina/Rom*, 221 vols. (Paris: Migne, 1844–64), 2:1077–80 (hereafter *PL*).

76. *Episcopi vero, domini apostolorum; presbyteri quoque, septuaginta duorum discipulorum locum tenent.* Anacletus, *Epistola* 3.1, in *PG* 2:812.

THE OFFICE OF BISHOP IN THE EARLY CHRISTIAN CHURCH 19

church.[77] Hatch points out that in the earliest churches only the bishop and deacons are mentioned, never the presbyters, indicating that the title of presbyter "had been for the time being shoved aside."[78] The reason for this, Hatch believed, was that the bishops and deacons were strictly functionaries, while the presbyters had more of a spiritual office but no part at all in *Kultus:* "They probably had no more than the place which the Jewish presbyters had in the synagogue—seats of honour and dignity, but no official part in the service."[79] Harnack seconded this episcopal-deaconal versus presbyterial distinction.[80] In the 1880s it was fashionable to believe that the episcopate and presbyterial offices were identical. Confusion of offices seems to be the rule, and nothing is easier than to designate any office bestowed by an apostle as "apostolic."

The discovery of the *Didache* in 1875 led Harnack to announce a realization which "was in opposition to everything that had ever been claimed before"—namely, that the primitive church was endowed not with one priesthood but with two.[81] Harnack pointed out what has since been universally accepted—the presence in the earliest church of traveling general authorities, an institution of great significance for the study of the existence of an original centralized church organization. These traveling agents, he noted, were not elected but were appointed to their office by "a mandate from God"; they were the apostles, prophets, and teachers, and they had, Harnack concluded, no administrative or judicial function.[82] The bishops and deacons, on the other

---

77. Acts 20:17, 28; Titus 1:7; Jerome, *Epistola* 146, in PL 22:1192–95.
78. Source unidentified.
79. Hatch, *Organization of the Early Christian Churches*, 78.
80. Adolf von Harnack, *Lehrbuch der Dogmengeschichte*, 5th ed. (Tübingen: Mohr, 1931), 1:237.
81. Source unidentified.
82. "... ein göttliches Mandat." Harnack, *Lehrbuch der Dogmengeschichte*, 1:236–37; see also *Die Lehre der Zwölf Apostel nebst Untersuchungen zur Ältesten Geschichte der Kirchenverfassung und des Kirchenrechts* (Leipzig: Hinrichs, 1884), 96, 103.

hand, had such functions, but they were exercised only in the local branches.[83] Having determined that administration was important in the early church and that general authorities were also important, Harnack left unanswered the question, Who would administer the whole church? It was the apostles, of course, but Harnack remained under the spell of Sohm's thesis that one could not function in a practical or regular way and still exercise spiritual powers.[84] That the Spirit is not directed or controlled does not mean that it cannot itself direct and control—that, we are told, is its specific function: the function of the Holy Ghost is to lead and direct in all things and not merely to give a vague emotional surge. If they operated wholly "in the Spirit," that is all the more reason for thinking the apostles were engaged in guiding and directing the affairs of the church among which they constantly traveled and not reason for denying them any official function at all. What we find in the *Didache* is, according to Harnack, "on the one side . . . the central ecclesiastical organization of those inspired teachers under the direction of the spirit, and on the other side the local organizations with their administrative officers." This is "the double organization of the primitive church."[85] It was soon pointed out that apostles also had function, while bishops, presbyters, and deacons were also expected to be full of the spirit; in other words, the division of church leadership positions into spiritual and nonspiritual offices was not valid. But this in no way challenges the existence of the double priesthood.

---

83. Harnack, *Lehrbuch der Dogmengeschichte*, 1:236; *Lehre der Zwölf Apostel*, 140–41.

84. Sohm, *Kirchenrecht*, 1:4.

85. "Auf der einen Seite steht also die gesamtkirchliche Organisation der charismatischen Lehrbegabten, auf der anderen die Gemeindeorganisation der Administrativbeamten. Das ist die berühmte Harnacksche Hypothese einer *doppelten Organisation* der Urkirche." Linton, *Das Problem der Urkirche*, 42, emphasis in original.

The Church of Jesus Christ of Latter-day Saints, claiming to have "the same organization that existed in the primitive church" (Article of Faith 6), has two priesthoods. One functions locally and the other administers the church as a whole; both are purely spiritual and there has never been any conflict between them. As in Harnack's system, "the basis of the entire system is the duality of the general church and the individual branches."[86] The latter, as we have noted, are organized on lines exactly similar to those of the church as a whole. So it was anciently, and that accounts for the ease with which the offices later became "identified" and also accounts for the possibility of claiming that the bishop was a successor to the apostle who ordained him—though the apostle might well outlive the bishop, and it was very common for bishops to hold their place only temporarily. Clement's first epistle does not say that a bishop is elected for life, even on good behavior, though the question asked had been exactly that. On the other hand, no one doubts that an apostle holds his office for life.

Unique apostolic gift. Though all officers of the church should be inspired, the great endowment of leadership is the prophetic gift. That was the great principle that set the Christians off from other religions. Justin Martyr, in defiance of modern Catholic teaching, says,

> Neither by nature nor by human intelligence is it possible for men to know great and divine matters, but by the gift that descends from above upon holy men, who do not need the learned arts, neither skills in controversy and debate, but rather to resign themselves to the power of the Holy Spirit, which if they are in tune will come down like a divine plectrum from heaven and play upon them

---

86. "Grundlegend blieb aber die Unterscheidung zwischen *zwei* Organisationen: der der Gesamtkirche und der der Einzelgemeinde." Linton, *Das Problem der Urkirche*, 42, emphasis in original.

as upon instruments, making use of righteous men and revealing to them the divine and heavenly gnosis.[87]

These men, unlike the philosophers, all tell the same story and all agree among themselves. Herein Christian leadership differed from that of other churches—it was led by prophets under direct, divine inspiration, whose wisdom was not the fruits of philosophy or training. In accusing the church of having lost the power while retaining the forms of godliness, Tertullian makes a sharp distinction between two clearly marked levels of religious operation: both are good and necessary, but the higher one has departed from the church. The higher type is apostolic and prophetic and its genius is power—*potestas*. Against this the present church, according to Tertullian, can only set up a succession of bishops with discipline, *officium*, in the place of *potestas*.[88] The old church had *imperium*—the authority to initiate organization, doctrine, etc.—while the new one had instead *ministerium*—a prescribed routine. The temple was the center of the old church, the synagogue the model of the new; the Spirit was the highest guide in the former, the scripture in the latter; *enthusiasmus* was the guiding principle of interpretation then, allegory now; revelation was the source of doctrine then, reason now; the gnosis, tongues, and prophecy have ceased as predicted, and in their place are left only faith, love, and hope; the high priest has departed, the bishop is

---

87. οὔτε γὰρ φύσει, οὔτε ἀνθρωπίνῃ ἐννοίᾳ οὕτω μεγάλα καὶ θεῖα γινώσκειν ἀνθρώποις δυνατόν, ἀλλὰ τῇ ἄνωθεν ἐπὶ τοὺς ἁγίους ἄνδρας τηνικαῦτα κατελθούσῃ δωρεᾷ, οἷς οὐ λόγων ἐδέησε τέχνης, οὐδὲ τοῦ ἐριστικῶς τι καὶ φιλονείκως εἰπεῖν, ἀλλὰ καθαροὺς ἑαυτοὺς τῇ τοῦ θείου Πνεύματος παρασχεῖν ἐνεργείᾳ, ἵν' αὐτὸ τὸ θεῖον ἐξ οὐρανοῦ κατιὸν πλῆκτρον, ὥσπερ ὀργάνῳ κιθάρας τινὸς ἢ λύρας, τοῖς δικαίοις ἀνδράσι χρώμενον, τὴν τῶν θείων ἡμῖν καὶ οὐρανίων ἀποκαλύψῃ γνῶσιν. Justin Martyr, *Cohortatio ad Graecos* 8, in PG 6:256–57.

88. Tertullian, *De Pudicitia* 21, in PL 2:1077–80.

THE OFFICE OF BISHOP IN THE EARLY CHRISTIAN CHURCH   23

in his place; the Holy Ghost has become an intellectual exercise; inspiration has yielded to tradition, oracles to councils. "To James the Just and to John and Peter, the Lord gave the gnosis after his resurrection," says Clement. "They gave it further to the other apostles, and the rest of the apostles in turn gave it to the seventy," but there is no account of its ever being passed on any further.[89] Why was it not handed to the bishops if they were to carry on the work?—that is what one would logically expect, as Irenaeus observed.[90] But could a bishop succeed an apostle?

When Bishops Became the Highest Officers in the Church

When it came about that the highest office in all the church was that of bishop, it was an absolute necessity to make the office the equivalent of the apostolate in order to avoid facing the terrible alternative of admitting that the apostolic power—the whole stay and support of the Church of Christ—had been withdrawn. If it had not been withdrawn, someone, of course, would have to have it, and who could that be but the one in highest authority, the bishop. Faced with this clear and desperate alternative, many simply said the bishops were the successors of the apostles and found there an end—this had to be because if they were not, the alternative was too dreadful to think of. Such is Batiffol's attitude. "The deacons should remember," wrote Cyprian, "that the apostles, that is to say, the bishops and those in charge, were chosen by the Lord, while the deacons were appointed by the apostles for themselves after the ascension of the Lord into heaven as ministers of the episcopate

---

89. Ἰακώβῳ τῷ Δικαίῳ καὶ Ἰωάννῃ καὶ Πέτρῳ μετὰ τὴν ἀνάστασιν παρέδωκε τὴν γνῶσιν ὁ Κύριος. οὗτοι τοῖς λοιποῖς ἀποστόλος παρέδωκαν. οἱ δὲ λοιποὶ ἀπόστολοι τοῖς ἑβδομήκοντα. Eusebius, *Historia Ecclesiastica* 2.1.4, in *PG* 20:136.

90. Irenaeus, *Contra Haereses* 4.33.7, in *PG* 7:1077–78.

and that of the church."⁹¹ This admission that the deacons, though ordained by apostles and therefore "apostolic," were actually of a lower order is significant. According to Clement of Alexandria, "The apostle Clement wrote the letter to the Corinthians."⁹² A note to this says that "apostolic men were sometimes called apostles by the ancient fathers."⁹³ This is a clear recognition on their part that the leaders of the church should be apostles, though they never come anywhere near proving that they were such. The normal "succession of the faith" among the fourth-century polemicists was patriarchs, prophets, apostles, and martyrs—none elective offices, as that of bishop always was. They are another sort of thing, the bearers of direct powers from the other world. If the apostles had departed, so had the prophets, and so the bishop naturally falls heir to their honor: "The bishops are the mouth of God," says the *Apostolic Constitutions*.⁹⁴ There are no more visitations of angels, so there is no other solution but that the bishop himself be God's second gift to the church—namely, the visitation of angels. A writing contemporary with this statement insists that the bishops are not merely successors to the apostles, but that they are apostles since they have inherited the power of baptizing and anointing. The great spiritual gifts of the ancients have also descended upon the bishops, with the power of loosening and binding that goes with them. Since the seventy were commonly regarded as taking over in place of the apostles, Hippolytus

---

91. *Meminisse autem diaconi debent quoniam apostolos, id est episcopos et praepositos Dominus elegit, diaconos autem, post ascensum Domini in caelos, apostoli sibi constituerunt episcopatus sui et Ecclesiae ministros.* Cyprian, *Epistola* 65.3, in *PL* 4:408.

92. ἐν τῇ πρὸς Κορινθίους ἐπιστολῇ ὁ ἀπόστολος Κλήμης. Clement of Alexandria, *Stromata* 4.17, in *PG* 8:1312.

93. Ἀπόστολος. *Superius dictum est, viros apostolicos nonnumquam apostolos ab antiquis Patribus appellatos fuisse.* PG 8:1312 n. 30.

94. στόμα θεοῦ εἶναι τοὺς ἐπισκόπους. *Constitutiones Apostolicae* 2.28.9, in *PG* 1:676.

THE OFFICE OF BISHOP IN THE EARLY CHRISTIAN CHURCH 25

lists the names of "the seventy apostles."[95] Though no proof is offered, this is a significant admission of a thing of which the fathers were well aware—that only an apostle could be the successor of an apostle and that the divine gifts could not be succeeded or replaced by anything—if they were to be handed down, it could only be the gifts themselves and not a substitute for them.

Local authority only. Bishops were not appointed or prepared to administer the affairs of the whole church since they were strictly local officers. We have noted Duchesne's perplexity at the absence of any machinery in Rome for the management of anything more than the local church there: the bishop of Rome was not set up to be a general authority.[96] "Follow ye all the bishop as Jesus Christ follows the Father," wrote Ignatius, "and follow the *presbyterium* as the apostles. . . . Wherever the bishop appears, there is the congregation, just as wherever Jesus Christ appears, there is the general [catholic] church."[97] The bishop is to the local church as no living officer is to the whole church. No one knows better than Ignatius that the general authorities have passed away—only Jesus Christ now presides over the whole church. "Shall I," writes the third bishop of Antioch after Peter, the head of the largest and, next to Jerusalem alone, the oldest church in Christendom, "reach such a pitch of presumption . . . as to issue orders to you as if I were an apostle?"[98] Plainly being "apostolic" did not give him the authority of an apostle.

---

95. Hippolytus, *De LXX Apostolis*, in *PG* 10:953–58.
96. Duchesne, *Origines du Culte Chrétien*, 15–16.
97. πάντες τῷ ἐπισκόπῳ ἀκολουθεῖτε, ὡς Ἰησοῦς Χριστὸς τῷ πατρί, καί τῷ πρεσβυτερίῳ ὡς τοῖς ἀποστόλοις . . . ὅπου ἂν φανῇ ὁ ἐπίσκοπος, ἐπεῖ τὸ πλῆθος ἔστω· ὥσπερ ὅπου ἂν ᾖ Χριστὸς Ἰησοῦς, ἐκεῖ ἡ καθολικὴ ἐκκλησία. Ignatius, *Epistola ad Smyrneos* 8.1–2, in *PG* 5:713.
98. ταῦτα οὐχ ὡς ἀπόστολος διατάσσομαι· τίς γάρ εἰμι ἐγώ ἢ τίς ὁ οἶκος τοῦ πατρός μου, ἵνα ἰσότιμον ἐμαυτὸν ἐκείνων εἴπω. Ignatius, *Epistola ad Philadelphenses* 4, in *PG* 5:828.

"It is impossible to dispute," wrote Jean Reville, "that the episcopate as represented in the Epistles of Ignatius is essentially a local function, the authority of which is limited to the community in which it was exercised. Never does Ignatius appeal to his title of bishop of Antioch to give more authority to his instructions."[99] This is the more remarkable since the whole subject of Ignatius's letters is episcopal authority. Certain churches are having trouble choosing and sustaining bishops, and Ignatius, appalled by the wild disorder and vicious atmosphere he finds in the churches everywhere, takes it upon himself to correct them. "Here we have a series of letters which are distinguished before all else by the ardor with which their author pleads the cause of the episcopate, demanding absolute submission of the faithful to their bishops: and the two main arguments, the two columns on which the very concept of the catholic episcopate itself has reposed from the beginning, do not appear!"[100] One of these columns is the axiom that the bishops were general authorities in the church, as they had to be if they were successors of the apostles. Yet Ignatius, searching desperately for a general authority to appeal to, finds none; he explicitly disclaims being one himself and says he speaks not because anyone has ordered or permitted him to, but simply because

---

99. "Il est impossible, du reste, de contester que l'épiscopat, tel que les Épîtres d'Ignace le représentent, est une fonction essentiellement locale et dont l'autorité est limitée à la communauté même où elle s'exerce. Nulle part Ignace ne se prévaut de son titre d'éveque d'Antioche pour donner plus d'autorité à ses enseignements." Jean Reville, "Études sur les Origines de l'Épiscopat: La Valeur du Témoignage d'Ignace d'Antioche," *Revue de l'Histoire des Religions* 21 (1890): 284.

100. "Voilà une série de lettres qui se distinguent surtout par l'ardeur avec laquelle leur auteur plaide la cause de l'épiscopat, réclame une soumission absolue des fidèles envers leurs évêques: et les deux arguments principaux, les deux colonnes sur lesquelles repose dès l'origine la notion même de l'épiscopat, catholique n'y figurent pas!" Reville, "Études sur les Origines de l'Épiscopat," 285.

his love will not let him hold his peace.¹⁰¹ "One cannot insist too much on this curious fact in the Ignatian literature . . . : the complete absence of any allusion to the apostolic nature of the episcopate, and to any justification of the episcopal power by the principle of apostolic succession."¹⁰² Could he have made such an appeal, Ignatius would have had the solution to his problems. But he will not make it, though he is perfectly aware of what a treasure it would be if he could only "give orders" like Peter and Paul: "They were apostles," he wrote to the Romans. "I am but a man."¹⁰³ Furthermore, Reville observes, "if the authority of the bishops had really been as well established as Ignatius wants it to be, it would not have been necessary to insist with such energy that people respect them."¹⁰⁴ No one viewed them with awe as apostolic officers in the end of the first century. Moreover there is in Ignatius "not yet the slightest trace of those conferences at which the bishops concerted, as in the second half of the second century. The bishop . . . not only does not yet have a sacerdotal character, but he does not even have the character of a general authority."¹⁰⁵

---

101. Ignatius, *Epistola ad Romanos* 4.3; 8–9, in *PG* 5:677, 680; *Epistola ad Trallianos* 3; 5–6, in *PG* 5:689, 693–96.

102. "On ne saurait trop insister sur ce trait si curieux de la littérature ignatienne . . . : l'absence complète de toute allusion à l'institution apostolique de l'épiscopat et de toute justification du pouvoir épiscopal par le principe de la succession apostolique." Reville, "Études sur les Origines de l'Épiscopat," 285.

103. ἐκεῖνοι ἀπόσολοι, ἐγὼ κατάκριτος. Ignatius, *Epistola ad Romanos* 4.3, in *PG* 5:689 (see also 5:808).

104. "Si l'autorité des évêques dans les communautés avait été réellement aussi bien établie que le demande Ignace, il n'aurait eu aucune raison d'insister avec autant d'énergie sur l'obligation d'une déférence respectueuse envers eux." Reville, "Études sur les Origines de l'Épiscopat," 287.

105. "On ne voit pas davantage une trace quelconque de réunions où les évêques se concertent, comme il y en aura dès la seconde moitié du IIe siécle. L'évêque . . . non seulement n'a pas encore de caractère sacerdotal, mais il n'a pas davantage le caractère catholique." Reville, "Études sur les Origines de l'Épiscopat," 285.

Bishops are not apostles. Exactly like Ignatius, Polycarp, writing to the churches, must confess that he is in no wise to be considered on a par with the apostles: "For neither I, nor any other such one, can come up to the wisdom of the blessed and glorious Paul. He, when among you, accurately and steadfastly taught the word of truth in the absence of those who were then alive. And when absent from you, he wrote you a letter ... which will build you up in that faith which has been given you."[106] Now this was written to the Philippians, and by all counts the letter to Philippi to which he refers is the weakest thing in the whole Bible—yet the most influential bishop of his day in the entire church, the man whose presence in Rome to settle the Easter controversy[107] was for Irenaeus the surest claim that that church had no apostolic guidance, thinks of his own authority as being infinitely below that of a brief and not very informative letter from a real apostle.

In pleading for episcopal authority, Clement preserves the same remarkable silence as Ignatius: he fails to mention any office of his own, to give any direct orders (he is much more apologetic than Ignatius in this), or to appeal to apostolicity in the office of the bishop, which might make the latter sacrosanct. He merely ventures as an opinion, and only because that opinion has been asked for, that there is nothing in the scriptures which says evil men should depose good, and so there is no reason for deposing a good bishop. But he is completely silent as to any principle of tenure, such

---

106. οὔτε γὰρ ἐγώ, οὔτε ἄλλος ὅμοιος ἐμοὶ δύναται κατακολουθῆσαι τῇ σοφίᾳ τοῦ μακαρίου καὶ ἐνδόξου Παύλου, ὃς γενόμενος ἐν ὑμῖν κατὰ πρόσωπον τῶν τότε ἀνθρώπων ἐδίδαξεν ἀκριβῶς καὶ βεβαίως τὸν περὶ ἀληθείας λόγον, ὃς καὶ ἀπὼν ὑμῖν ἔγραψεν ἐπιστολάς, εἰς ἃς ἐὰν ἐγκύπτητε, δυνηθήσεσθε οἰκοδομεῖσθαι εἰς τὴν δοθεῖσαν ὑμῖν πίστιν. Polycarp, *Epistola ad Philippenses* 3.2, in *PG* 5:1008.

107. The controversy concerned the designation of the appropriate date for Easter celebrations. *Catholic Encyclopedia* (New York: Appleton, 1909), 4:228.

THE OFFICE OF BISHOP IN THE EARLY CHRISTIAN CHURCH 29

as we find in the holy office of the apostles. "Christ came from God," writes Clement, "and the apostles from Christ." We wait for the next step, but it is not forthcoming. Clement, like Ignatius, resolutely refuses to say what in later ages would be so obvious as to be mechanical: "and the bishops from the apostles."[108] Instead, he makes a statement later that the apostles set up the bishops after the old Jewish pattern, and knowing that there would be trouble about this office of bishop, they passed an *epinome* (i.e., a bylaw or special order) arranging for worthy men to take over and worthy successors to follow—that is all.[109] The *epinome* puts everything on a level far below that of a general authority.

Consider here that all along the bishops and apostles existed side by side as contemporaries; we never hear of bishops traveling with apostles to be trained up as their successors, for the activities of the two were totally different. Very early orders penalize a bishop for leaving his city; a bishop could not travel, and an apostle, as an emissary, had to travel.[110] The fact that the two offices existed as full-time functions side by side for many years without overlap shows that each was doing its own work. Was the strenuous work of an apostle added to that of a bishop when the apostles fell asleep? "The apostles were a type, preserving the image of an archetype," says Chrysostom, but he does not carry it on to the bishops.[111] Since the bishops are shepherds and Christ is the Archshepherd, says the Catholic Schermann, their offices are analogous[112]—but so are they analogous with the

---

108. ὁ Χριστὸς οὖν ἀπὸ τοῦ θεοῦ [ἐξεπέμφθη], καὶ οἱ ἀπόστολοι ἀπὸ τοῦ Χριστοῦ. Clement, *Epistola Primera ad Corinthios* 42.2, in *PG* 1:292.
109. Clement, *Epistola Primera ad Corinthios* 44.1–2, in *PG* 1:295–96.
110. *127 Canons of the Apostles* 2.12, in François Nau and René Graffin, eds., *Patrologia Orientalis* (Paris: Librairie de Paris, Firmin-Didot, 1903–), 8:668–69 (hereafter *PO*).
111. ἄρα τύπος ἦσαν οἱ ἀπόστολοι, ἀρχέτυπόν τινα εἰκόνα διασώζοντες. John Chrysostom, *In Epistolam ad Philippenses* 3.12.3, in *PG* 62:273.
112. Schermann, *Die allgemeine Kirchenordnung*, 2:45.

kings of the East who often called themselves shepherds, and for that matter had the functions of real shepherds. Analogy is not enough, even if it has scriptural justification.

"All who were ordained to any office by the laying on of hands of an apostle formed the *episkope* [the body of overseers]," says Schermann, "and could therefore have the name of bishop."[113] "As long as the apostles lived, ... they personally performed the liturgical functions, founded Christian congregations, and set apart presbyters, who carried on their official functions there.... These local liturgists and officiants of the local churches were also called, according to their office, *episkopoi*."[114] This is the common and understandable but typically myopic view that an apostle could not ordain anyone to any office at all without giving him thereby apostolic authority!

Irenaeus makes much of the fact that the bishops were "instituted by the apostles in the various churches, where their successors have come down to our time."[115] Like the passage in Clement, this makes it clear that when successors are first mentioned they are not stated to be successors of the apostles, but only officials installed by apostles. "The tradition," says Irenaeus, "has been handed down from the apostles and preserved in the churches by successions of presbyters."[116] Tertullian, the greatest

---

113. "Alle ... von den Aposteln durch Handauflegung Bestellte teilten sich in die ἐπισκοπή und konnten daher den Namen ἐπίσκοπος haben." Schermann, *Die allgemeine Kirchenordnung*, 2:39.

114. "Solange die Apostel lebten ... die liturgischen Funktionen selbst ausgeübt und in den Städten, wo sie Christengemeinden gründeten, πρεσβύτεροι aufgestellt, welche ihr Amt dort weiterhin vertraten.... Diese ortsansässigen Liturgen und Vorsteher der Gemeinde wurden auch nach ihrem Amte ἐπίσκοποι benannt." Schermann, *Die allgemeine Kirchenordnung*, 2:38–39.

115. *Habemus annumerare eos qui ab apostolis instituti sunt episcopi, et successores eorum usque ad nos.* Irenaeus, *Contra Haereses* 3.2.2, in *PG* 7:848.

116. *Cum autem ad eam iterum traditionem, quae est ab apostolis, quae per successiones presbyterorum in Ecclesias custoditur, provocamus eos.* Irenaeus, *Contra Haereses* 2.2.2, in *PG* 7:847.

authority of the third century on the nature and institutions of the primitive church, was impatient with this loose equating of everything that came from the apostles with a full grant of apostolic power. The keys and the promise were given to Peter, he says, but to Peter only; there is not a word said to indicate that they were at a later date to be transferred to someone else. What good are your "successions?"[117] he asks: the real church is "the Spirit working through an inspired [*spiritalem*] man; the church is not a succession of bishops."[118]

Yet so important was it to tie up Peter somehow with the office of bishop that at an early date the attempt was producing a rich outpouring of contradictions and absurdities. We have seen the preposterous results of trying to make Peter both an active apostle and the bishop of Rome. Some people believe, says Chrysostom, that there must have been two Peters! The *Gospel of the Twelve Apostles* simply has Christ ordain Peter an archbishop, though such an office did not exist before the fourth century.[119] But what else could you do? According to the *Apostolic Constitutions,* when the church was being formally organized, Peter suggested first of all ordaining a bishop in the presence of all the apostles, including Paul and James, bishop of Jerusalem—pouring all their united authority into one vessel, and then doing homage to him.[120] Absurd it may sound, but is it not what the later Christian claim amounts to?

Seeing James as the Presiding Bishop of the Church

The mention of James the brother of the Lord—whose title Catholic writers usually put in quotation marks, controlling the texts to conform to their theories rather than correcting

---

117. Tertullian, *De Praescriptionibus* 32, in *PL* 2:52–54.
118. Tertullian, *De Pudicitia* 21, in *PL* 2:1077–80.
119. *Gospel of the Twelve Apostles*, in *PO* 2:147.
120. *Constitutiones Apostolicae* 8.4–5, in *PG* 1:1069–76.

those theories by the texts—reminds us of the unique and important position he held in the church. Here was a bishop who was actually a general authority. How does one account for that? According to the most respected authorities, one does not—James was a freak, a mistake, a flash in the pan. After all, he had no successors, did he, in his strange and exalted office? But then, neither did the apostles. How strange that all the general authorities should simply disappear—not only the traveling ones, but the sedentary ones as well. One of the earliest church writers, Hegesippus, quoted by Eusebius in *Historia Ecclesiastica* 2.23, says, "The brother of the Lord, James, took over the church along with [μετά + genitive] the apostles,"[121] which is true, since he was strictly contemporary with the apostles and did not succeed them but was killed before any of them. Yet Jerome translates this passage: *"suscepit ecclesiam Hierosolymorum post* [μετά + accusative] *apostolos frater Domini Jacobus"*[122]—which totally changes James's position, making him a successor to the apostles, whom he did not succeed at all. Yet such violence is necessary if we are to establish an apostolic succession through bishops.

Eusebius, seriously afflicted by doubts and misgivings as a result of his experiences at Nicaea, set himself to establishing official ties between his own church and the apostles. He did it, as Irenaeus had, by tracing lines of bishops. All Irenaeus wanted in his arguments with the heretics was to establish proof that certain doctrines went back to the apostles, so Eusebius is able to announce at the outset of his study: "I have not found until now a single writer on ecclesiastical affairs who has concerned himself with this question" of episcopal succession.[123] Setting about "to record the

---

121. διαδέχεται δὲ τὴν Ἐκκλησίαν μετὰ τῶν ἀποστόλων, ὁ ἀδελφὸς τοῦ Κυρίου Ἰάκωβος. Eusebius, *Historia Ecclesiastica* 2.23.4, in *PG* 20:197.
122. Jerome, *De Viris Illustribus* 2, in *PL* 23:639.
123. μηδένα πω εἰς δεῦρο τῶν ἐκκλησιαστικῶν συγγραφέων διέγνων περὶ τοῦτο τῆς γραφῆς σπουδὴν πεποιημένον τὸ μέρος. Eusebius, *Historia Ecclesiastica* 1.1.5, in *PG* 20:52.

THE OFFICE OF BISHOP IN THE EARLY CHRISTIAN CHURCH 33

lines of succession of the holy apostles . . . and those who led and presided in the most conspicuous positions in the church"[124]—i.e., looking for some succession to the apostles not in any particular office but assuming, for the sake of argument, that any important function in the church must be apostolic if it can be traced to an apostle as the "instigator"—Eusebius reviews the bishops lists of Jerusalem, Rome, Antioch, and Alexandria. These are mere samplings, chosen, he tells us, because of their relative importance, but only a few among many.[125] In exactly this sense Irenaeus cites Rome as one of many examples—a good example to use, he explains, because of its outstanding antiquity and leadership, but by no means the only one.[126] Addressing himself to his task, Eusebius quickly discovers that the documents are totally inadequate even in those great churches to prove direct derivation of office from the apostles: the beginnings of these churches, he finds, are a complete mystery. As to the apostles, "they are like men standing on the other side of a huge gulf, from whom we catch only a few faint syllables, vague, incoherent—snatched away by the wind."[127] What a powerful and significant image! It reminds one of Polycarp's equally grave and significant pronouncement: "In Asia the great lights went out."[128]

In the sixth book of Clement's lost *Institutions*, a work on the organization of the church, Eusebius found the famous announcement that Peter, James, and John did not dispute for first place, but made James the Just bishop of Jerusalem

---

124. τὰς τῶν ἱερῶν ἀποστόλων διαδοχάς . . . καὶ ὅσοι ταύτης διαπρεπῶς ἐν τοῖς μάλιστα ἐπισημοτάταις παροικίαις. Eusebius, *Historia Ecclesiastica* 1.1.1, in *PG* 20:48.
125. Eusebius, *Historia Ecclesiastica*, in *PG* 20. Jerusalem is discussed in 3.11, 4.5, 5.12; Rome in 5.6; Antioch in 3.22; and Alexandria in 3.21.
126. Irenaeus, *Contra Haereses* 3.3.3, in *PG* 7:849–50.
127. Source unidentified.
128. καὶ γὰρ κατὰ τὴν 'Ασίαν μεγάλα στοιχεῖα κεκοίμηται. Eusebius, *Historia Ecclesiastica* 5.24.2, in *PG* 20:493.

without debate.¹²⁹ Of what "first place" is he speaking? Can there possibly have been any such dispute or question among the three as to the presidency of the church? Of course not—the Lord had already settled that long before. There is no mention here of their disputing among themselves for any first place: "Peter and James and John, after the ascension of the Savior, as those set at the head by the Savior, did not set themselves to establishing their relative degrees of authority, but chose James the Just to be bishop of Jerusalem."¹³⁰ Here we are told that they were already the presidency and acted unitedly as such. They did not appoint James the Just to take over their office or be their successor—they all outlived him. Yet that is the absurd interpretation that is put on the passage to make it seem that a bishop is a successor to apostles. James, having received a high office, was still not president of the church—Peter, James, and John were. Here we have two supreme offices coexisting. How is that possible? Very easily—James was the presiding bishop of the church, not its president, for that was Peter.

Consider the history of the early church, writes Chrysostom, how "James the brother of the Lord was at that time overseer of [ἐπεσκόπευεν, oversaw] the church at Jerusalem in the beginning, and also presided over all the other faithful Jews. When Jews in Antioch also started to believe, because of the long distance from Jerusalem and the fact that some Gentiles there were also believing, Peter went and lived among them as a member of their race [*ethnikos*]."¹³¹ This is an attempt to explain how there could be two heads

---

129. Eusebius, *Historia Ecclesiastica* 2.1.3, in PG 20:136.

130. Πέτρον γάρ φήσιν καὶ Ἰακώβου καὶ Ἰωάννην μετὰ τὴν ἀνάληψιν τοῦ Σωτῆρος, ὡς ἂν καὶ ὑπὸ τοῦ Κυρίου προτετιμημένους, μὴ ἐπιδικάζεσθαι δόξας, ἀλλ' Ἰάκωβον τὸν Δίκαιον ἐπίσκοπον ἱεροσολύμην ἐλέσθαι. Eusebius, *Historia Ecclesiastica* 2.1.3, in PG 20:136.

131. Ἰάκωβος ὁ ἀδελφὸς τοῦ Κυρίου τὴν ἐκκλησίαν τότε ἐπεσκόπευεν ἐν ἀρχῇ, τὴν ἐν Ἱεροσολύμοις, καὶ τῶν ἐξ Ἰουδαίων πιστευσάντων προει-

of the church, but Chrysostom cannot claim what would appear to be a simple and logical explanation, that James presided over the Jewish element in the church while Peter took care of the Gentiles, for that was simply not so, Peter himself "representing the Jewish element." Chrysostom himself gives us the clue to the answer when he describes James's functions as those of a bishop—but a presiding bishop, indeed, one who "looked after the affairs" not only of his city, but of all of them. He was, as is well known, not a traveling authority like the apostles and not a missionary. He "held the fort," so to speak, in Jerusalem and managed the general offices. To him the apostles sent in written reports. To him, as a bishop, Clement must report his doings and his pseudo-claims to the presidency; at general conferences it was James who acted as master of ceremonies, as it was James who kept the records—all for the sake of order and regularity.

Since this office of presiding bishop of the church disappeared as completely as that of apostle and of the first presidency, it is not surprising that students of succeeding ages have all been perplexed by it and thought it a freak, a mistake, a fifth wheel—with Peter, James, and John alive and well, why should they choose yet another chief in the church? Not to supplant them certainly—the nature of the work for which the Master had chosen them from the beginning had not changed and they had no intention of turning over that work to another—but to preside along with them over the lower priesthood.

We have seen that the discovery of two priesthoods in the ancient church came as a complete surprise when it was announced in the mid-1880s. The implications of the discovery

---

στήκει πάντων. συνέβαινε δὲ εἶναι καὶ ἐν Ἀντιοχείᾳ Ἰουδαίους, οἵτινες πιστεύσαντες τῷ Χριστῷ, διὰ τὸ τῶν Ἱεροσολύμων εἶναι πόρρω, καὶ πολλοὺς ὁρᾶν τοὺς ἐξ ἐθνῶν πεπιστευκότας ἀδεῶς. . . . κατελθὼν τοίνυν ὁ Πέτρος . . . ἐθνικῶς ἔζη λοιπόν. John Chrysostom, *In Illud, in Faciem Ei Restiti* 14, in *PG* 51:382–83.

have not yet been fully realized since it requires a complete readjustment of our whole concept of the organization of the early church, an adjustment which established churches are, of course, extremely reluctant to make. But once that necessary readjustment is made in the light of the discoveries of recent years, the office of James at last makes perfectly good sense. He presided over the lower priesthood—the priesthood of Aaron.

The Bishop as an Office in the Lower Priesthood

After his resurrection, according to one of the oldest fragments, Christ gave something very special, something the Jews did not have, to Peter, James, and John, and they in turn transmitted it to the rest of the apostles, who transmitted it to the seventy[132]—but there is no mention of its getting any further than that. Where do the bishops come in? Their office was not something brought to earth first by the Lord—the Jews already had it as literal descendants of Aaron. The oldest mention of the episcopal offices states explicitly that this was no new thing but was had among the Jews: "The apostles have preached the gospel to us by command of the Lord Jesus Christ, Jesus Christ by command of God. Christ was therefore sent forth by God, and the apostles from Christ."[133] At this point one naturally expects the next link in the chain, for some claim that this letter is being written by the bishop of Rome specifically to assert his primacy in the rule of the church—somehow he forgets to mention this, the whole point of his letter, and goes on, without mentioning any central directive office in the church. "Preaching through the countries and cities,

---

132. Eusebius, *Historia Ecclesiastica* 2.1.4, in *PG* 20:136.

133. οἱ ἀπόστολοι ἡμῖν εὐηγγελίσθησαν ἀπὸ τοῦ Κυρίου Ἰησοῦ Χριστοῦ, Ἰησοῦς ὁ Χριστὸς ἀπὸ τοῦ θεοῦ ἐξεπέμφθη. ὁ Χριστὸς οὖν ἀπὸ τοῦ θεοῦ, καὶ οἱ ἀπόστολοι ἀπὸ τοῦ Χριστοῦ. Clement, *Epistola Primera ad Corinthios* 42.1–2, in *PG* 1:293.

THE OFFICE OF BISHOP IN THE EARLY CHRISTIAN CHURCH 37

they appointed the firstfruits, having tested them in the spirit, to be the *episkopoi* and helpers [*diakonoi*] of those who should later believe."[134] Nothing at all is said about there being apostles in office or function or in directing the affairs of the church—they are the local overseers to stay on the spot and take general charge. "There was nothing new in that," Clement continues. "From of old it had been written of bishops and deacons, for somewhere the scripture saith: I shall establish their bishops [LXX *episkopoi, pequadathek*] in righteousness and their deacons [LXX *diakonoi, nogeshek*] in faith [Isaiah 60:17]."[135] This shows that the episcopal office is a continuation of a Jewish institution, and there is much to bear that proposition out.

The upstart sects that claimed to preserve the primitive church intact and attempted without authorization to reproduce its powers, gifts, and offices did not fail to note that the office of bishop could not be the highest office in the true church—and the great and learned Tertullian was convinced of that also,[136] to the point of joining one of those sects. One of their most powerful arguments against the main church was that it no longer had any offices higher than bishop. "Among us," wrote Jerome, "the bishops hold the place of the apostles, but they put the bishop in third place."[137] Yet Jerome recognized their doctrines and practices as thoroughly orthodox save on that one point—they insist

---

134. κατὰ χώρας οὖν καὶ πόλεις κηρύσσοντες καθίστανον τὰς ἀπαρχὰς αὐτῶν, δοκιμάσαντες τῷ πνεύματι, εἰς ἐπισκόπους καὶ διακόνους τῶν μελλόντων πιστεύειν. Clement, *Epistola Primera ad Corinthios* 42.4, in *PG* 1:292–93.

135. καὶ τοῦτο οὐ καινῶς, ἐκ γὰρ δὴ πολλῶν χρόνων ἐγέγραπτο περὶ ἐπισκόπων καὶ διακόνων· Καταστήσω τοὺς ἐπισκόπους αὐτῶν ἐν δικαιοσύνῃ καὶ τοὺς διακόνους αὐτῶν ἐν πίστει. Clement, *Epistola Primera ad Corinthios* 42.5, in *PG* 1:293.

136. Tertullian, *De Pudicitia* 21, in *PL* 2:1077–80.

137. Apud nos apostolorum locum episcopi tenent; apud eos episcopus tertius est. Jerome, *Epistola* 41.3, in *PL* 22:476.

on prophecy and recognize spiritual offices higher than those of a bishop.[138] Some of those revivalist groups went so far in imitating the early church as to have twelve apostles. Such bold but unauthorized claims met everywhere with enthusiastic reception, indicating a general awareness that something was lacking in the main church. This feeling of loss and dissatisfaction expressed itself in many ways.

When the historical approach to the problem of the organization of the early church supplanted the conventional dogmatic approach in the 1880s, it became apparent, says Linton, "that the episcopate is not a continuation of the apostolate,"[139] and this led to all sorts of theorizing and speculation. Though the theories have changed through the centuries, the basic premise remains unshaken. While it is obvious enough that the apostles appointed bishops and presbyters, Lake observed—and who would doubt it?—"it is not less clear that the functions of an apostle were quite different from those of a presbyter or bishop, and that functionally the apostle is akin to the prophet, not to the presbyter."[140] This is proven, Lake points out, by the *Didache*.[141] Strange that one of the most celebrated and devout scholars of the day could have announced as late as 1911 as a notable contribution to knowledge a thing that the Latter-day Saints had known for generations: that the functions of bishops and priests are quite different from those of prophets and apostles, and the fact that the former were ordained to their offices by the latter does not make their office "apostolic." "If we ask who were the most important people in the Christian church in the first generation," Lake writes further, "the answer undoubtedly is, the Apostles and Prophets. If we go on farther, and ask who was the most important person in

---

138. Jerome, *Epistola* 41, in *PL* 22:474–76.
139. Source unidentified.
140. Lake, "Christian Life in Rome," 38.
141. Ibid., 38–39.

THE OFFICE OF BISHOP IN THE EARLY CHRISTIAN CHURCH 39

the church at Rome at the end of the second century [not, observe, in the whole church], the answer unquestionably is that it was the Bishop. But the difficulty comes when we inquire how this change took place; for that is precisely the problem to which no undoubted or unquestionable answer can be given."[142]

The great Eduard Schwartz designates the theory of the "monarchical episcopate as bearer of the apostolic succession" as a "legal fiction," the true nature of which is apparent in many things.[143] In the earliest church, says Theodor Brandt in a recent study, "'Apostolic' and 'Diakonat' had as yet nothing to do with the official degrees of the later hierarchy," which were another thing entirely.[144] "The bishops recognized the superior authority of the apostles," wrote the Catholic Duchesne, ". . . [as] founders and spiritual masters . . . of all the Christian societies in general,"—i.e., over against the bishops he sets their superiors—the general authorities. "As these great leaders disappear," Duchesne continues, "one sees appearing a definitive hierarchy," in other words, the local organization of bishop, priest, and deacon.[145] This is the old Jewish system, he says, which was already on the ground and is a natural hierarchy for any such organization to fall into.[146] But these offices do not appear to take over

---

142. Ibid., 37.
143. "[Die Theorie] der monarchisch gewordene Episkopat als Träger der apostolischen Sukzession; es kam die Rechtsfiktion auf." Eduard Schwartz, *Kaiser Constantin und die Christliche Kirche* (Stuttgart: Teubner, 1969), 24.
144. "Apostolat und Diakonat haben noch nichts mit der Rangordnung der späteren Hierarchie zu tun." Theodor Brandt, Kirche im Wandel der Zeit (Wuppertal: Brockhaus, 1977), 2:37.
145. "[Les] évêques . . . reconnaissent l'autorité supérieure des apôtres . . . fondateurs et maîtres spirituals . . . de toutes les chrétienés en general. . . . A mesure que disparaissent ces grands chefs, on voit apparaître la hiérarchie definitive." Duchesne, *Origines du Culte Chrétien*, 8.
146. Duchesne, *Origines du Culte Chrétien*, 7–9.

in place of the general authorities—they had been there all along doing a full-time job with no thought of qualifying for apostolic functions. How can Duchesne say they appear when they were there already? Because he must say it if there are to be any successors to the apostles. But who says there have to be? What Duchesne should have been able to write, had the church continued and had the apostasy not come, as they themselves announce, is: "As these leaders disappear, other such leaders took their place as happened anciently with the election of Matthew." But instead, all he can point to is that when the great lights went out there were lesser lights still shining—but that has been the case in every dispensation of the gospel.

As we have seen, even among this lower priesthood there was the greatest confusion when the apostles departed, as the writings of all the apostolic fathers attest. We have noted the inextricable confusion of the office of presbyter with that of bishop to the degree that many scholars have thought the two offices to be one and the same. In Alexandria, one of the very oldest Christian foundations, "all churches were under one bishop, but each presbyter [priest] had his own church in which to assemble his own people."[147] As late as A.D. 300 the Council of Elvira declares that "If a deacon who is ruling [*regens*] a congregation baptizes people without a bishop or a priest, the bishop must pronounce a blessing over those thus baptized to make it valid, though if he fails to do so and those baptized should die, they will not go to hell as if unbaptized."[148] The bishop should be present at ordinances, Ignatius wrote, so that everything may be done "firmly

---

147. Source unidentified.
148. *Si quis diaconus regens plebem sine episcopo vel presbytero aliquos baptizaverit, episcopus eos per benedictionem perficere debebit; quod si ante de saeculo recesserint, sub fide qua quis credidit poterit esse justus.* Council of Elvira, Canon 77, in Karl Joseph von Hefele, *Histoire des Conciles d'Après les Documents Originaux,* trans. a Benedictine monk of St. Michael's Abbey in Farnborough, 10 vols. (Paris: Letouzey et Ané, 1907), 1:261–62.

and securely."¹⁴⁹ Such instances illustrate great vagueness and doubt on matters concerning the authority of the lower priesthood even when functioning in its proper field. This complete confusion—not only among the various claims and theories tying the offices of bishop, priest, and deacon to those of apostle, prophet, and seventy, but also among the various officers of the local churches as to their office and authority, and finally among the bishops for a claim to be general authorities—can only have come about if and when the lower priesthood was also lost to men. After all, James the Just and his mysterious office of presiding bishop disappeared just as completely and suddenly as did the apostles—and none was left in his place. It is true that thousands of public and religious officials in the city of Jerusalem survived him, but that does not mean that they succeeded him.

Batiffol has stoutly argued the descent from the apostles of a single, unchanging, unique episcopal authority. He grandly announces that in the ancient church priests could not have cathedras: "The *cathedra* [bishop's chair, seat, "see"] is the exclusive *insignium* of the bishops—the symbol of his authority, the symbol of the unity of the church."¹⁵⁰ Yet Hugo Koch points to Constantine's references to presbyters' thrones in 314 and cites many ancient texts to show that priests as well as bishops have chairs or thrones.¹⁵¹ Duchesne discovered that for a long time there was only one bishop in all of Gaul—the other churches were governed by other officers.¹⁵²

---

149. ἵνα ἀσφαλὲς ᾖ καὶ βέβαιον πᾶν ὃ πράσσεται. Ignatius, *Epistola ad Smyrneos* 8.2, in *PG* 5:713 (see 5:852).

150. "Mais la *cathedra* est l'insigne exclusif de l'évêque, le symbole de son autorité, le symbole de l'unité de l'Église." Pierre Batiffol, *Cathedra Petri: Études d'Histoire ancienne de l'Église* (Paris: de la Tour Maubourg, 1938), 108.

151. Hugo Koch, "Bischofsstuhl und Priesterstühle zu Canon 58 von Elvira," *Zeitschrift für Kirchengeschichte* 7 (1925): 172–75.

152. Louis Duchesne, *Fastes Épiscopaux de l'Ancienne Gaule*, 2nd ed. (Paris: Fontemoing, 1907), 1:39–40.

Dependence on Jewish Sources for Church Practices Relevant to the Bishop

The famous dictum of Tertullian that the church grew up "in the shadow of the synagogue"[153] is the point of departure for much discussion and investigation. It is the key to the understanding of conventional Christianity. There is nothing mysterious in the survival and integrity of the local branches after the passing of the apostles: they had been organized around the synagogues from the first. In the synagogue they had a pattern both for local organization and for "spiritual Israel." The word *church* itself, as has often been noted, is the equivalent of the Hebrew *qāhāl,* the congregation of all Israel, of which the meetings in the synagogue were merely a scale-model reproduction. The synagogues scattered throughout the world were a result of the Diaspora—they did not represent the real assemblies of Israel, which had to take place at the temple in Jerusalem and had to embrace the entire holy nation, but they were merely regarded as temporary expedients. To this idea, Lietzmann attributes the singular practice of the early Christians of referring to their local churches as temporary foundations on the earth: "The church of God, which is temporarily visiting [*zu Gaste*] in Rome, greets the church of God, which is temporarily visiting in Corinth," which means, explains Lietzmann, "the church is on this earth only as a temporary guest—it is a stranger and a pilgrim."[154]

"The Christian church took from the Jews two basic ideas," according to Schwartz: "(1) that of the people of God, and (2) that of the spiritual gifts." The "people of God" are

---

153. . . . sub umbraculo insignissimae religionis. Tertullian, *Apologeticus Adversus Gentes pro Christianis* 21, in *PL* 1:450. See Hugh Nibley, *The World and the Prophets* (Salt Lake City: Deseret Book and FARMS, 1987), 221.

154. "Die Kirche Gottes, die im Rom zu Gaste ist, grüßt die Kirche Gottes, die in Korinth zu Gaste ist. . . . Und sie ist auf Erden nur zu Gaste, ist ein Fremdling." Lietzmann, *Geschichte der Alten Kirche,* 2:42.

identical with the Christian idea of the church: "From the very first beginnings the gospel is preached and believed not by a sum total of individuals, but by an organized community [*Gemeinschaft*], originally constituted by the Resurrected One through direct revelation, and later by the belief that the Spirit of the Lord continued to operate in its midst."[155] This sort of thing, Schwartz believes, is part of an unbroken tradition carried forth among the Jews,[156] though not by all the Jews. Official Jewry did not like it, but as we have seen there were at all times numbers of ardent Jews who thought in messianic terms and whose language was that of the New Testament.

There has been much discussion as to whether the apostolate was originally a Jewish institution. In every age there have been men "sent" from God—that is, apostles, in the literal sense of the word; and by the very nature of their calling, they had to be prophets. The Twelve certainly come under this category, though scholars have been troubled because they were not exactly like other prophets in all respects but were very special missionaries, special witnesses with a special assignment. Should we look for fraud and imitation if they resemble the ancient prophets in so many things? Of course not. The Lord himself describes the sending of prophets from time to time into the vineyard, and among them he includes himself—another one sent from the presence of the Lord of the vineyard—but the fact that he places himself in the category along with other workers

---

155. "Es sind zwei aus dem Judentum übernommene Glaubensgedanken, der des Volk Gottes und der des geistlichen Charisma. . . . Vom ersten Anfang wird dies Evangelium nicht von einer Summe von Individuen gepredigt und geglaubt, sondern von einer Gemeinschaft, die ursprünglich durch die direkte Offenbarung des Auferstandenen, dann durch den Glauben, daß der Geist des Herrn in ihr fortlebt, konstituiert wird." Schwartz, *Kaiser Constantin und die Christliche Kirche*, 17.

156. Schwartz, *Kaiser Constantin und die Christliche Kirche*, 18.

sent into the vineyard in no wise precludes his describing himself as a unique and special representative.

The finding of the Dead Sea Scrolls makes us less and less surprised at the close resemblance between the church Jesus founded and the sort of thing that was to be found among faithful Jews of the time: the one was the realization of what the others merely anticipated. At all times the churchmen had sought to establish ties between the church and the prophets, patriarchs, and apostles of old—and always they have had to fall back on sentimental abstractions and allegorical extravagances. This has been annoying and unsatisfying, and the fathers have not been able to leave the mysteries of royal priesthood and Melchizedek alone. "The church receives royal power from Christ in two ways," according to St. Ephraim, who is typical in his speculation: "Through David, who was an eternal divine king—it receives the priestly power through him directly as high priest." And how does the church get it? "Through the ordination of James, called the brother of the Lord and apostle, the first bishop and a natural son of Joseph, and consequently a legitimate brother of the Lord. . . . This James was of the line of David; he was a Jewish high priest, and Eusebius tells us much about him."[157] Long out of touch with ancient sources and even traditions, Ephraim is trying to make out a case, and he is hopelessly confused: he is typical.

The once-popular Hellenistic theory of the independent origin of the liturgy, organization, and missionaries of the separate Christian churches has now been left behind in favor of viewing "the organization of the primitive church as an extension of the pattern of salvation laid down in the Old Testament."[158] The Dead Sea Scrolls and the Damascus fragment have borne out this viewpoint. In a study of these, J. L. Teicher has recently suggested a reconstruction of events:

---

157. Source unidentified.
158. Source unidentified.

> After the martyrdom of James in 67 and shortly before the fall of Jerusalem in 70 C.E., the leaders of the Hebrew Christians in Jerusalem received by divine revelation a warning of the imminent catastrophe and escaped to Pella. Soon after the fall of the city an electoral assembly, composed of the *desposynoi* [Jesus' blood relations] and apostles and disciples of Jesus, met in Pella and chose a successor to James, Symeon son of Clopas and cousin of Jesus.... Symeon's election was contested and his success in face of the stronger rights of Jesus' closer relative—since it is generally agreed that the rule in the early church was "monarchical"—must be regarded as the ... sign of victory of the Pauline trend in the Church.... The secession of the Hebrew Christians from the Church began after the election of Symeon.[159]

These Jewish Christians, Teicher suggests, "organised themselves as a separate Jewish Christian sect in the Syrian desert, probably adopting as a model ... certain Essene institutions." The leaders of this movement were "sons or grandsons of Jude."[160] On the other hand, Ethelbert Stauffer says that Simeon (Symeon) was chosen as "the only living relative of the Lord who had seen Christ in a special revelation" and thus breaks down Teicher's threadbare explanation of all oddities and discrepancies in the ancient church by appeal to "Pauline Christianity."[161] Stauffer notes that a successor to James was actually ordained and that the whole thing was done on the ancient Jewish pattern.[162] In the roll discovered at Jericho he finds the title of bishop as an official Jewish religious office.[163] The word *didache* is also found in pre-Christian use with exactly the meaning it later had in the church, as is the word *paroikia*,

---

159. J. L. Teicher, "The Damascus Fragments and the Origin of the Jewish Christian Sect," *Journal of Jewish Studies* 2/3 (1951): 140.

160. Ibid.

161. "Der einzige noch lebende Herren verwandte, der sich auf eine Sonderchristophanie berufen kann." Ethelbert Stauffer, "Zum Kalifat des Jakobus," *Zeitschrift für Religions- und Geistesgeschichte* 4/3 (1952): 212.

162. Ibid., 208.

163. Ibid., 206.

"sojourn," which was used to describe the temporary nature of the local religious communities. Thus new words are being added to the already large vocabulary of standard terms that are characteristically Christian, yet have their origin among the local communities of the Jewish Diaspora.

Stauffer emphasized that James was the most important man in Jerusalem in A.D. 62 and that Simeon had that distinction after James's martyrdom.[164] But he does not offer a word as to either running any kind of competition to the apostles, even though by all later calculations the apostles must certainly have bestowed their office on James when they made him presiding bishop. Between bishop and apostle there is plainly no overlapping, no confusion. Stauffer notes in all the earliest records of episcopal succession the operation of the old Jewish laws and customs, which allowed the whole thing to be kept as much as possible within a family. The Jews, he notes, kept careful genealogies and followed "the high-priestly rule of succession," which meant that all their priesthood should be traced back to Aaron. This is the rule for bishops, Stauffer tells us, and it is in marked contrast to the succession of apostles—special witnesses chosen by the Lord himself.[165]

This close tie-in of the office of bishop with the office and blood of Aaron was a permanent heritage in the church—vague and confused as the traditions all became, it nevertheless keeps turning up in every age. "Everyone must confine himself to his own office," says the *127 Canons of the Apostles,* a work discovered in the early twentieth century, in a passage complaining that the office of high priest is not being taken seriously in the church:

> Those who make up their own rules are opposing Christ, the Bishop of All Creatures, the Son of God the Great High Priest Jesus. By Moses were established the high priests,

---

164. Ibid., 214.
165. "Das hohepriesterliche Sukzessionsprinzip." Ibid., 197–98, 207.

priests, and Levites; by the Saviour were established the Twelve Apostles and by the apostles we, Clement and James, were instituted, along with others too numerous to mention. Christ is the first true, only sovereign, priest; after his ascension we established the bishops, priests, and deacons to the number of seven.[166]

All the Clementine writings, those closest to Peter, see in the Old Testament the norms and patterns for the offices of bishop and below. According to the *Apostolic Constitutions*, a bishop should hear charges, judge crimes, and assign penalties following the Jewish pattern.[167] Those who preside in the churches should be supported financially by the membership "as the priests, Levites, presidents, and officiants of God, as prescribed in Numbers 18:1–8. . . . Formerly," this passage notes, "the congregation [*laos*, laity] were called the people of God and a holy nation."[168] They are no longer called that, but nonetheless the catholic church is now the people of the Decalogue, the chosen people, etc.[169] "[The bishops] are now your high priests, and your priests are the elders; and your Levites are now deacons, and your readers, cantors, and doorkeepers are your deaconesses and widows and virgins and orphans."[170] This seems rather confusing, but the thing to note is the strict adherence to the imitation of the Aaronic priesthood.

The *Apostolic Constitutions* continues: the Old Testament tabernacle is the church. "Therefore you who are our bishops

---

166. *127 Canons of the Apostles* 1.17, in *PO* 8:661.
167. *Constitutiones Apostolicae* 2.16.1–4, in *PG* 1:625–28; Numbers 12:14.
168. ἅτε ἱερεῖς, λευίτας, προέδρους, λειτουργοὺς θεοῦ, καθὼς ἐν βίβλῳ τῶν ᾿Αριθμῶν γέγραπται περὶ τῶν ἱερέων . . . καὶ γὰρ ὁ λαὸς πρότερον θεοῦ λαὸς καὶ ἔθνος ἅγιον ὠνομάζετο. *Constitutiones Apostolicae* 2.25–2.26.1, in *PG* 1:664.
169. *Constitutiones Apostolicae* 2.25, in *PG* 1:664–65.
170. οὗτοι γὰρ εἰσιν ὑμῶν οἱ ἀρχιερεῖς· οἱ δὲ ἱερεῖς ὑμῶν, οἱ πρεσβύτεροι· καὶ οἱ λευῖται ὑμῶν, οἱ νῦν διάκονοι, καὶ οἱ ἀναγινώσκοντες ὑμῖν, καὶ οἱ ᾠδοί, καὶ οἱ πυλωροί, αἱ διάκονοι ὑμῶν, καὶ χῆραι, καὶ αἱ παρθένοι, καὶ οἱ ὀρφανοὶ ὑμῶν. *Constitutiones Apostolicae* 2.25.18, in *PG* 1:665.

today be to your people priests, Levites—of the ark, of the holy catholic church, standing at the altar and bringing the intellectual and bloodless sacrifices through Jesus the Great High Priest. Be ye prophets, princes, leaders, kings, mediators between God and the faithful, knowers of the scriptures, voices of God, witnesses of his will, bearing the sins of all and answering for all."[171] And to the people: "As the Jews could not offer without Levites, so you may do nothing without the bishop. Anything done without that office is void, as the doings of Saul were without the approval of Samuel. Christ without the Father cannot glorify himself. . . . It is fitting for the bishop to bring the sacrifice as the high priest, whether by themselves or by the deacons."[172]

As to the ordination of a deaconess, "Let the bishop anoint her head with oil, in the manner in which the priests and kings of old were anointed."[173] That, in view of the fact that the deaconess holds no office and no authority at all! It is all a type and a pattern: "The deacons must refer everything to the bishop as Christ does to God; but such things as the

---

171. ὑμεῖς οὖν σήμερον, ὦ ἐπίσκοποι, ἐστὲ τῷ λαῷ ὑμῶν ἱερεῖς λευῖται, οἱ λειτουργοῦντες τῇ ἱερᾷ σκηνῇ, τῇ ἁγίᾳ καθολικῇ ἐκκλησίᾳ, καὶ παρεστῶτες τῷ θυσιαστηρίῳ κυρίου τοῦ θεοῦ ἡμῶν καὶ προσάγοντες αὐτῷ τὰς λογικὰς καὶ ἀναιμάκτους θυσίας διὰ Ἰησοῦ τοῦ μεγάλου ἀρχιερέως· ὑμεῖς τοῖς ἐν ὑμῖν λαϊκοῖς ἐστε προφῆται, ἄρχοντες καὶ ἡγούμενοι καὶ βασιλεῖς, οἱ μεσῖται θεοῦ καὶ τῶν πιστῶν αὐτοῦ, οἱ δοχεῖς τοῦ λόγου καὶ ἀγγελτῆρες, οἱ γνῶσται τῶν γραφῶν καὶ φθόγγοι τοῦ θεοῦ καὶ μάρτυρες τοῦ θελήματος αὐτοῦ, οἱ πάντων τὰς ἁμαρτίας βαστάζοντες καὶ περὶ πάντων ἀπολογούμενοι. *Constitutiones Apostolicae* 2.25.7, in *PG* 1:661.

172. ὡς οὖν οὐκ ἦν ἐξὸν ἀλλογενῆ, μὴ ὄντα λευίτην, προσενέγκαι τι ἢ προσελθεῖν εἰς τὸ θυσιαστήριον ἄνευ τοῦ ἱερέως, οὕτως καὶ ὑμεῖς ἄνευ τοῦ ἐπισκόπου μηδὲν ποιεῖτε. εἰ δέ τις ἄνευ τοῦ ἐπισκόπου ποιεῖ τι, εἰς μάτην ποιεῖ αὐτό· . . . ὡς γὰρ ὁ Σαοὺλ ἄνευ τοῦ Σαμουὴλ προσενέγκας ἤκουσεν. . . . εἰ οὖν ἄνευ τοῦ πατρὸς ὁ Χριστὸς οὐ δοξάζει ἑαυτόν. . . . προσήκει οὖν καὶ ὑμᾶς, ἀδελφοί, τὰς θυσίας ὑμῶν ἤτοι προσφορὰς τῷ ἐπισκόπῳ προσφέρειν ὡς ἐρχιερεῖ, ἢ δι' ἑαυτῶν ἢ διὰ τῶν διακόνων. *Constitutiones Apostolicae* 2.27.1–3; 2.27.5–6, in *PG* 1:669–72.

173. τὴν κεφαλὴν αὐτῆς χρίσει ὁ ἐπίσκοπος, ὃν τρόπον οἱ ἱερεῖς καὶ οἱ βασιλεῖς τὸ πρότερον ἐχρίοντο. *Constitutiones Apostolicae* 3.15.3, in *PG* 1:797.

THE OFFICE OF BISHOP IN THE EARLY CHRISTIAN CHURCH 49

deacons can manage themselves, having received authority from the bishop, as the Lord did from the Father: public administration and relief."[174] All rules of marriage and sex life are cited from the Jewish law.

The ordination prayer for bishops is significant: After an invocation following the Old Testament pattern comes the prayer: "Give in thy name, O God who is known in the heart, to this thy servant, whom I have chosen for bishop that he may blamelessly ... care for the flock. ... Give to him, all ruling Lord, through thy Christ, the participation in the Holy Spirit; that he may have authority to [bind and] loose ... according to the authority which thou gavest to thine apostles."[175] A letter (falsely) attributed to Anacletus says that a bishop must be anointed "after the [Old Testament] example of the prophets and kings; ... the invisible virtue of the Holy Ghost is mixed in the holy chrism. James the brother of the Lord was ordained bishop of Jerusalem by Peter, James, and John at Jerusalem; thereby, as they bestowed ordinations upon his successors with the approval of all others present, similarly he was ordained a bishop.... It follows that those who hold the highest priesthood, i.e., bishops, are to be judged by God and not by men."[176] "If the sons of Aaron represent the presbyters in their

---

174. καὶ πάντα μὲν ὁ διάκονος τῷ ἐπισκόπῳ ἀναγερέτω, ὡς ὁ Χριστὸς τῷ Πατρί· ἀλλ' ὅσα δὲ δύναται, εὐθυνέτω δι' ἑαυτοῦ, λαβὼν παρὰ τοῦ ἐπισκόπου τὴν ἐξουσίαν, ὡς ὁ Κύριος παρὰ τοῦ Πατρὸς τὸ δημιουργεῖν, τὸ προνεῖν· τὰ δ' ὑπέρογκα ὁ ἐπίσκοπος κρινέτω. *Constitutiones Apostolicae* 2.44.3, in *PG* 1:704.

175. δὸς ἐν τῷ ὀνόματί σου, καρδιογνῶστα θεέ, ἐπὶ τὸν δοῦλόν σου τόνδε, ὃν ἐξελέξω εἰς ἐπίσκοπον, ποιμαίνειν τὴν ἁγίαν σου ποίμνην καὶ ἀρχιερατεύειν σοι, ἀμέμπτως λειτουργοῦντα. ... δὸς αὐτῷ, δέσποτα παντοκράτορ, διὰ τοῦ Χριστοῦ σου τὴν μετουσίαν τοῦ ἁγίου πνεύματος, ὥστε ἔχειν ἐξουσίαν ... λύειν δὲ πάντα σύνδεσμον κατὰ τὴν ἐξουσίαν, ἣ ἔδωκας τοῖς ἀποστόλοις. *Constitutiones Apostolicae* 8.5.6–7, in *PG* 1:1073.

176. *Ordinationes episcoporum ... exemplo prophetarum et regum ... virtus invisibilis sancto chrismati est permissa ... Hierosolymitarum ... Jacobus ... Domini nuncupatus est frater, a Petro, Jacobo et Joanne apostolis est ordinatus, successoribus videlicet dantibus formam eorum ... reliquisque omnibus assensum praebentibus, ullatenus episcopus ordinetur.* Anacletus, *Epistola* 2.1, in *PG* 2:802.

office," says this letter, "and Aaron represents that of the high priest, that is, the bishop, then Moses indubitably stands for the figure of Christ; like Christ, he is a direct mediator between God and men, the true leader of the people and the true head of the priesthood."[177]

Note here that the bishop is of Aaron, while Moses, guiding the people as a prophet by direct revelation, is something higher. Anacletus here always calls the office of bishop the highest priesthood, because in his day it truly was. In the *Damascus Covenant* there is in each camp an "inspector [*mebaqqer*]": "He will love them as a father his children ... as a shepherd his flock." Above them there is also "an inspector of all the camps"—the bishop of bishops as it were. The bishops must retire at sixty, the presiding bishop at fifty: "No officers for life!"[178] It has often been noted that the office of bishop has no life tenure as the higher offices do. Even Clement, when the problem was brought up, could not point to any such rule for ancient bishops. As described in the *Jewish New Covenant*, "here and there at the head of each community there is an overseer, the 'bishop.' And the ideal of both churches (Christian and pre-Christian) is that of unity, communion in love—even going so far as to share common property."[179]

"At first," wrote Duchesne, "the local ecclesiastical group was constituted and organized on the model offered by the Jewish communities."[180] "Whether by imitation of the syna-

---

177. *Si ergo Aaron filii, presbyterorum figuram gestabant, et Aaron summi sacerdotis, id est episcopi, Moyses indubitanter Christi tenebat formam; quoniam fuit similitudo mediatioris Dei, qui est inter Deum et hominem Jesus Christus, qui est verus dux populorum, et verus princeps sacerdotum.* Anacletus, *Epistola* 2.4, in *PG* 2:810.

178. *Damascus Document* 13.9; 14.8–9.

179. Source unidentified.

180. "Le groupe ecclésiastique local s'est d'abord constitué et organizé sur le modèle offert par les communautés juives." Duchesne, *Origines du Culte Chrétien*, 11.

gogues, or simply through the dictated force of essential need in every community, the first Christians soon found themselves provided with a hierarchy of three degrees. This hierarchy took its powers, directly or indirectly, from the apostles themselves, sometimes from the local bishop and sometimes from the superior ecclesiastical authority, representing the succession of the apostles."[181] Here again is the unwarranted but necessary assumption that any officers having their powers from the apostles must represent a line of apostolic succession. Duchesne can tell us absolutely nothing about this "superior authority" through which the local churches' officers received their powers, save that it disappeared very early and very completely. The apostolic fathers all compare the local hierarchy with that of the main church and with that of Christ, the Father, and the apostles, but this is, as we have seen, strictly analogy: sometimes an office is treated as the equivalent to that of the apostles; another time the holder of the same office is compared with Christ himself, or with the Holy Ghost, or with Moses, or with Abraham, or with the high priest, or with Aaron, or with God the Father, etc. It is all simply an analogy to illustrate not the absolute powers of the relative offices of the priesthood, but their relative powers and the need of subordination one to another. If Christ is subject to the Father, why should not a deacon be subject to the bishop? A powerful argument for order and proper subordination—but with

---

181. "Soit par imitation des synagogues, soit par la simple influence des besoins essentials à toute communauté, les premières chrétientés se trouvèrent bientôt pourvues d'une hiérarchie à trois dégreès. Cette hiérarchie tenait ses pouvoirs, directement ou indirectement, des apôtres eux-mêmes. La communauté désignait ordinairement les personnes, mais l'investiture leur venait, soit de l'éveque local, soit, quand il s'agissait de cette fonction elle-même, de l'autorité ecclésiastique supérieure, représentant la succession des apôtres." Duchesne, *Origines du Culte Chrétien*, 10.

no thought of making the deacon the equal to Christ or the bishop to the Father.

Duchesne surmises that in this Jewish system, "nowhere does one find a local religious center analogous to Jerusalem and to its temple. This last fact, which so sharply marked off the difference between Jews and Christians, was prompt, it is true, to disappear" when the Christians lost their central organization as the Jews had lost theirs.[182] This is a very important fact in understanding the nature and genius of the Christian church, for it answers the question: What became of the ancient Christian church? The same thing that became of the Jewish church and priesthood—they were taken away. The synagogue is not the temple; the rabbis are not the Levites; the ancient rites and ordinances are not now being practiced; the Jewish religion as set forth in the inspired books is today in abeyance. But that does not mean that nothing on earth remains of it. Paul told the Corinthians that the greatest of all gifts, the gnosis, would be taken away, that prophecy, even to the limited degree then enjoyed, would be silenced, and that the gift of tongues would be found no more. Does nothing remain then? In their place, says Paul, will be left behind faith, hope, and love. And this is exactly what faithful Jews retain of their old religion: they live in hope, they live in faith, and they live in charity; they keep the memory and the hope alive; if they do not any more have the glories of the temple, they never cease to recall them; forbidden even to set foot in Jerusalem, they swore never to forget what Jerusalem had been. Their synagogues were local churches led by a council of "elders": "to every Jewish society belong the elders; even in the Hellenistic and

---

182. "Nulle part on n'y trouve un center religieux local, analogue à Jérusalem et à son temple. Ce dernier trait, qui accuse si nettement la différence entre juifs et chrétiens, ne tarde pas, il est vrai, à disparaître." Duchesne, *Origines du Culte Chrétien*, 7.

Roman period they make the core of the Synhedrion." This seems to be the origin of the Christian *presbyteroi*.[183]

In the *Apostolic Constitutions* the prayer of John for the ordination for a presbyter asks God to "fill him with the spirit of grace and counsel even as Moses was ordered to choose assistants." For the deaconess he prays, let her be as Miriam, Deborah, Anna, and Huldah—all Old Testament characters.[184] The presence of numerous offices in the early church having no specific standing or authority, which were all dropped in various times and places, is a heritage of a loosely controlled local organization. The synagogues kept alive the Jewish religion. They did not preserve the ancient rites and ordinances nor the authority to perform them; they kept warm the memory of other dispensations and above all kept alive the hope of Israel. Thus, though deprived of the glories of the temple and the priesthood, they nonetheless performed a valuable service, religious and prophetic. They are not a thing to be held in contempt. So too with these Christian churches that grew up "in the shadow of the synagogues." They were synagogues too. When the apostolic authority was withdrawn, when the rites and ordinances were taken away, they kept alive the memory of the Savior and the apostles. By its own confession the unique function of the Christian church is to preserve without increase or diminution a definite "deposit," to hold it and keep it warm while looking forward to the second coming. This is precisely the function of the synagogue, and it deserves our honor and respect. The synagogue was admittedly but a feeble reflection of the religion of the Jews: scattered and uprooted communities kept the flame burning.

---

183. "Zu jeder jüdischen Gemeinschaft gehören die Ältesten; noch in der hellenistischen und römischen Periode sind sie der Kern des Synhedrions." Schwartz, *Kaiser Constantin und die Christliche Kirche*, 24.

184. *Constitutiones Apostolicae* 8.20.1, in *PG* 1:1116–17.

How then should the new revelation follow such a sad pattern unless it found itself in a like case? Joseph Lechner, in the latest authoritative work on the Catholic liturgy, finds its origin "before all in Judaism, the liturgy of the synagogue."[185] If the least be said for it, we find here closely parallel institutions. Only if the Christians were as lost and deserted as the Jews would they turn to them for the rites and practices of their worship. The Mass, of which Lechner is speaking, owes more of its ritual and liturgy to the rites of the synagogue than to any other source. The synagogue rites, however, are not the rites of the temple, but of a people separated from and deprived of all the ordinances and authority that had once been given their fathers from heaven. Now, when the Christians must go to this sad source for the entire substance of the liturgy, we can only assume that they too, as Duchesne points out, lost all official ties with their own divine origins and had to carry on, as the Jews, in faith, hope, and charity through the centuries.[186] The whole religious life of the Middle Ages, as we shall see later, was a quest and a hope: a search for something lost. The teachings and ordinances of the apostles appear in the very earliest Christian sources as deep, dark mysteries. But the ritual and liturgy carried out by the bishop, priest, and deacon can be examined in every stage of their development—and Lechner has done that—and found to be borrowings from human institutions on every side. Lechner not only admits the fact but goes even further, making the best of an inescapable position by exalting it to a principle: "If the above-named pre- and non-Christian influences have played the most evident role in shaping the cult practice of the church, they are by no means the only such influences, nor the last, and it is by no means out of the question that in the future still

---

185. "Vor allem das Judentum, die Liturgie der Synagoge." Joseph Lechner, *Liturgik des römische Ritus*, 6th ed. (Freiburg: Herder, 1953), 5.
186. Duchesne, *Origines du Culte Chrétien*, 47–48.

other cultural and ethnic zones shall contribute elements to our liturgy, displacing older forms, and that the cult of the church shall adapt itself to still other peoples and concepts as it already has to those of the West."[187] Since according to Catholic teaching, the raison d'être of the priesthood is the performance of cult offices, it must be admitted that priesthood and cult are here seen to be hopelessly adrift in the world—anything like fast apostolic ties and controls is out of the question in a church that has borrowed its rituals from the pagans—"displacing older forms" and acquiring new ones as desired. Batiffol rightly says, speaking for his own church, "Ecclesiology reaches its completion with the dogma of the pontifical primacy."[188] In a church founded by the Lord there would be no science of "ecclesiology" to study the development of organizational dogma—for the organization would be complete at the outset.

From the Dead Sea Scrolls we learn that something very close to the office and title of bishop was had among the Jews in pre-Christian times. The historic background of the episcopal office has never been completely explored. Once its pre-Christian and Jewish background is recognized, many doors are opened. The marked dependency of the whole church order on that of the synagogue makes the dependence of the office of bishop on the Jewish models unavoidable. We are referring to the conventional office of bishop, however, not to that office as it existed in apostolic times: for, like everything else in the church, the lower priesthood was lost as completely

---

187. "Wenn auch die bisher genannten vor- und außerchristlichen Beeinflussungen den kirchlichen Kult am augenscheinlichsten mitgestaltet haben, so sind es durchaus nicht die einzigen oder letzten, und es ist keineswegs ausgeschlossen, daß in der Zukunft nicht auch andere Kultur- und Volksbereiche unserer Liturgie, ältere Formen ausscheiden und daß diese Gestaltungen den kirchlichen Kult wie einst den abendländischen so nun ihn anderen Völkern und Vorstellungen anpassen könnten." Joseph Lechner, *Liturgik des römische Ritus*, 6.
188. Source unidentified.

as the higher. The apostles indeed founded churches, but the bishops "stood in doubt of them" and regretted that they could only handle their affairs properly when an apostle was at hand to instruct them; they noted that with the withdrawal of apostolic authority the churches wilted like flowers cut from a stock.[189] All is confusion and perplexity in the apostolic fathers. Not only did the churches instantly begin disputing with each other in the absence of an apostolic authority to appeal to, but within each church factions arose putting forth rival candidates for bishop. Such a state of things, the apostolic fathers warn again and again, can and, if it does not soon cease, most certainly will destroy the church. But they also know that without a head to turn to there is no hope of improving things, and they themselves, insisting they have no such general authority, know of no one else to turn to. Only one outcome was possible—the predicted one: the famine for the word of the Lord.

The Jewish and Worldly Origins of the Office and Title of Bishop

If the office of bishop in the later church came directly from the apostles, it is very strange, and a fact on which we cannot insist too emphatically, says Reville. Ignatius is entirely unaware of the fact,[190] as is *1 Clement,* and these two are the earliest writers after the apostles and are completely and intimately concerned with the problem of establishing episcopal authority. Neither of them appeals to the apostolic nature of the episcopal office in pleading its importance and dignity! It is plain that in their time it did not have that dignity. On the other hand there is no doubt at all that the apostles did establish bishops. This must have been another order entirely. Where then did the bishops of the second pe-

---

189. Shepherd of Hermas, *Liber Tertius qui inscribitur Similitudines* 3.4, in *PG* 2:955–58.

190. Reville, "Études sur les Origines de l'Épiscopat," 285.

riod come from? Nothing could be simpler: if the churches were modeled after the synagogue, so naturally would be their officers. The Jews had had apostles, but the early church had something very special: *the* Apostles, the Twelve. Every Jewish community had its council of elders—the presbyters; but the early Christians never for a moment confused them with those they called *"the* elders," that is, the elders of the apostles' time, whose deeds and sayings reach us in Irenaeus, Polycarp, Clement, and Eusebius as traditions from a special order of beings the likes of which have completely disappeared from the earth. In the later Christian church the number of deacons in every church was supposed to be exactly seven (Acts 6), to represent in some way *the* Seventy, who had vanished and whose office and calling was one of the mysteries.

The office of teacher is identified with that of reader. As such it was a part of every synagogue, but the early fathers knew that a teacher in the primitive church was something entirely different—just what, they could not say. In every synagogue one might find officers bearing the names of bishop, priest, teacher, and deacon. These names were also employed in the early church but in a very special sense. It was not this early sense, but the Jewish one, that the later church preserved along with rites and ordinances that were also not of the earliest times but much later acquisitions taken from many sources by a church that would never have been under the painful necessity of building up its rituals through the years had the original rites and practices, quite sufficient for all purposes, not been completely lost. The excuse (i.e., the standard explanation) that more practical, popular, and otherwise expedient procedures had to be worked out to suit altered circumstances is worthless since ritual is not a practical thing anyway. It is not adapted to the convenience of a society, but rather requires of the society—any society—the discipline of conformity to it.

Everything about the later episcopal office betrays its Jewish and worldly origin. The idea of a religious overseer in a community is very ancient, and very anciently that function is "episcopal." Thus Solon assures his fellow Athenians at the beginning of the sixth century B.C. that God will never destroy the city as long as it is watched over by Athena, *episkopos*.[191] While the Egyptian god is hidden and secret, says Eduard Meyer, the Greek god is *episkopos* because he oversees the land from his high castle seat. This is a common Aryan concept—prominent in Norse mythology—of necessarily Asiatic origin: it belongs to the economy of the mountain palace, the super lookout from which the ruler surveys all the deeds that are done in his domain and sends out the arrows of his wrath to destroy those who think to escape his will. The concept is most at home among the Persians, whence the Jews seem to have derived it. Strangely enough, the episcopal office is not a distant derivative but is endowed with certain astonishing fixtures which show its direct Asiatic contacts. The oldest bishop's staves were the caduceus and thunder arrow, and they bore on them such dread inscriptions as "Strike" and "Destroy," appropriate only to the divine weapon.

There was no Persian institution better known to the West in ancient times than that of the "King's Eyes" and the "King's Ears"—the royal spies who told the divine king all that was going on in the world. Ancient literature is full of references to like institutions. In the same passage in which he describes these officers, Xenophon discourses on the Persian king as the Good Shepherd—one need not, therefore, think the terminology is purely accidental or far-fetched.[192] According to a very early epistle attributed to Evaristus, "the deacons are the bishop's eyes in every city; there should be seven on duty when the bishop preaches, lest anyone of the song

---

191. Solon, elegaic fragment 4.
192. Source unidentified.

[literally of his own people!] speak disrespectfully or make any move against him, or treat lightly the divine word."[193] In turn, the bishop himself is described in a letter attributed to Alexander of Rome as "the eyes of the Lord," and the conclusion from that is very significant—namely, that anyone who crosses a bishop is guilty of the crime of lèse-majesté.[194] That is, we have here the bishop holding the power of a temporal king, modeled on accepted Oriental concepts. "Bishops are to be judged by God alone," says a letter supposedly of Pius I, "who has chosen them as his eyes."[195] After describing the functions of the bishop in terms of Numbers, i.e., the Old Testament pattern, the *Apostolic Constitutions* notes: "Since therefore you are *skopoi* [literally "lookouts," "inspectors," or "spies"], you yourselves are under the inspection [*skopos*] of Christ."[196] Later the same source announces that "the deacons are the bishop's eyes, ears, mouth, heart, souls ... as Jethro took the load from Moses."[197]

K. G. Goetz has surmised that the Gentile Christians adopted the name of *episcopus* in preference to the old Jewish title, *archisynagogus*, in precisely the same way in which they took over *ekklesia* in preference to the usual Jewish *synagogue*.[198] This would confirm our contention that the origin of the

---

193. *Diaconi, qui quasi oculi videntur esse episcopi in unaquaque civitate, iuxta apostolorum constituta septem debent esse, qui custodiant episcopum praedicantem, ne aut ipse ab insidiatoribus quoque modo infestetur, aut laedatur a suis, aut verba divina.* Evaristus, *Epistola* 1.1, in *PG* 5:1047.

194. ... *oculi Domini.* Alexander I, *Epistola* 1.1, in *PG* 5:1060.

195. *Episcopi autem a Deo sunt judicandi, qui eos sibi oculos elegit.* Pius I, *Epistola* 1.2, in *PG* 5:1121.

196. ὥσπερ οὖν ὑμεῖς σκοποί ἐστε, οὕτως καὶ σκοπὸν ἔχετε τὸν Χριστόν. *Constitutiones Apostolicae* 2.25.12, in *PG* 1:664.

197. πλὴν ἔστω ὁ διάκονος τοῦ ἐπισκόπου ἀκοὴ καὶ οφθαλμὸς καὶ στόμα, καρδία τε καὶ ψυχή ... ὥσπερ ὁ Ἰοδὼρ τῷ Μωϋσῇ διετάξατο. *Constitutiones Apostolicae* 2.44.4, in *PG* 1:704–5.

198. K. G. Goetz, "Ist der מבקר der Genizafragmente wirklich das Vorbild des christlichen Episkopats?" *Zeitschrift für die neutestamentliche Wissenschaft und die Kunde der älteren Kirche* 30 (1931): 89–93.

conventional Christian bishopric is to be found in the same place as the origin of its rites and liturgies—with the Jews and pagans, and not with the apostles. Granted that James the brother of the Lord was "a unique phenomenon without survival," Linton asks, where did the local churches get their bishops and their organization? There are two answers to this, he explains: (1) the Jewish origin theory, which everyone accepted until in the 1880s when Giovanni Battista de Rossi, the papal archaeologist, and others suggested (2) pagan models, to be found in those collegia—clubs and social common-interest groups—which swarmed in the world of late antiquity.[199] In neither case was the origin "apostolic." Every possible type of ancient society was then put forward by this or that school to explain the emergence of the later church organization, but no agreement was reached.

First Clement says the apostles themselves set up bishops based on Old Testament models, and from the language the author uses, he appears to be engaging in a little personal speculation: certainly he quotes no official doctrine to that effect.[200] Matthew succeeded Judas, says the *Apostolic Constitutions*, according to the dictates of Psalm 109:8: "Let another take his oversight [*episkopeia*]."[201] In the *Testaments of the Twelve Patriarchs*, the apostle and bishop appear in Jewish garb: "Until the time when the most high shall send out [*aposteilei*] his salvation, in the oversight [*episkopei*] of his Only Begotten."[202] The survival of Israel was a thorn in the side of the Christian church, blighting all its claims to being the last and ultimate development in the unfolding of God's plan on earth. The organization of Jewish society in the Middle Ages can hardly have been an imitation of the

---

199. Linton, *Das Problem der Urkirche*, 19–21.

200. *1 Clement* 42.5.

201. τὴν ἐπισκοπὴν αὐτοῦ λάβοι ἕτερος. *Constitutiones Apostolicae* 6.12.1, in *PG* 1:940.

202. ἕως οὗ ὁ Ὕψιστος ἀποστείλῃ τὸ σωτήριον αὐτοῦ, ἐν ἐπισκοπῇ Μονογενοῦς. *Testamenta Duodecim Patriarchorum* 12.9, in *PG* 2:1148.

THE OFFICE OF BISHOP IN THE EARLY CHRISTIAN CHURCH 61

Christian, yet we have attempts at a centrally organized Jewish church documented in the writings of Benjamin of Tudela, who describes how "permission is granted by the Prince of the Captivity to all the Jewish congregations of these different countries to elect rabbis and ministers, all of whom appear before him in order to receive consecration [it was by laying on of hands] and the permission to officiate, upon which occasions presents and valuable gifts are offered to him even from the remotest countries."[203] But who ordains the Prince of the Captivity? The caliph, successor to Muhammad as head of Islam! Of the Jewish congregations of Europe, Benjamin says, "they send letters to one another by which they exhort themselves to hold firm in the mosaic law."[204]

The exact parallel to Christian institutions is here no more striking than that to the usages of Asiatic kingship. The emergence of papal institutions throughout the world follows hard upon the establishment of the office of religious overseer, or bishop—we find them both wherever we look, with no indication that they began with the Christian church. One is not left here to vague surmise, however, as the study of church vestments quickly reveals the priority of pagan institutions, especially Asiatic, over the Christian ones. This we will treat below.

Changes in the Office of Bishop

There is no dearth of early texts describing the functions of the lower priesthood. Immediately after comparing them with the apostles, Ignatius describes the work of the presbyters. It is strictly of a local, temporal nature—they are to visit the sick, help the poor, preserve good order generally in the church. That is all.[205] So much for their "apostolic"

---

203. Benjamin of Tudela, *The Itinerary of Rabbi Benjamin of Tudela*, trans. and ed. A. Asher, 2 vols. (New York: Hakesheth, n.d.), 103.
204. Ibid., 163.
205. Source unidentified.

calling. The ancient office of deacon was the same—to help the bishop generally in the performance of the strictly temporal tasks and odd jobs of the church. Later on the priests and deacons become inspired teachers—a function totally foreign to their original calling—and in that they illustrate a like change in the office of bishop. As the bishop's assistants, they must be spiritual if he is spiritual, yet nothing is more certain than the fact that in the beginning their office was temporal. Also nothing is more certain than that their calling was never separated from that of the bishop—they are always and everywhere a single team. Therefore in the undoubted nature of their work, we have the key to the bishop's own calling, and in the radical theoretical change of orientation that their offices underwent we see evidence for a like change of orientation in the episcopal calling.

But we need not confine ourselves to such secondary evidence, however convincing. For the nature and function of no ecclesiastical office is so well, so often, and so fully described, both directly and indirectly, as that of bishop. Out of many studies of the word *episcopus* emerges a consensus: the bishop is an inspector sent by a higher authority to examine local conditions. He examines and reports; to do that he must stay on the ground. From the inscriptions "no fixed meaning of the word's content has been found; . . . just as the word *apostle*, it is *ein inhaltleeres Beziehungswort* [meaningless epithet]."[206] It was the Christians who gave it a definite content. For them the bishop was chief local officer, but it is very significant that he was not elected by the society of which he was in charge—they merely sustained him by a show of hands. It was a higher authority that put him in charge.

---

206. "Man [hat] eine feste *inhaltliche* Bedeutung für das Wort ἐπίσκοπος nicht nachweisen können. . . . Auch das Wort ἐπίσκοπος ist demgemäss, genau so wie das Wort ἀπόστολος, ein *inhaltleeres Beziehungswort*." Linton, Das Problem der Urkirche, 107, emphasis in original.

Change in qualification and selection. The local election theory has now been given up. One of the most actively discussed questions has been that of the plurality of bishops: why the plurality? It seems strange that this should have been a question at all. There was a plurality of bishops because there was a multiplicity of places requiring direction and administration. The question would never have arisen were it not for the determination of churchmen to see the bishops as apostolic general authorities, which by their very number they could not have been. The office and function of bishop is clearly marked from the first, but if we accept what is shown us, then the later concept of bishops as rulers of the whole church rather than of local churches alone is completely discredited. And so we are not allowed to accept the record as it stands but must seek for great and hidden mysteries to explain a glaring contradiction. The contradiction is not in the record—there is no contradiction here at all—but in the need and determination of the churches to make out of the bishop something that he was not. Bishops took over the work of apostles, who could not stay in one place more than three nights, while as bishops they could not leave one place more than three weeks.

While pointing out that the office of bishop was a spiritual, religious, peculiarly Christian one, Harnack noted that it was vastly different in its busy practicality from the functions of those prophets, teachers, evangelists, etc., whose concern was to teach the church by revelation from heaven. Many texts on the qualifications and training of bishops bear that out fully. The "inspired men" whom Justin Martyr describes as the true teachers and leaders of the early church differed from the great men of the world precisely in having no formal education and in relying at no time on any skill in rhetoric or logic.[207] This point is exploited by Tertullian, Origen, Clement of Alexandria, the *Clementine Recognitions,* etc. Yet formal education

---

207. Justin Martyr, *Cohortatio ad Graecos* 8, in *PG* 6:256–57.

and skill in rhetoric and logic are the very things most consistently prescribed for bishops. In the pseudo-Clementine letters to James, Clement tries to avoid the office of bishop with its heavy worldly preoccupation and concern.[208] Many priests in the fourth century tried to avoid the office on the significant grounds that it meant giving up the spiritual life. It is for that reason that Peter was said to have handed over the office to Linus, Clement, and Cletus. The spiritual life was the very essence of apostleship. To return to the pseudo-Clementine letters, Peter insists that Clement take over the office: You are the best qualified of all, he says, you lead a moral life, you are well instructed in the doctrine, and you have been with me and heard me preach more than anyone else. . . . So the sooner you agree, the quicker you will relieve me of a great worry.[209] This is not the way God calls a man to an office: here is no mention of the will of God, no mention of revelation. Note the strictly practical and worldly ground on which Clement is chosen: he is qualified by character, training, and experience. The qualifications for a bishop set forth by the apostolic fathers are the same: they are all the very qualities one would demand of any public leader—and no more. Above all, their concern is for "public order." This we shall consider closer when we view the bishop in civil life. As to his strictly religious concerns, a letter attributed to Telesphorus says the bishop's faith must be *"in apostolorum eruditione fundatam* [having been founded upon the learning of the apostles]."[210]

"A bishop," says the *Apostolic Constitutions* "must be trained and experienced in speech [*logos*]. . . . He must not be over fifty years old"[211]—can one imagine such a limitation

---

208. Clement, *Epistola ad Jacobum* 3, in *PG* 2:36–37.
209. Clement, *Epistola ad Jacobum* 3, in *PG* 2:37.
210. Telesphorus, *Epistola ad Omnes Universaliter Christi Fideles,* in *PG* 5:1081.
211. ὅτι χρὴ τὸν ἐπίσκοπον εἶναι πεπαιδευμένον, καὶ ἔμπειρος τοῦ λόγου . . . οὐκ ἔλλαττον ἐτῶν πεντήκοντα. *Constitutiones Apostolicae* 2.1.1, in *PG* 1:593. [See Numbers 8:25.]

on an apostle, prophet, evangelist, or any inspired office? He must be especially competent to handle "the blasphemies of certain pseudo-brethren which are being inflicted upon many" and so "must be trained and experienced in the word, as befits his age."²¹² It reminds us, however, that there are exceptions, that Solomon and Josiah were chosen when young—as ever, the examples are drawn from the Old Testament record and not from apostolic sources. As the description in the *Apostolic Constitutions* goes on, it becomes apparent that the only peculiarly Christian qualification of a bishop is training in Christian doctrine: nothing is said of inspired gifts. "He must be the husband of one wife. . . . He must be sober, reliable [*pistos*], and neat [*kosmios*—one thinks of the wonderful unneatness of certain prophets]."²¹³ Since the Lord said to Moses, be no respecter of persons, the bishop should act accordingly—note that when an identical passage appears both in the Old Testament and the New Testament, no mention is made of the New Testament: everything indicates the Mosaic system as the pattern. Of course the bishop should teach by example, as Christ did: "first do, then teach." His title, according to this source, comes from Ezekiel 33:2–3: the bishop sits as a judge and teacher, exactly as the *pəqûdhîm* of ancient Israel. He is a disciplinary officer. He is the leader, not the follower; he does not yield to the rebellious layman but takes his orders from God alone. He receives those orders, as he does his doctrine, through the scriptures. He is not an infallible prophet, but a fallible man, and must remember that "everybody makes mistakes."²¹⁴ "The bishop must take thought and consider

---

212. πρὸς τάς τινων ψευδαδέλφων εἰς πολλοὺς ἐπιφεραμένους βλασφημίας. . . . ἔστι οὖν πεπαιδευμένος καὶ ἔμπειρος τοῦ λόγου, καθήκων τῇ ἡλικίᾳ. *Constitutiones Apostolicae* 2.1.1–2, in *PG* 1:596.

213. τοιοῦτον δὲ δεῖ εἶναι τὸν ἐπίσκοπον, μιᾶς ἄνδρα γεγενημένον γυναικὸς μονογάμου . . . εἰ ἔστι σέμνος, πιστός, καὶ κόσμιος. *Constitutiones Apostolicae* 2.2.2–3, in *PG* 1:597.

214. *Constitutiones Apostolicae* 2.18.12, in *PG* 1:632.

how to keep the people from getting off the track since he is their supervisor."²¹⁵ As shepherd, he will be held responsible. How is a bishop to be judged? Ezekiel 34:17 is the key: bishop to bishop, layman to layman, prince to prince.²¹⁶ And the people themselves will be responsible for following a bad shepherd: "As rational beings, the sheep are answerable for their own behavior and obliged to avoid pernicious pastors."²¹⁷ There is much written about the judging of bishops—by whom and how it is to be done. This is in marked contrast to the rule of the *Didache*, that an apostle or prophet, being under the direct working of the Spirit, is not to be judged by anyone.²¹⁸

Change in functions and duties. The bishop stands in a contractual relationship to a society. Not so the higher officers, who are social officers: Bishops shall minister to the traveling general brethren as their superiors, according to the *Didache*.²¹⁹ Bishops, the *Apostolic Constitutions* continues, should be gentle, not imperious, shepherds, for they are physicians of the church of the Lord.²²⁰ The bishop is an officer of peace: the preservation of peace and order in his community is a prime concern. They must judge as God judges—charitably. The examples cited are David, Manasseh, the case of Nineveh, and others—all from the Old Testament.²²¹ A bishop who expels a righteous man from the community is worse than a murderer, for he does not take a proper *skopos* [view, study] of the situation.²²² Always

---

215. ὅτι χρὴ τὸν ἐπίσκοπον φροντίζειν, ὅπως ὁ λαὸς μὴ πλημμελῇ, διὰ τὸ εἶναι αὐτὸν σκοπόν. *Constitutiones Apostolicae* 2.18, in *PG* 1:629.

216. τουτέστιν, ἐπίσκοπον πρὸς ἐπίσκοπον κρινῶ, καὶ λαϊκὸν πρὸς λαϊκόν, καὶ ἄρχοντα πρὸς ἄρχοντα. *Constitutiones Apostolicae* 2.19.1, in *PG* 1:633.

217. διὸ φευκτέον ἀπὸ τῶν φωρέων ποιμένον. *Constitutiones Apostolicae* 2.19.3, in *PG* 1:633.

218. *Didache* 11.11.

219. *Didache* 11.3–12.2.

220. *Constitutiones Apostolicae* 2.20.9–11, in *PG* 1:633–37.

221. *Constitutiones Apostolicae* 2.20, in *PG* 1:633–37.

222. *Constitutiones Apostolicae* 2.21.7–8, in *PG* 1:640–41.

the text plays on the word *episkopos*—inspect, consider, study, examine, etc. J.-P. Migne, the editor of the *Patrologiae Graecae*, thinks the *Apostolic Constitution* is very inept.[223] This doctrine of the episcopal office itself comes from Christ, we are told, "being commensurate with his glorious utterances."[224] This is what is meant by direction from heaven.

The "spiritual" nature of the bishop's office is illustrated by the declaration: If we should honor our physical parents, "how much more our spiritual ones ... who baptized us, filled us with the Holy Ghost, nourished us with the word of salvation ... forgave our sins," etc.[225] And again, if we honor and support kings and rulers, how much more so the bishop? How much more should we pay to feed him and his clerics whom God has established: "Priesthood is greater than kingship in the exact proportion as the spirit is greater than the body."[226] Now these are well-known, maybe threadbare, commonplaces of the schools: nothing is more immediate to the vice of allegorizing than that of "spiritualizing" all things, and allegory is not failing in the above passage. Nothing was more natural, easy, inevitable than to "spiritualize" the episcopal calling by these Platonic clichés. In the same beautifully figurative sense, "the bishop in the judgment hall has the Christ of God to sustain and vote with him."[227] "The bishop

---

223. Migne, *PG* 1:519–22.

224. ὁμόστοιχον ταῖς ἐνδόξοις φθογγαῖς αὐτοῦ. *Constitutiones Apostolicae* 1.1, in *PG* 1:557.

225. εἰ γάρ περὶ τῶν κατὰ σάρκα γονέων φησὶν τὸ θεῖον λόγιον· τίμα τὸν πατέρα σου καὶ τὴν μητέρα σου, ἵνα εὖ σοι γένηται, καὶ ὁ κακολογῶν πατέρα ἢ μητέρα θανάτῳ τελευτάτω, πόσῳ μᾶλλον περὶ τῶν πνευματικῶν γονέων ὑμῖν ὁ λόγος παραινέσει τιμᾶν αὐτοὺς καὶ στέργειν ... τοὺς δι' ὕδατος ὑμᾶς ἀναγεννήσαντας, τοὺς τῷ ἁγίῳ πνεύματι πληρώσαντας, τοὺς τῷ λόγῳ γαλακτοτροφήσαντας ... τοὺς τῶν ἁμαρτιῶν λύσαντας. *Constitutiones Apostolicae* 2.33.1–3, in *PG* 1:680–81.

226. ὅσῳ τοίνυν ψυχὴ σώματος κρείττων, τοσούτῳ ἱερωσύνη βασιλείας. *Constitutiones Apostolicae* 2.34.4, in *PG* 1:681.

227. καθότι καὶ ἐν τῷ δικαστηρίῳ συμψήφον ἕξει καὶ συνίστορα τῆς δίκης τὸν Χριστὸν τοῦ θεοῦ. *Constitutiones Apostolicae* 2.47.2, in *PG* 1:708.

is like the pilot of a great ship: the deacons are the crew, the members the well-behaved cargo full of careful scruples and decent behavior. The church building must be long and face the East . . . like a ship. The bishop's throne must be in the middle with the presbyters' sects on either side with the deacons standing at attention like sailors lightly clad," etc.[228] Let visiting deacons sit with the deacons, visiting presbyters with the presbyters, and a visiting bishop with the bishop.[229] No layman shall perform priestly work: baptism, sacrifice, the laying on of hands, or the *eulogia*. The bishop, and he alone, shall lay on hands. Imitating Solomon, the bishop shall instruct the people to deal kindly with the poor.[230] The bishop must be ordained by three bishops, or at the very least by two. A presbyter must be ordained by one bishop and the rest of the clergy. A presbyter can teach, baptize, offer sacrifices, and *eulogein* [exhort] the people; a deacon can minister for the bishop and presbyters but not for the people.[231]

A bad bishop, we are further told, is not really a bishop, having been appointed not by God but by men.[232] In support

---

228. ὅταν δὲ συναθροίζῃς τὴν τοῦ θεοῦ ἐκκλησίαν, ὡς ἂν κυβερνήτης νηὸς μεγάλης μετ' ἐπιστήμης πάσης κέλευε ποιεῖσθει τὰς συνόδους, παραγγέλλων τοῖς διακόνοις ὡσανεὶ αὐταις τοὺς τόπους ἐκτάσσειν τοῖς ἀδελφοῖς καθάπερ ἐπιβάταις μετὰ πάσης ἐπιμελείας καὶ σεμνότητος. καὶ πρῶτον μὲν ὁ οἶκος ἔστω ἐπιμήκης, κατὰ ἀνατολὰς τετραμμένος . . . ὅστις ἔοικεν νηΐ. κείσθω δὲ μέσος ὁ τοῦ ἐπισκόπου θρόνος, παρ' ἑκάτερα δὲ αὐτοῦ καθεζέσθω τὸ πρεσβυτέριον, καὶ οἱ διάκονοι παριστάσθωσαν εὐσταλεῖς τῆς πλείονος ἐσθῆτος· ἐοίκασι γὰρ ναύταις καὶ τοιχάρχοις. *Constitutiones Apostolicae* 2.57.2–4, in *PG* 1:724–25.

229. *Constitutiones Apostolicae* 2.58.2, in *PG* 1:740.

230. *Constitutiones Apostolicae* 3.15, in *PG* 1:793–97.

231. ἐπίσκοπον προστάσσομεν χειροτενεῖσθαι ὑπὸ τριῶν ἐπισκόπων· ἢ τὸ γοῦν ἔλλαττον, ὑπὸ δύο·. . . πρεσβύτερον δὲ διὰ διάκονον ὑπὸ ἑνὸς ἐπισκόπου, καὶ τῶν λοιπῶν κληρικῶν· . . . ἀλλὰ μόνον, τὸν μὲν πρεσβύτερον διδάσκειν, ἀναφέρειν, βαπτίζειν, εὐλόγειν τὸν λαόν· τὸν δὲ διάκονον ἐξυπηρετεῖσθαι τῷ ἐπισκόπῳ καὶ τοῖς πρεσβυτέροις· τουτέστι, διακόνειν· οὐ μὴν καὶ τὰ λοιπὰ δι' εὐεργεῖν. *Constitutiones Apostolicae* 3.20.1–2, in *PG* 1:804–5.

232. οὔτε ἐπίσκοπος ἀγνοίᾳ ἢ κακονοίᾳ πεπιεσμένος ἔτι ἐπίσκοπός ἐστιν, ἀλλὰ ψευδώνυμος, οὐ παρὰ θεοῦ, ἀλλὰ παρὰ ἀνθρώπων προβληθείς. *Constitutiones Apostolicae* 8.2.4, in *PG* 1:1068.

THE OFFICE OF BISHOP IN THE EARLY CHRISTIAN CHURCH 69

of this, many Old Testament examples are cited of kings and rulers who were punished for going beyond their authority. Interestingly, the remark is made that though Silas and Agabus were prophets they did not claim to be equal to the apostles[233]—showing that apostolic men, even inspired ones, were not thought thereby to have the authority of apostles. The lector "is to serve the church as Esdras of Old, reading thy laws to the people."[234] Widows are to be ordained "after the type of Judith and Anna."[235] But virgins, as such, are not to be ordained, "since the Lord left no instructions" to that effect.[236] But where did he instruct about ordaining widows? One attributes what one wishes to the Lord, and when one does not wish, points to his silence on the subject. In the *127 Canons*, the Lord is represented as instructing the apostles: "Determine the order of the bishops, the seating of the priests, the duties of the deacons, the capacities of the readers, widows without sin, and the activities necessary to the founding of the church"—so they "did it after the pattern of what is in heaven."[237] Here it is possible to attribute to the Lord what was traditionally regarded as strictly the work of apostles. Such a convenient extension of things is seen in the same text, which improves on the scriptures: "It is good that he be not married, but if he already is married, that he be 'the husband of one wife.'" Thus the later episcopal office was written into the scriptures by a revamping of 1 Timothy 2:2–3 and Titus 1:6–12, which is patently absurd but which shows how easy it was to "control" the apostles.

Such liberties are even more apparent in what follows. The apostle John says, "The bishop should have two priests

---

233. Σίλας μὲν οὖν καὶ Ἄγαβος ἐφ' ἡμῶν προφητεύσαντες οὐ παρεξέτειναν ἑαυτοὺς τοῖς ἀποστόλοις. *Constitutiones Apostolicae* 8.2.8, in *PG* 1:1068.

234. ὁ σοφίσας Ἔσδραν τὸν θεράποντά σου ἐπὶ τὸ ἀναγινώσκειν τοὺς νόμους σου τῷ λαῷ σου. *Constitutiones Apostolicae* 8.22.4, in *PG* 1:1120.

235. χήρα οὐ χειροτονεῖται ... ὡς Ἰουδὶθ καὶ Ἄννα αἱ σέμνονται. *Constitutiones Apostolicae* 8.25.2, in *PG* 1:1121.

236. ἐπιταγὴν γὰρ κυρίου οὐκ ἔχομεν. *Constitutiones Apostolicae* 8.24.2, in *PG* 1:1121.

237. *127 Canons of the Apostles* 1.1, in *PO* 8:574.

for assistants," but all the other apostles object, saying that not two but three are required, since there are twenty-four elders: twelve on the right hand and twelve on the left. "That is right," says John, "those on the right hand will take the cup from the chiefs of the angels and carry it to the Lord, and those on the left are over all the angels. The priests must be of advanced age, beyond the age of marriage and united in the love of their chief."[238] So angels may be drawn into the system at will. The deacons, says this source, hold no priesthood: the bishop only lays his hands upon his head but utters no words, because a deacon does not stand among the priests but is simply a helper to the bishop. His business is to do odd jobs and keep the bishop informed as to what is going on. The deacon is not supposed to be a teacher, for "he is not allowed to share in the spirit of greatness in which the priests have share." He is to try to do everything to please the bishop—that is why the bishop puts his hands upon his head. The priest, on the other hand, receives the laying on of hands of the bishop and all the priests that are with him, at which time the Holy Ghost descends upon him. But still the priest, though receiving the same spirit as the bishop, has no right to give orders as the bishop does; therefore he only ordains priests in cooperation with the bishop.[239] In the early church, deacons were ordained not by bishops but by apostles, along with and at the same time as the bishops, but now have either lost their authority or never had it. But they did have it. They must have lost it, therefore, as did those who were coordained: bishops and presbyters. Confessors, in recognition of their merits, were said to receive an honorary diaconate and/or priesthood without any laying on of hands, such being necessary only if those parties became bishops.[240] By what right are these concessions made? What

---

238. *127 Canons of the Apostles* 1.13, in *PO* 8:584.
239. *127 Canons of the Apostles* 1.23, in *PO* 8:592.
240. *127 Canons of the Apostles* 1.24, in *PO* 8:593–94.

general authority has been consulted? If anyone claims the gift of healing, says the *127 Canons*, he shall not be established by laying on of hands, but prove his claim by the event.[241] Though tithes go to the support of clerics and others, firstfruits are exclusively for priests and ministers, following the old Jewish law.[242]

The earliest letter from the hand of the Christian is that of Pope Maximos of Alexandria (264–282). In this we find the bishop actively engaged in commercial affairs—not his own but those of the church. "Egyptian provincial Christians employ the highest ecclesiastic in the country as their confidential agent in money affairs,"[243] comments Adolf Deissmann with amazement. "The link between the Christian corn-sellers in the Fayûm and their agent in Rome is . . . the Papas of Alexandria!"[244] When one considers that this is the earliest description of a bishop's activity, it is most significant. Both Justin Martyr and Tertullian speak of elders (*seniores*) presiding or acting as presidents at meetings[245]—plainly such an officiant did not need to be a bishop, as we have seen above. Cyprian, in the third century, advises deacons always to remember that "the Lord chose apostles, that is to say, bishops and leaders, while deacons were established by the apostles only after the ascension of the Lord to heaven for their episcopate and for the ministry of the church."[246] The sweeping "that is to say" is as significant as the denial of priesthood

---

241. *127 Canons of the Apostles* 1.26, in *PO* 8:595.
242. *127 Canons of the Apostles* 1.59, in *PO* 8:643.
243. Adolf Deissmann, *Light from the Ancient East: The New Testament Illustrated by Recently Discovered Texts of the Graeco-Roman World*, trans. Lionel R. M. Strachan (New York: Doran, 1927), 213.
244. Ibid.
245. Justin, *Apologia* 1.65, in *PG* 6:428. Tertullian source unidentified.
246. *Meminisse autem diaconi debent quoniam apostolos, id est episcopos et praepositos Dominus elegit, diaconos autem, post ascensum Domini in caelos, apostoli sibi constituerunt episcopatus sui et Ecclesiae ministros.* Cyprian, *Epistola* 65.3, in *PL* 4:408.

to the deacons because they were only installed by apostles. Only! Cyprian is trying to save the bishops from the same fate as the deacons and he does it by the most obvious word juggling. Both have lost their authority, but while he must admit the fact for the deacons, he can only save the bishops by identifying them completely, and without question or discussion, with the apostles whom the Lord chose.

Eusebius says that "James first received the throne of the church of Jerusalem and the episcopate from the Lord himself, and from the apostles, according to the divine words."[247] Eusebius was determined to make the bishops the successors of the apostles, yet like the others he can produce no proof but only an awkward assumption. The claim that James got his office from the Lord himself is in conflict with all other sources, yet Eusebius sees that it must so be if James is to have the same kind of authority as the apostles, who were all personally appointed.

The first duty of the bishop, says Ambrose, is to teach. "But there is but one true master," and bishops like everyone else must study and learn before they are ready to teach.[248] Then in his writing entitled *On the Offices of the Ministry*, Ambrose makes the surprising statement that his whole essay could be written using nothing but phrases taken "from the schools of philosophy" since they teach the same as the scriptures.[249] By the fourth century, *scripture* meant a very special and peculiar reading of the scripture—not its literal sense. This is the strange twist the church gave to a promise which

---

247. τὸν γὰρ Ἰακώβου θρόνον τοῦ πρότου τῆς ἱεροσολύμων Ἐκκλησίας τὴν ἐπισκοπὴν πρὸς αὐτοῦ τοῦ Σωτῆρος καὶ τῶν ἀποστόλων ὑποδεξαμένον, ὃν καὶ ἀδέλφον τὸν Χριστοῦ χρηματίσαι οἱ θεῖοι λόγοι περιέχουσιν. Eusebius, *Historia Ecclesiastica* 7.19.1, in *PG* 20:681.

248. *Unus enim verus magister est, qui solus non didicit quod omnes doceret: homines autem discunt prius quod doceant, et ab illo accipiunt quod aliis tradant.* Ambrose, *De Officii Ministribus* 1.3, in *PL* 16:27.

249. *Et etiam hoc nomen philosophorum tantummodo scholae aptum sit, an etiam in Scripturis reperiatur divines.* Ambrose, *De Officii Ministribus* 2.4, in *PL* 16:34.

the ancient church understood in a diametrically opposite sense. Since there is only one teacher for the church, the ancients said, the one qualification for those who would teach the church is not study and learning, but direct dictation from the One who knows.[250] Starting from the same premise, Ambrose now comes to the opposite conclusion: since there is only One Teacher, he says, no one else can speak with his voice, but every bishop must study and learn to speak as men must—in the school.[251] "Ecclesiastical men," says Ambrose's great contemporary, Jerome, "who meditate on the law of God day and night cannot be deceived."[252] This came in reply to Pelagius's claim that revelation was an indispensable prerequisite to infallibility. Nonsense! says Jerome, if men only meditate hard enough, they will always be right. This was the bland assurance of the schools—it would have made a primitive Christian smile. But Jerome also assures us that "not all bishops are bishops. . . . Ecclesiastical dignity does not make a Christian."[253] In fact, in a later discussion Jerome sees through the flimsy argument easily enough: "I know that this question has been variously disputed by the most learned men," he writes of a point in Daniel 9, "and everyone of them decides it, saying what he thinks on the basis of his own cleverness. Since therefore it is dangerous to judge between the opinions of the magisters of the church, and to prefer one to the other, I will say what each one thinks and leave it to the reader which opinion he feels he should follow."[254] The early apologists all

---

250. Source unidentified.
251. *Unus enim verus magister est, qui solus non didicit quod omnes doceret: homines autem discunt prius quod doceant, et ab illo accipiunt quod aliis tradant.* Ambrose, *De Officii Ministribus* 1.3, in *PL* 16:27.
252. *Sed ecclesiasticos viros, qui in lege Dei, die ac nocte meditantur, decipere non valent.* Jerome, *Epistola* 132.3, in *PL* 22:1149.
253. *Non omnes episcopi episcopi sunt. . . . Non facit ecclesiastica dignitas Christianum.* Jerome, *Epistola* 14.9, in *PL* 22:353.
254. *Scio de hac quaestione ab eruditissimis viris variae disputatum, et unumquemque pro captu ingenii sui dixisse quod senserat. Quia igitur periculosum*

made much of the fact that there was a perfect unity of opinion among the ancient apostles, precisely because they did not judge matters "on the basis of their own cleverness," as the teachers of the church do in Jerome's day. Surely bishops lack whatever it was that made an apostle an apostle.

Roman Origin of a Divine Office?

It is a truism that the establishment of Christianity as the big popular church at the end of the ancient world was largely due to the influence of city bishops, who emerged during the time of troubles that accompanied the fall of the empire as the natural leaders of their societies. Their courage, devotion, and enterprise are too well known to need a description or encomium at this point. But such men were not a new thing in the cities of the Mediterranean. The pious, inspired leader who gives his all for his city and guides it by his wisdom, courage, and skill is a stock figure in the Greek tragedy, where he is already designated as *episkopos*. Like the kings of the East such an one is called the "shepherd," and the people, the citizens, are his flock.[255] The leading man of the town had an influence that went beyond that of his office: "Whom have the people to imitate," Epictetus asks of a friend, a high official in a provincial city whom he is rebuking for undignified behavior, "except you their superior, the governor, friend of Caesar, and his procurator?"[256] "The city teaches the man," said Simonides[257]—and that in the broadest sense.

---

est de magistrorum Ecclesiae judicare sententiis, et alterum praeferre alteri, dicam unusquisque senserit, lectoris abritrio derelinquens, cuius expositionem sequi debent. Jerome, *Commentariorum in Danielam Liber 9,* in *PL* 25:542.

255. Anacreon, lyric fragment 348, from Hephaestion, *Poem* 4.8.

256. τίνας γὰρ ἔχουσιν μιμήσασθαι οἱ πολλοὶ ἢ . . . σε . . . τὸν αὐτῶν ἄρχοντα, τοῦ Καίσαρος φίλον καὶ ἐπίτροπον. Epictetus, *Arrian's Discourses of Epictetus* 3.4.2–3.

257. πόλις ἄνδρα διδάσκει. Simonides, elegaic fragment 15.

The world of late antiquity was a city-world; each city was an island universe, completely engrossed in its own affairs and wholly under the rule and sway of leading personalities. The local kings had sunk to ritual figures, but the need and hunger for leadership was as great as ever. The whole society crystallized around its leaders, but by what right did they lead? By popular choice—that was the democratic principle. But popular choice has rather vague rules of succession that brought ceaseless unrest and the chronic disease of the antique world—faction, stasis.

Because Rome was the most important city in the ancient world, the nature of its popular government is of particular significance and is very well documented. The basis of all Roman politics, writes Theodor Mommsen, is of three principles: (1) that an official gives direct commands, (2) that the Senate is the highest authority in the state, and (3) that all things must be sanctioned by a sovereign popular assembly.[258] All office was magistracy, and all magistrates were priests in Rome: the political structure was also the state church. The great significance of priesthood in public life, says Georg Wissowa, lay in the fact that "its bearers all held at the same time the highest civil offices and so played the decisive role in the Senate."[259] Certain rights and privileges the common people claimed for themselves at all times: they claimed the right to spontaneous, direct, uncontrolled demonstrations for some outstanding person. Such demonstrations were the antithesis of the orderly subordination which was the ideal of the ruling families and went back to the old days of the kings. Thus when Publicola died, he was publicly buried and honored by a year-long mourning of the matrons.[260] Menenius

---

258. Source unidentified.
259. "... seine Träger [bekleideten] zugleich die höchsten Staatsämter und damit im Senat [spielten] die entscheideten Rolle." Georg Wissowa, *Religion und Kultus der Römer* (Munich: Beck, 1971), 480.
260. Dionysius of Halicarnassus, *Antiquitatum Romanarum* 5.48.

was buried by passing the hat among the plebes while the Senate, not to be put to shame, contributed land for his sepulchre.[261] It was a rule laid down by the aristocrats, once they had abolished the popular kingship, "that wherever a multitude was, there should be a lawful governor of that multitude present"[262]—appointed by themselves.

The spirit of the aristocratic rule always fighting to hold its own, always moralizing and appealing to fake traditions to inspire loyalty and submission, is shown in the story of the Alban migration to Rome. All the poorer people went to the king, says Dionysius of Halicarnassus, and clamored to settle in Rome and divide up the new land equally. But the more illustrious and the more important of the people, whether by merit or by chance, resented leaving their holdings and their ancestral hearths, so the Senate planned to check the business by a call to arms. There was an uproar in the popular assembly at this, and the nobles immediately had the assemblage surrounded by soldiers—their own retainers with drawn swords. Then Tullus gave them a speech: Tomorrow, he said, your city will be destroyed and you must all go to Rome and take what you find there.[263] Expedience and self-interest inspired that firm sense of rule and right, which the Romans always flattered themselves was an abstract moral principle. Against it there were the ancient folk practices which no declarations of law or philosophy could suppress: when a man was popular with the Roman people, nothing on earth could keep them from demonstrating in his favor and escorting him through the streets. In the end the highest and holiest office in the state, that of the *imperator*, rested wholly on one thing alone—spontaneous popular acclaim. An ancient grave inscription from the Appian Way is typical of the public spirit of Rome: "Stranger, stop and look. Here the city holds the bones of a good merciful son,

---

261. Dionysius of Halicarnassus, *Antiquitatum Romanarum* 6.96.
262. Source unidentified.
263. Dionysius of Halicarnassus, *Antiquitatum Romanarum* 3.30.

THE OFFICE OF BISHOP IN THE EARLY CHRISTIAN CHURCH

a lover of the poor. I beseech thee, wayfarer, do no injury to this monument."[264] Cicero praises "Tuditanus, who in pallium and high boots used to throw out coins to the people from the rostrum."[265] Such a generous soul would receive, in recognition for his public spirit, the title of father. A man might give such a public donative in memory of his father, "in his father's name." "The Roman people disapprove of private luxury," wrote Cicero, "but admire public magnificence"; therefore, he argues, "candidates to public office ought not to be forbidden the exercise of that kindness which is liberality rather than bribery."[266] Naturally the seeds of abuse lay in such a system, which finally destroyed itself.

In imperial times only the emperor was allowed to give popular donatives—the right was jealously forbidden to all others, for to give a public gift was to vie with the emperor in popularity.[267] The emperor on his part, however, was under constant and heavy obligation to keep up a steady outpouring of donatives. "As *Ersatz* for the political rights of which the emperors robbed the Roman people," said Viktor E. Gardthausen, "we may consider the duty of providing public sustenance which the emperors took over, not as their victorious general . . . but as the richest man in the city," following a very ancient tradition.[268] The obligation of

---

264. Source unidentified.
265. *Tuditanus nempe ille, qui cum palla et cothurnis nummos populo de rostris spargere solebat.* Cicero, *Philippicae* 3.6.
266. *Odit populus Romanus privatam luxuriam, publicam magnificentiam diligit . . . nec candidatis ista benignitas adimenda est quae liberalitatem magis significat quam largitionem.* Cicero, *Pro Murena* 76.4–77.1.
267. Hugh Nibley, *The Ancient State: The Rulers and the Ruled* (Salt Lake City: Deseret Book and FARMS, 1991), 152.
268. "Als Ersatz für die politischen Rechte, welche das Kaiserthum dem römische Volke raubte, kann die Verpflegung Roms angesehen werden, welche die Kaiser übernahmen; es war nicht der Kriegsherr des römischen Reiches . . . sondern vielmehr der mächtigste Mann der Hauptstadt." Viktor E. Gardthausen, *Augustus und seine Zeit*, 2 vols. in 5 (Leipzig: Teubner, 1891–1904), 1.2.587.

the best-fixed citizen to be a leader in the community was supported by ample rewards in a world in which "every municipal government could be summarized in two terms: the honor of the city (a second religion with the Romans), and the dignity of the citizen. The first of these meant constant rivalry among the cities to outshine each other; the second, among the individuals of any one city."[269]

From this it is easy to see that the ascendancy of a particular man in the city as a bishop would not be a new or sensational thing. Any man holding such an office would naturally be expected to be a model of dignity and deportment, but also of kindness, generosity, and popularity. Religious communities within cities—the ubiquitous colleges—followed the same pattern. Thus, during a festival, people in the great cities made fun of the Roman origin of the Emperor Alexander Severus by calling him a *Syrum archisynagogum* [high synagogue] and an *archierum* [high priest].[270] In the time of Belisarius, Procopius tells us, the chief men of African towns were nearly all priests. Sidonius's account to a friend of how "there you stood, with a fine grace . . . half torn to pieces by the people madly rushing to salute you, but so loyally responsive to this popular devotion that those who took the greatest liberties seemed surest of your most generous acknowledgments" might have been written by Cicero, but it describes the popular acclaim not of a hero of the Republic, but of a local bishop.[271]

When a debtor came to him seeking sanctuary in the church, Augustine took up a public collection and thus paid off the debt. But such a public collection was an accepted Roman practice, and Augustine as a bishop was simply fulfilling the office as would normally be expected of the head man of the city. Augustine's own election to his high office,

---

269. Source unidentified.
270. Scriptores Historiae Augustae, *Alexander Severus Aelii Lampridii* 28.7.
271. Source unidentified.

like that of his friends, was strictly a popular gesture: the people chanted his name over and over again in front of his house and would have torn him to pieces had he not accepted the honor which it was their right to bestow.[272] For every bishop had to be elected by the people of the city and their vote took the old form of the popular *acclamatio*. Ambrose was thus made bishop of Milan before he was even a Christian. It is no wonder that for him the words *populus* and *fideles* are absolutely interchangeable—he makes no distinction between the old city *populace* and the Christian *congregation*—they are one and the same, and the man who leads them is no gift of apostolic insight to the world. Jerome makes layman the equivalent of *plebes,* and Leo the Great uses only *plebes,* never *populi,* which shows that he recognizes the pagan implications as well as Ambrose did a hundred years before him; but whereas Ambrose admits the fact, Leo would sooner avoid it. But Hermann Usener has pointed out that "In the record of the daily schedule of the papal chancellery, the *liber diurnus,* edited at the beginning of the eighth century, it is still customary, after mentioning the clergy expressly, to include the nobility and the populace of the city as factors in the choosing of the pope."[273] And exactly as distinguished ancients had competed bitterly for the highest honors of the city by rival largesses and all sorts of political tricks and popular appeals, so rival candidates for the office of bishop continued to play the same game with the same pieces and for identical stakes.

Of course, such a thing as a candidate to an apostolic office is unthinkable—the Lord alone chooses apostles, but

---

272. Possidius, *Vita Sancti Augustini Episcopi* 4, in *PL* 32:36–37.
273. "Noch die Formulare der päpstlichen Kanzlei, der 'liber diurnus,' dessen Redaktion man in den Anfang des VII. Jahrh. setzt, pflegen nach der Erwähnung des Klerus ausdrücklich Adel und Volk der Stadt Rom als Faktoren der Papstwahl zu nennen." Hermann Usener, "Das Verhältnis des römischen Senats zur Kirche in der Ostgothenzeit," *Kleine Schriften,* 4 vols. (Osnabrück: Zeller, 1965), 4:145.

these men were candidates in every sense of the word. "The defensor of the Roman Church has informed us," wrote Cassiodorus, "that lately, when a president was sought for the papal chair, so much were the usual largesses to the poor augmented by the promises which had been extorted from the candidate, that, shameful to say, even the sacred vessels were exposed to sale in order to provide the necessary money."[274] The riots in Rome among the pagans concerning the qualities of Clement were quickly succeeded by identical disputes within the Christian congregation of the city—identical in nature, but much worse—and the rivalry between Damasus and Liberius was not settled until the corpses of 137 of the faithful had been removed from the scene of the controversy in St. Peter's. The first epistle of Clement deals with these very conditions in Corinth, which the writer finds "loathsome, disgusting, and devilish."[275]

The elected bishop would often make the most of his popularity in the approved pagan manner. Thus Bishop Firmilianus had all the fixtures of a Roman noble: he would dictate letters as he walked along in the marketplace, followed by a large troop of hangers-on. He erected for himself as a tribune the high throne and *secretum* [judge's chamber] of a Roman judge, and in speaking, he slapped his thigh and stamped his foot just like any popular orator.[276] This was not the exception, but the rule. The priests of God are, before all things, magistrates, Eusebius reminds us. "Whenever I have a case to try," says his great contemporary, Gregory Naziansus, "I do so, even when the accused is one of my best friends or belongs to the highest nobility, for nothing is superior to the law of God and

---

274. *Nuper siquidem ad nos defensor Ecclesiae Romanae flebili allegatione pervenit, cum apostolicae sedi peteretur antistes quosdam nefaria machinatione necessitatem temporis aucupatos ita facultates pauperum extortis promissionibus ingravasse, ut, quo dictu nefas est, etiam sacra vasa emptioni publicae viderentur exposita.* Cassiodorus, *Historia Ecclesiastica* 9.15, in *PL* 69:779.
275. *1 Clement* 1.1, in *PG* 1:206.
276. Eusebius, *Historia Ecclesiastica* 7.30.8–9, in *PG* 20:712–13.

THE OFFICE OF BISHOP IN THE EARLY CHRISTIAN CHURCH   81

of his church."[277] Note the patronizing attitude, expressing as a noble sentiment what anyone in a democratic state would take for granted. The bishops are plainly aristocrats, as we shall presently see. "He would win my favor, I the people's and he and I together, yours," writes Sidonius in a Ciceronian vein.[278] The method of winning favor in this case utilized shiploads of wheat and honey: "We should have these cargoes ready in no time for the expectant crowds."

"The episcopal epoch, exactly like the imperial epoch is, before all else, an epoch of municipal civilization. When the imperial machine collapsed, the cities remained standing, solid pieces of the ancient defense structure."[279] Note the exact parallel between the emergence of the city supreme and the local church supreme: in both cases it was the passing of a central authority that left local authority the only and therefore the highest in the *oecumene* [entire inhabited world]. But just as a city prefect does not have the authority of an emperor because an emperor installed him and then passed away, neither does a local bishop have the authority of an apostle because an apostle installed him and then passed away. "The Christian population in each city," according to Duchesne, once the ubiquitous, traveling general authorities were no more, "raised itself from the position of an imperceptible minority to that of a respectable minority; it finally became the majority, and then the unanimity.... The fourth century saw the last acts of this transformation almost everywhere, as least as far as concerns the city masses."[280] Now when these "im-

---

277. Source unidentified.
278. Source unidentified.
279. Source unidentified.
280. "La population chrétienne s'éleva, dans chaque ville, de la situation de minorité imperceptible à celle de minorité respectable; elle devint ensuite la majorité, puis l'unanimité.... Le quatrième siècle vit à peu près partout les derniers actes de cette transformation, au moins en ce qui regarde les masses populaires des villes." Duchesne, *Origines du Culte Chrétien*, 11.

perceptible minorities" were bade farewell by the apostles, they were, to say the least, in a bad way; in the days of the apostolic fathers they had become even worse—utterly corrupt within themselves. Yet from that point they grew to complete domination without the guide of any apostles or general authorities. How could they win over the urban masses without being like them? They could not: "They were Christians," writes Duchesne of the newly converted masses of the fourth century, but they were Christians in the only way such people could be—in name only.[281] The early Christians had wanted none of this sort of thing, as the world had wanted none of them: *Unam omnium rempublicam agnoscimus—mundum* [We acknowledge a single republic for everyone—the world], Tertullian declared.[282] This indeed was the Jewish heritage—Moses taught that all the world was a single state, writes Philo.[283] It was always popular for bishops to deplore the busy preoccupations of the world in which they found themselves, yet the whole nature of their office was just such busy preoccupation. "Following the voice of God," wrote Nicephorus to Leo III, "I turned from all honors and authority and from the restless ambition of the royal court and city affairs."[284] But he soon found out that actually to leave those things in deed as well as word could only mean ceasing to be a bishop. After all, such denunciation of the noise and distraction of empty affairs was ever stock with the schools, and the Sophists worked it to death as a means of furthering their public careers.

---

281. "La masse était chrétienne comme le pouvait être la masse, de surface et d'étiquette." Louis Duchesne, *Histoire Ancienne de l'Église*, 5th ed., 3 vols. (Paris: de Boccard, 1929), 3:5.
282. Tertullian, *Adversus Gentes* 38, in *PL* 1:528.
283. Source unidentified.
284. Source unidentified.

The Importance of Each Bishop Becomes Tied to the Prominence of His City

The preeminence of Rome. Every bishop in Christendom has his office designated by the name of a city. No one doubts that the office of bishop is primarily a city office. The perpetual leadership of the church, according to the bull *Unam Sanctam,* is in the succession of Peter,[285] "which succession is to be found in the bishop of the city of Rome."[286] Early Christianity was a city religion. It had to be if the apostles were to carry out their great assignment. It spread, says Norman H. Baynes, "from the provincial capital . . . to the country-side," so that "the provincial capital came to be regarded as the mother church."[287] The last expression is strictly in the heathen tradition. Polycarp wrote that "faith is the Mother of all of us,"[288] and Eusebius says "all men had God for a Father, and for a Mother, true piety."[289] The idea of mother church is something else—it is simply the mother city. A center from which settlements were spread in a colony was always called the "mother city" or metropolis. Chrysostom calls the church of Antioch "our mother and the mother of all the churches. Mother, not only because she is first in age, but because she was built up by apostolic hands."[290] Which is he praising, the church of Antioch or the city of Antioch? They

---

285. Heinrich Denzinger, *Enchiridion Symbolorum Definitionum et Declarationum de Rebus Fidei et Morum,* 31st ed. (Rome: Herder, 1957), items 468–69.
286. Ibid., item 466.
287. Norman H. Baynes, "Alexandria and Constantinople: A Study in Ecclesiastical Diplomacy," *Journal of Egyptian Archaeology* 7 (1926): 146.
288. [πίστις] ἐστὶ μήτηρ πάντων ἡμῶν. Polycarp, *Epistola ad Philippenses* 3.2–3, in *PG* 5:1008.
289. αὐτίκα γοῦν ὥσπερ ἐξ ἑνὸς φύντες πατρὸς, ἑνός τε θεοῦ οἷα παῖδες, καὶ μητρὸς μιᾶς τῆς ἀληθοῦς εὐσεβείας. Eusebius, *De Laudibus Constantini Oratio* 16.7, in *PG* 20:142.
290. τὴν μητέρα ἡμῶν καὶ τῶν ἐκκλησιῶν ἁπασῶν. μήτηρ μὲν γὰρ, οὐχ ὅτι τῷ χρόνῳ πρεσβυτέρα μόνον ἐστίν, ἀλλ' ὅτι καὶ ὑπὸ ἀποστολικῶν ἐθεμελιώθη χειρῶν. John Chrysostom, *In Inscriptionem Actorum* 2.1, in *PG* 51:77.

are inseparable. In the best known of all pagan hymns, Horace prays that the sun may never shine on anything greater than Alma Roma.[291] One of the earliest bishops of Rome is represented as signing himself "Hyginius in Christ's name *episcopus* of Almae Urbis Romae," using Horace's own expression.[292] Note, he is not "bishop of the mother church," but "bishop of the mother city of Rome"—that title having been used long before the Christians. Because he was bishop of such an important city, he must have been an important bishop, and his glory derives from his city, not from his apostolic calling. As we have seen, the earliest bishops made no appeal to any apostolic authority. "From the moment when Christianity aspired to embrace the *Orbis Romanus* in its entirety," writes Duchesne, "it could have no other capital [than Rome]. It was, besides that, consecrated as it were by the preaching and death of the two great apostles. ... Rome, capital of the empire, seat of St. Peter, holy place of the apostles, became without dispute the metropolis—the mother city—of the church."[293]

Now, though there is no proof that Peter was ever a bishop at Rome, and nothing at all to indicate that the apostles thought of the city as holy (it was indeed abominable Babylon for the early Christians, as Duchesne often reminds us in other passages discretely distant from this one),[294] there is one point none will dispute, and Duchesne wisely begins his argument with it, so that the other very dubious points

---

291. Horace, *Carmen Saeculare* 9–12.
292. *Hyginius in Christi nomine almae urbis Romae episcopus.* Hyginius, *Epistola* 1, in *PG* 5:1087.
293. "Du moment où le christianisme aspirait à embrasser l'Orbis Romanus tout entièr, il ne pouvait avoir d'autre capitale. Elle était d'ailleurs comme consacrée par la predication et le martyre des deux plus grands apôtres. . . . Rome, capitale de l'empire, siege de saint Pierre, lieu sacré des apôtres, devient sans conteste la métropole de l'Église." Duchesne, *Origines du Culte Chrétien*, 14–15.
294. Duchesne, *Origines du Culte Chrétien*, 14.

THE OFFICE OF BISHOP IN THE EARLY CHRISTIAN CHURCH   85

will seem to follow from it as corollaries: that is the point that Rome was the first city of the world.[295] When the importance of a bishop came to be measured directly by the importance of his city, the bishop of Rome would of course come first. But Duchesne should never have used such an argument at all. The primacy of the pope is supposed to rest on the claim to a special office inherited directly from Christ through Peter and not (of all things) on the bigness and importance of a city. Yet it was not Duchesne who first saw in the importance of the city the foundation of its bishop's claim to primacy. Eusebius honors Julius of Rome as "the leader of the imperial (or ruling) city" in a discussion wherein he argues that the leader of the church is Constantine.[296] Everyone knew that Rome was the imperial city, and everyone knew that Julius was its bishop—but not a word as to his having any primacy in the church. According to the Byzantine writers, "the governor [*eparchos*] of Rome is not the Roman emperor (who had long ceased to live in Rome), but the chief man in Rome, the pontifex," a political figure.[297]

A flawed principle. The principle that a bishop was exactly as important as his city is certainly not a holy one and certainly was not known to the ancient church, but by the fourth century it became the guiding principle of general church organization. According to Baynes, when a traveling apostolate proved far more inadequate than anything subsequently invented, "we hear during the latter half of the second century of the gathering of bishops in councils."[298] Does the traveling apostolate, inadequate and outdone, raise any objections? Is

---

295. Duchesne, *Histoire Ancienne de l'Église*, 1:536–38.
296. τῆς δέ γε βασιλευούσης πόλεως ὁ μὲν προεστὼς ὑστέρει διὰ γῆρας. Eusebius, *Vita Constantini* 3.7, in *PG* 20:1061.
297. Source unidentified.
298. "When a travelling apostolate, when the web of a far-flung correspondence both proved inadequate, we hear during the latter half of the second century of the gathering of bishops in councils." Baynes, "Alexandria and Constantinople," 146.

there any whisper of jealousy, of rivalry, or of overlapping areas of authority? What does the inadequate apostolate have to say on the matter? Who consults it before going about setting up the new system? What Baynes conveniently overlooks is not that the apostolate was inadequate—it was nonexistent. From the first, the organization of these meetings of bishops is very significant: it is always the bishops of a particular province that come together, and they always meet in the capital of that province. That is natural enough. The restored church has always organized its missions corresponding to geographical and linguistic boundaries—after all, it was the nations to which the apostles preached, and they preached to them as nations, fully recognizing the convenience of established political boundaries and divisions. By about the middle of the third century, regular meetings of bishops were being held in each province once a year. The general Council of Nicaea made this practice compulsory. What was more natural than that the bishop of the capital city to which all the other bishops had to come for the conference should be the one to make all arrangements for the meeting, the housing of the bishops, the exact time and place of the sessions, and should be the one to send out the notices? And what is more natural than that such functions should bestow upon him a kind of headship over the others? Upon nothing did the early church insist more emphatically than the absolute equality of bishops, but there was a strong historical force at work.

The more important the city, the more important the bishop, was a principle which was not necessary while the church enjoyed the guidance of traveling general authorities, and the early emergence of the principle is thus another witness of the absence of general authority in the church. Had there been a need in the church, that head with general authority of course would have determined the importance of any office and of the divisions of the church and not left it to the purely mechanical and secular calculations of the census taker. Churchmen have recognized this and have tried to deny anything but a perfect resemblance between the two systems. Thus Duchesne insists that in delimiting the areas of ecclesiastical authority, the provinces of the church, though having the same name and the same area as the provinces of the empire, did not copy those provinces but were identical with them by virtue of having the same cause or origin.[299] This argument is as absurd as it is disingenuous.[300] There had been plenty of historical accidents to influence the final configuration of provincial boundaries, which were by no means the result of purely physical considerations, and those historical accidents were not duplicated hundreds of years later as the church spread. "At the Council of Nicaea," he observes, "the grouping of bishops by provinces and their subordination to the bishop of the civil metropolis are already an accomplished fact. . . . The provinces to which the council refers are those of the time, those which Diocletian had formed."[301] So they were formed by Diocletian, not the apostles. There is nothing apostolic about this—but is there anything wrong with it? There is, for the inevitable hierarchy among the bishops not only wiped out the basic principle of episcopal equality, but introduced an "order of the priesthood" in which rank was assigned purely by the census taker, and this rank inevitably and quickly was taken as a degree of holiness. The bigger the city, the holier its head. God does not work that way.

We readily agree with Duchesne that the bishop of Rome would of course be a top man in the church,[302] but could it be

---

299. Duchesne, *Origines du Culte Chrétien*, 17, 20, 24.

300. Duchesne says elsewhere they simply followed civil bodies. Duchesne, *Origines du Culte Chrétien*, 12, 22.

301. "Au concile de Nicée, le groupement des évêques par provinces et leur subordination à l'évêque de la métropole civile sont déjà choses acquises. . . . Les provinces visées par le concile sont celles du temps, celles que Diocletian avait formées en subdivisant les anciennes." Duchesne, *Origines du Culte Chrétien*, 22.

302. Duchesne, *Origines du Culte Chrétien*, 24; Duchesne, *Histoire Ancienne de l'Église*, 2:661–62.

the true church if he owed his primacy to the preeminence of his city, as the Council of Constantinople in 381 made clear he did? Originally the *prima sedes* [the senior episcopal see] was the oldest, not the biggest, bishopric in a province. By all accounts Jerusalem would be the *prima sedes*—James the Just being always taken as the type and model of all bishops, as well as the first bishop. He was ordained not by two apostles ("double apostolate"), but by three—the three highest; and his city was sanctified not by the preaching and death merely of apostles, but of the Lord himself. The Council of Nicaea had to take special recognition of Jerusalem: "Since it is the prevailing custom and the ancient tradition, that the bishop of Aelia [Jerusalem] be honored, so let his successor be in the future ... while the metropolis retains its dignity intact."[303] This is a laborious special concession—on the present principle Jerusalem has no claim, but is offered this concession out of respect for tradition. Jerusalem is not called by the scriptural name which alone proclaims its unrivaled primacy as the Holy City, and it is held in respect only by virtue of a special decree to sustain its all but vanished dignity. Jerusalem as a city was nothing.

A few years later at Antioch the principle was laid down that "the bishop in the metropolis has charge of the entire province because all those who have any business come together from all directions in the metropolis; therefore, it was decided that he should accordingly be afforded a superior honor and that the other bishops should undertake nothing further without him."[304] How neatly things have been reversed: once the

---

303. ἐπειδὴ συνήθεια κεκράτηκα καὶ παράδοσις ἀρχαῖα, ὥστε τὸν ἐν Αἰλίᾳ ἐπίσκοπον τιμᾶσθαι, ἐχέτω τὴν ἀκολουθίαν τῆς τιμῆς τῇ μητροπόλει σωζομένου τοῦ οἰκείου ἀξιώματος. Council of Nicaea, Canon 7, in Hefele, *Histoire des Conciles d'Après les Documents Originaux*, 1:569.

304. "L'évêque placé à la tête de la métropole est également chargé du soin de la province, car, c'est à la métropole que se rendent tous ceux qui ont des affaires à traiter. En conséquence il a été réglé qu'il occuperait aussi le premier rang pour les honneurs et que les autres évêques ne

place was important because of the office, and the office was important because of the prophet who held it. Now the office is important because of the place, and the man is important because of the office. Note that an archbishop is more holy than others not because God has established such an office, but specifically because he happens to live in the capital where people come to do business. But if the metropolitan was the highest bishop in the affairs of a province, what about the relative ranks of metropolitans? Were not some provinces more important than others, just as some cities were, and should not the holy principle of size and number be consistently applied to them? It should indeed. Constantine remarked once to Eusebius that while bishops within provinces could always appeal to their metropolitan for judgment when there were differences among them, there would have to be one yet higher to appeal to when the metropolitans disagreed among themselves—and he, Constantine, was that man.[305] But after Constantine died there was trouble in agreeing upon a head of the church, and the Council of Constantinople in 381 recognized reality by proclaiming five dioceses "as resorts of an ecclesiastical jurisdiction superior to that of the provinces or provincial synods."[306] Needless to say, these were the four world cities, plus little Jerusalem—the fifth wheel, the uncomfortable reminder of another day and another order.

Following the civic pattern. The hierarchy of bishop, metropolitan, and patriarch was no more an invention of the church than dioceses and provinces were. It was taken over from the civil pattern, as Baynes has shown: the metropolitan, called "patriarch," corresponds to the *vicarius* over the imperial

---

pourraient rien faire sans lui." Council of Antioch, Canon 9, in Hefele, *Histoire des Conciles d'Après les Documents Originaux,* 1:717.

305. Source unidentified.

306. "Comme resorts d'une juridiction ecclésiastique supérieure à celle des métropolitains et des conciles provinciaux." Duchesne, *Origines du Culte Chrétien,* 24.

dioceses.[307] The patriarch of Alexandria had unusual power over all Egypt because the Hellenistic administration of Egypt had always been from a single center—Alexandria—and the system had been preserved by the Romans. "The importance and precedence of a bishopric depended upon the importance and precedence within the Empire of the bishop's city."[308] That was the rule: the famous third canon of the Council of Constantinople in 381 declared that the bishop of Constantinople should stand second in honor to the bishop of Rome *"because the city of which he is bishop is New Rome."*[309]

"The rank of churches," says Baynes, "is determined by the prominence of cities as *civil* capitals."[310] Letters attributed to the earliest popes, though not genuine, state the principle again and again, which is binding on the church by at least the fourth century. Bishops are not to be established in *castellis* [military posts] or in smaller cities or villas, according to a decree of Anacletus—such places should be managed by presbyters only, for "the name of bishop should be used as title and denomination only of an honorable city."[311] Here a big city is by definition an "honorable" one, and only such an one can have a bishop. What a significant norm for apostolic holiness! The same letter notes that though "the provinces existed long before the time of Christ's advent," and are therefore of non-Christian origin, "the division was renewed by the apostles and by the blessed Clement, our predecessor," so they are Christian after all.[312]

---

307. Baynes, "Alexandria and Constantinople," 147.
308. Ibid.
309. Ibid., emphasis in original.
310. Ibid., emphasis in original.
311. *Episcopi autem non in castellis aut modicis civitatibus debent constitui, sed presbyteri per castella et modicas civitates atque villas debent ab episcopis ordinari et poni. . . . et, ut dictum est, non ad modicam civitatem, ne vilescat nomen episcopi, aut aliubi, sed ad honorabilem urbem titulandus et denominandus est.* Anacletus, *Epistola* 3.2, in PG 2:812.
312. *Provinciae autem multo ante Christi adventum tempore divisae sunt maxima ex parte, et postea ab apostolis et beato Clemente praedecessore nostro ipsa divisio est renovata.* Anacletus, *Epistola* 2.4, in PG 2:807.

Plainly our author feels there is something wrong with ecclesiastical organization that follows along strictly civil heathen lines: the perfect parallel of the two led to the belief, held by such respected authorities as John Chrysostom, that the apostles actually took over and administered the civil government of the whole world in their day! A fantastic picture, but how is one otherwise to account for the fact that a church government that is supposed to have been set up in its perfection by the apostles copies all its forms from the pagans? Bishops are to appeal to patriarchs or primates, says our text, though they are called by different names.[313] There was considerable looseness in the nomenclature and the rank. An archbishop, we are told, is the same as a metropolitan, who gets his title from the fact that he presides in a metropolis, which is defined as a city in which are located the lower courts of law.[314] The civil pattern decides all these degrees of glory.

Another letter attributed to Anacletus says that primates or patriarchs can only be bishops of a city which is both a metropolis and has a church dating from the earliest times. Lacking churches *priscis temporibus* [dating from the earliest times], all the other big-city bishops are only archbishops or metropolitans "because this corresponds to the principles laid down in the civil law."[315] "No archbishops are to be called primates," according to a letter attributed to Anicetus, "unless they hold *primas civitates*," by which is meant not the first cities to receive the gospel, but the biggest cities: "they are called patriarchs and primates because of their multitude," this being, our letter brazenly announces, "the

---

313. *Ipsis quoque in civitatibus vel locis nostris, patriarchas vel primates, qui unam formam tenent, licet diversa sint nomina, leges divinae et ecclesiasticae poni et esse iusserunt, ad quos episcopi (si necesse fuerit) confugerent, eosque appellarent, et ipse primatum nomine fruerentur, et non alii.* Anacletus, *Epistola* 2.4, in *PG* 2:807.
314. Anacletus, *Epistola* 2.4, 3.3, in *PG* 2:807–8, 813.
315. *Quia haec eadem et leges saeculi in suis continent principibus.* Anacletus, *Epistola* 3.3, in *PG* 2:813.

rule of the apostles and their successors."³¹⁶ Jerusalem was contemptuously pushed aside; it lacked one thing—size. The holiest sees of Christendom remained the four world cities of the time: "Evidently the importance of these respective churches due to their size and to the dignity of their cities was the chief factor in winning for them this exceptional recognition."³¹⁷

Another letter of Anicetus tells how the apostles Peter, James, and John ordained the most blessed James, who was called the Just, and was even called the brother of the Lord after the manner of the flesh.³¹⁸ If three archbishops were necessary to ordain James, our writer continues, "a bishop should certainly not be ordained by less than three other bishops," while an archbishop should be ordained by even more.³¹⁹ In view of the nature and origin of the office of archbishop, to call Peter, James, and John archbishops is a supreme declaration of bankruptcy: this very letter states that originally there was no difference among bishops, archbishops being a later development.

A principle of power. The principle that made the glory of a bishopric a direct function of the size and importance of

---

316. *Nuli archiepiscopi primates vocentur, nisi illi qui primas tenent civitates, quarum episcopos apostoli et successores apostolorum regulariter patriarchas et primates esse constituerunt . . . propter multitudinem eorum, primatum constitui.* Anicetus, *Epistola ad Galliae Episcopos* 2, in *PG* 5:1131.

317. Source unidentified.

318. It is strange that though the Roman Catholic Church today explains this as meaning that he was a half brother or stepbrother, being the son of Joseph by an earlier marriage, none of the ancient sources uses any word for half brother or stepbrother in describing James—though there was no shortage of such words in the old languages and people were careful and specific in designating family relationships.

319. *Si autem non minus quam a tribus apostolis tantus vir fuit ordinatus episcopus, patet profecto eos formam, instituente Domino, tradidisse, non minus quam a tribus episcopis, episcopum ordinari debere. Sed crescente numero episcoporum . . . debent etiam plures augeri, id est, si archiepiscopus dein obierit.* Anicetus, *Epistola ad Galliae Episcopos* 1, in *PG* 5:1129–30.

its city was scrupulously observed in practice. There was, of course, an important exception to the rule that bigness and importance were the same; the capital was the exception, as in the modern world. The Byzantine historian Socrates (ca. A.D. 380–450) tells us that many of the bishops recognized the superiority of the bishop of Nicomedia "because Diocletian had set up the imperial headquarters at that place."[320] This is perfectly consistent with the statement of the council that the bishop of a metropolis was more important than other bishops because the business of the province was done in his city and because of the statement of the Council of Constantinople defining a metropolis as a city where the provincial courts of law were located. "As early as the year 42, Antioch had dethroned Jerusalem," according to Albert Dufourcq. "Antioch appeared as the metropolis of infant Christianity; it was from there that the apostles gradually spread the gospel throughout the world."[321] Duchesne has discoursed at length on how Milan ruled the church as long as Milan was the capital: it was there under the supervision of the bishop of Milan that councils were held to settle questions of priority and subordination. It was to Milan and not to Rome that the churches of the West appealed for advice and instruction in matters of organization and ritual; Milan, not Rome, plays the leading role in the story of the ritual and liturgy of the Western churches and to this day celebrates Mass after a rite different from that of Rome. Why this overwhelming, if only

---

320. ἴσχυε δὲ κατ' ἐκεῖνο τοῦ καιροῦ μάλιστα ὁ Εὐσέβιος, ὅτι κατὰ τὴν Νικομέδειαν ὁ βασιλεὺς τότε διέτριβε. καὶ γὰρ ἐκεῖ τὰ βασίλεια μικρὸν ἔμπρεσθεν οἱ περὶ Διοκλετιανὸν ἐπεποίηντο. διὰ τοῦτο οὖν πολλοὶ τῶν ἐπισκόπων τῷ Εὐσεβίῳ ὑπήκουον. Socrates Scholasticus, *Historia Ecclesiastica* 1.6, in *PG* 67:52.

321. "Vers l'an 42, Antioche a détrôné Jérusalem. Antioche apparaît comme la métropole du christianisme naissant; c'est de là que les Apôtres répandent peu à peu l'Evangile dans le monde." Albert Dufourcq, *Histoire de la Fondation de l'Église: La Révolution Religieuse*, 5th ed., L'Avenir du Christianisme 1 (Paris: Bloud, 1909), 220.

passing, preponderance of Milan? "The true reason," writes Duchesne, "is that Milan was the official imperial residence, the capital of the empire of the West. . . . Milan was the great center of the Western church only because she was the capital of the empire."[322] This seems to explain away an embarrassing phenomenon—the bishop of Milan was not the real head of the church; he only acted as such while Milan was the capital. But that raises as grave a question as it answers: If Rome were the rightful apostolic head of the church, then the size and importance of Milan would have absolutely nothing to do with the question, and the church would not for a moment have taken orders from Ambrose as it did. Much later, Rome was accepted as the head of the church no matter where the capital was or how big it was. But in the fourth century and long after, the capital city always laid claim to being the headquarters of the church—a claim that was universally respected. Duchesne has another explanation of the embarrassing phenomenon: "[Many churches] appealed to Milan . . . in preference to Rome," he notes, but that was "only because Milan was nearer."[323] A few miles difference in geographical proximity outweighs all the claims of Rome! What a feeble argument! In later centuries, when everyone believed in Rome's apostolic calling, such a consideration would have been thought ridiculous, if not blasphemous. When, during the Council of Sardica in 347, Julius, bishop of Rome, emerges as the most important bishop, it is because Rome is again, temporarily, the capital.

"By basing its claim to precedence on its apostolic foundation," writes Father John Bligh, "the Roman see avoided the

---

322. "La vraie raison, c'est que Milan était la residence impériale officielle, la capitale de l'empire d'Occident. . . . Milan était ainsi . . . le grand center des relations ecclésiastiques occidentals, et cela uniquement parce qu'elle était la capitale de l'empire." Duchesne, *Origines du Culte Chrétien*, 36.

323. "[Beaucoup d'églises] recouraient à Milan . . . de préfèrence à Rome . . . uniquement parce que Milan était plus voisine." Duchesne, *Origines du Culte Chrétien*, 37–38.

humiliating position of the Patriarchate of Constantinople, which frankly admitted that its claim to the Primacy of Honor rested on its connexion with the seat of Empire."[324] What else could Constantinople do? Everybody knew that it had not been founded by the apostles, though Constantine tried to set up there the common tomb of all the apostles. But Alexandria and Antioch based their claims to precedence on apostolic foundation just as much and quite as rightly as Rome. When Alexandria matched Rome's claim by announcing her foundation by two apostles, Rome countered in 362 with the doctrine of the double apostolate—which led to embarrassing complications and was later dropped. But as F. J. Badcock observes,[325] there was no mention of apostolic succession in the orders of 325, which maintained the customary privileges of Rome, Alexandria, and Antioch, the sees being in the order of their civic importance, but not of apostolic foundation. To evidence this, Jerusalem remained a suffragan see of Caesarea (a much larger city) in spite of its being the mother of all the churches. Later attempts to build up in retrospect a theoretical apostolic foundation for the Roman claim (discussed by Badcock) do not obscure the eagerness with which the Roman Church describes herself as the mistress of the world by virtue of having inherited the glory of ancient Rome—papal Rome gloried in being the successor of imperial Rome from whom she took what was peculiar and distinctive in dress, ritual, and ideas of government.

Nancy Lenkeith has most recently dealt with this much-treated subject. So close were the ties between mother church and mother city that "if Rome were destroyed, the physical basis of the legitimacy of both popes and emperors would be lost altogether: if its power grew out of control, popes

---

324. John Bligh, "The 'Edict of Milan': Curse or Blessing?" *Church Quarterly Review* 153 (1952): 307.

325. F. J. Badcock, *The History of the Creeds,* 2nd ed. (New York: Macmillan, 1938), 165–79.

and emperors might lose their claim to the city. Hence the hostility of a population which found itself thwarted every time it tried to do what Milan, Florence, and the others were doing."[326] The dependence of religious priority and authority on the occupation of a particular piece of ground, even if that ground is Jerusalem itself, has no place in a church that is led from heaven. In the case of Rome it becomes a fanatical obsession. Chrysostom, totally at a loss for any sure and reliable principle of authority on which to refute the heretics, finally falls back on the ultimate argument: we must assume and teach, he says, that whatever church holds possession of the holy places is the true church. True, he says, some protest that we hold those places by force—with the air of imperial arms—but it is unthinkable that God should allow the holy places to remain in the hands of heretics. In the end this remains for Chrysostom the one and only sure and simple argument that can convince the world of the truth of the church to which he adheres. It was not very long before those holy places were to fall into the hands of the Muslims.

Competing claims of power. It was only by the authority of civil claims that it was possible to set Constantinople up as a "Second Rome," holier even than the first. Had the claims of Rome been purely apostolic, there could have been no thought of duplicating them at will simply by establishing another city to resemble old Rome. The city has become the foundation of general authority in the church, in recognition of the historic fact that now this city and now that city is in very truth the queen of the world, the mother city—metropolis. The city that ruled the world was the city that could, as a matter of course, claim to be the head of the church, and in turn Antioch, Rome, Milan, and Constantinople put forth the claim and exercised the power in

---

326. Nancy Lenkeith, *Dante and the Legend of Rome*, Mediaeval and Renaissance Studies, Supplement 2 (Leiden: Brill, 1952), 18.

reality. Constantinople counted for "more than Rome, more than any of the centers of the ancient Oriental monarchies," writes N. Iorga.[327] "Constantinople was always a sort of Kremlin."[328] By the dedication of Constantinople on 17 May 330, writes Andreas Alföldi, Constantine "gave his Christian organization of the state a centre free from any touch of paganism."[329] The emblems on his coins show that "the new capital is the ideal centre of Christian world-empire. On Constantine's own confession God appeared to him in a dream and ordered him to found the new residence."[330] Constantinople was to be the Christian Rome because the old Rome was too pagan. What about its apostolic claims? If they were being made, they certainly bore no great weight. "When Constantinople openly became the ideal centre of the Christian Empire, Rome, the old capital, renounced by the Emperor, was *ipso facto* bound to be left the citadel of the old traditions."[331] And though the old traditions, as Lenkeith has demonstrated, never died out,[332] Constantinople became "the city," untainted by paganism, the pure and holy capital, not only of the church, but of the world.

To counter the growing power of Milan, the bishops of Rome lent their support to the rival dioceses of Ravenna and Arles. In Arles, intrigues resulted in the expulsion of Hero, an excellent bishop; in his place Pope Zosimus supported one Patroclus, who abused his power and lost it. So did attempts

---

327. "Plus qu'à Rome, plus que dans n'importe quels centres des vieilles monarchies de l'Orient, la capitale importe." N. Iorga, *Histoire de la Vie Byzantine: Empire et Civilisation*, 3 vols. (Bucarest: l'École Roumaine en France, 1934), 1:119.
328. "Constantinople fut toujours un peu un Kremlin." Iorga, *Histoire de la Vie Byzantine*, 1:120.
329. Andreas Alföldi, *The Conversion of Constantine and Pagan Rome*, trans. Harold Mattingly (Oxford: Clarendon, 1948), 110.
330. Ibid.
331. Ibid., 116.
332. Lenkeith, *Dante and the Legend of Rome*, 1–32.

at power politics, featuring active correspondence with the Gallic bishoprics in attempts to weaken their ties with rivals, all come to an end with the setting up of new barbarian kingdoms in which "the court of the king became the center of ecclesiastical affairs as of all others."[333] This, as we have seen, is no new system invented by barbarians. Rome was remarkably uninterested in the local rituals and liturgies that sprung up everywhere on the Oriental-Milanese pattern. Even when asked for instructions, the popes showed little interest in prescribing their own form of the Mass. Nowhere does the rise of national churches appear as a threat or challenge, let alone an insult, to Rome. In dealing with rival cities, however, it was, as it had always been, another matter. The city that could not sleep until Carthage, Corinth, Veii, etc., were leveled to the ground was not lightly to be challenged by anyone. But as far as religion was concerned, other cities had equal or better claims.

Throughout the Middle Ages, Rome bitterly resented the existence of Jerusalem with its undeniable claim to be *the* Holy City, the exact center of the earth, the supreme hierocentric point where the cross of redemption stood over the exact spot where Adam's skull lay buried, and where the holy sepulchre stood at the pivotal point not only of the earth but of the universe. Jerusalem was the one supreme goal of every pilgrim, the place of the life, death, resurrection, and ascension of the Lord, the mount of the Lord's house and site of the sacrifice of Isaac, the home of the apostles, etc. And how Rome hated Constantinople! Constantinople is for Claudian the *altera* Rome, the false copy of the true Rome, which it has basely forced into second place. Why does Claudian take this so to heart? Not for the sake of the apostles, certainly, but because he idolizes pagan Romanites and their *pietas* [devotion to the gods, to the family, and to the

---

333. "La cour du roi devint le centre des affaires ecclésiastiques comme de toutes les autres." Duchesne, *Origines du Culte Chrétien*, 40.

state]—it is not as a Christian but as a proud citizen of the city of Rome that he boils with resentment against the new upstarts and feels within every fiber of his being that Rome and Rome alone should rule the world—*and* the church.

When a barbarian king writes to the bishop of Rome for help, he does not appeal to him as Peter's successor but simply as the custodian of "the laws of Rome and of Caesar."[334] For shame, cries the pope. You should have referred to the laws of God instead, "for you are truly God's vicar in the kingdom by the side of his royal prophet. . . . Try to be able to rule with him in eternity, whose vicar you are in the reign that is foretold."[335] The good king's ignorance of the status of Rome is no more striking than the bishop's designation of the king as vicar and coruler with God.

The Fight for Power

As soon as the "rank of churches is determined by the prominence of cities as *civil* capitals,"[336] a clash between the rivals for top place is inevitable. Nothing is less surprising than Duchesne's observation that "the bishops of the capital did not content themselves for long with being the ecclesiastical heads of a single diocese."[337] Could one expect anything else of human nature?

When the episcopal seat became the highest office in the city, it became at that moment the goal of the ambitious and the unscrupulous; and when it became but a step to a higher place, the rivalry and the bitterness among the top cities knew no bounds. Examples are legion. "It is not the

---

334. *Leges Romanas et Caesaris.* Eleutherius, *Epistola* 2, in *PG* 5:1143.

335. *Vicarius vero Dei estis in regno iuxta Prophetam regem . . . ut possis cum eo regnare in aeternum, cuius vicarius estis in regno praedicto.* Eleutherius, *Epistola* 2, in *PG* 5:1144.

336. Baynes, "Alexandria and Constantinople," 147, emphasis in original.

337. "Les évêques de la capitale ne se contentèrent pas longtemps d'être les chefs ecclésiastiques d'un seul diocèse." Duchesne, *Origines du Culte Chrétien,* 24.

priestly office that is to blame," writes Chrysostom, commenting on the culmination of the evil in his time, but those who abuse it, as every intelligent person admits.[338] Yet we go right on electing unqualified men so that "in our day it has reached the point where, unless God very quickly snatches us from the danger and saves us and his church [all will be lost]. Pray tell me, where do you think all these riots come from that now fill the churches? From nothing in the world but the false teachings of those at the head, and from these haphazard and uncontrolled elections."[339] All this corruption comes from the head: if the head is sick, of course the whole body will suffer. "Some are actually filling the churches with murder, leading whole cities to riot and revolt, all because they are fighting [to get themselves elected bishops]."[340] A more disastrous lack of central control in the church could hardly be imagined.

This passage gives us a glimpse of an important phenomenon that can be documented at enormous length, that is, the mass participation of the city mobs in the affairs of the church, usually centering around the person of the bishop. Since the destruction of the old monarchies in the great revolutions of the eighth century B.C., the Mediterranean world had been governed by men whose claims to the right to rule had to rest on trickery, force, and flattery. Tyrants were a necessary evil, democracies another. Authority rests on the will of heaven,

---

338. ὅτι οὐχ ἡ ἱερωσύνη τούτων αἰτία, ἀλλ' ἡ ἡμετέρα ῥαθυμία. John Chrysostom, *De Sacerdotio* 3.10, in *PG* 48:639.

339. ἐφ' ἡμῶν μικροῦ δεῖν ἔμελλε γίνεσθαι, εἰ μὴ ταχέως ἡμᾶς ὁ Θεὸς τῶν κινδύνων ἐκείνων ἐξείλκυσε, καὶ τῆς ἐκκλησίας τῆς αὐτοῦ καὶ τῆς ἡμετέρας φειδόμενος ψυχῆς. ἐπεὶ πόθεν, εἰπέ μοι, νομίζεις τὰς τοσαύτας ἐν ταῖς ἐκκλησίας τίκτεσθαι ταραχάς; ἐγὼ μὲν γὰρ οὐδὲ ἄλλοθεν πόθεν, οἶμαι, ἢ ἐκ τοῦ τὰς τῶν προεστώτων αἱρέσεις καὶ ἐκλογὰς ἁπλῶς καὶ ὡς ἔτυχε γίνεσθαι. Chrysostom, *De Sacerdotio* 3.10, in *PG* 48:647.

340. ὅτι γὰρ καὶ φόνων τὰς ἐκκλησίας ἐνέπλησάν τινες, καὶ πόλεις ἀναστάτους ἐποίησαν ὑπὲρ ταύτης μαχόμενοι τῆς ἀρχῆς. Chrysostom, *De Sacerdotio* 3.10, in *PG* 48:647.

THE OFFICE OF BISHOP IN THE EARLY CHRISTIAN CHURCH 101

but how was that will to be determined when the principle of royal priestly succession had been abolished for the state? The authority of the Pythian oracle became enormous. The traveling sophos, a great and disinterested spirit endowed with divine perspicacity and ever seeking knowledge, became the ultimate advisor to the nations, who humbly sought his services. But still there was nothing hard and fast to go by, and so stasis became the chronic and fatal malady of the ancient world. A knack and tendency for taking sides and slugging it out on all issues filled all the cities of late antiquity with constant riot and disorder—some of it of a ritual nature, some of it recognized as a necessary evil, and all of it disquieting to the point of driving men wild with a desire for ataraxia, and willing to pay any price to get it. When the church became the world church, it did not put an end to these disorders: under the direction of church leaders, stasis, faction, and rioting (like public oratory) took a new lease on life. The Christians had been in imperial favor for the first time for hardly more than a week when Christian mobs, urged on by clergy, fell upon each other in the streets of all the great cities with a savagery and abandon which scandalized and scared the pagans and drove the emperor to bed with sick headaches. A fierce partisan spirit has been the breath of life to the clergy ever since.

In the time of the apostolic fathers we meet everywhere with "fierce, loathsome, riotous sedition" within the Christian communities.[341] The object of their warfare is the support of rival candidates to the office of bishop. This had in every century been the principal cause of trouble in the Christian church. This is because the office of bishop, unlike that of an apostle or of any general authority, is an elective one. To be a bishop, one must gain the support of the multitude and that multitude must outshout the opposition, for the bishops were elected after the old pagan pattern of the *acclamatio*.

---

341. *1 Clement* 1.1, in *PG* 1:206.

If the episcopal office was not originally a political one, it could not be anything else once it became the gift of popular election. One can think of nothing less "apostolic" than such a state of things. In recent years defenders of the faith have loudly declared the monarchical and undemocratic nature of church office—but to recognize that this should be the nature of church office is a far cry from proving that it has been such through the years.

In Search of a General Authority

The burning question in the time of the apostolic fathers was, Who is in charge around here? No one, including the apostolic fathers themselves, knew the answer. In their days, the churches were writing letters to each other to be read and considered and then handed on: the bishop of Smyrna writes to the church at Philippi; the bishop of Antioch does the same, also sending letters of advice and council to churches at Tralles, Ephesus, Rome, Philadelphia, and Magnesia—explaining that he has no right to give orders but finds himself unable to keep silence in the face of the way things are going. Irenaeus, bishop of Lyons, gives Victor of Rome a severe dressing-down in the Easter controversy—and Victor backs down; "the church sojourning at Rome" sends an opinion to "the church sojourning in Corinth" because the latter has asked for it but boasts that it has received apostolic instruction by a visit from Polycarp, bishop of Smyrna, who came to Rome to correct some false ideas of Anicetus, the bishop there.[342] None of these advisors sets himself up as an authority or a superior and, what is more significant, none of them, though desperately pressed for leadership, knows of any higher authority to which he can recommend those whom he is instructing. The perfect equality of the bishops is evident enough, but it is also repeatedly stated as a basic principle.

---

342. Eusebius, *Historia Ecclesiastica* 5.24, in *PG* 20:493–508.

In all the lively interchange of letters and ideas between the bishops of the third century, the church at Rome "naturally" has a place of prime importance, Hugo Koch notes;[343] but in all this correspondence "there is always expressed the consciousness of the equality of all churches and bishops, and when their opinion differs from that of Rome they do not change it."[344] It was inevitable that certain bishops should from very early times have claimed superior ratings, and Tertullian pours withering contempt on the one "who calls himself the bishop of bishops,"[345] and later Cyprian says "we recognize no bishop of bishops."[346] The church of the third century, says Koch, believed that Matthew 16:18 proclaimed the authority of the episcopal office, but not of any one super-bishop.[347] When a bishop visits another church, according to the *Apostolic Constitution,* he must sit beside the bishop of that church, "sharing with him the same identical honor; and he shall be asked to address the people with words of instruction. If he modestly refuses, he shall be forced."[348] This is to emphasize the absolute equality of bishops. The concluding speech of the great Council of Nicaea was an appeal by the emperor to the bishops to remember a thing which they had forgotten, that "the decision of which bishop

---

343. Hugo Koch, *Cyprian und der römische Primat: Eine kirchen- und dogmengeschichtliche Studie,* Texte und Untersuchungen zur Geschichte der altchristlichen Literatur 5.1, 3rd ser. (Leipzig: Hinrichs, 1910), 152.
344. Source unidentified.
345. *quod est episcopus episcoporum.* Tertullian, *De Pudicitia* 1, in *PL* 2:1032–33.
346. This is only found in the notes of *PL* 4:1153 (*Nemo se episcopum episcoporum constituat*). See also 4:1330.
347. Hugo Koch, *Cathedra Petri,* 47–58; Cyprian und der römische Primat, 53.
348. τῆς αὐτῆς ἀξιούμενος ὑπ' αὐτοῦ τιμῆς· καὶ ἐρωτήσεις αὐτόν, ὦ ἐπίσκοπε, προσλαλῆσαι τῷ λαῷ λόγους διδακτικούς ... ἐὰν δὲ δι' εὐλάβειαν, ὡς σοφός, τὴν τιμήν σοι τηρῶν, μὴ θελήσῃ ἀνενέγκαι, κἂν εἰς τὸν λαὸν εὐλογίαν αὐτὸν ποιήσασθαι καταναγκάσεις. *Constitutiones Apostolicae* 2.58.2–3, in *PG* 1:740.

is really superior to another must rest with God. You must yield gracefully to each other," says Constantine, "and so avoid all this terrible dissension."[349] For it was nothing but fighting among the bishops for places of superior power—a fight in which doctrinal issues served, as all well knew, only as pretexts. This fight had brought on the need for the emperor's intervention and the calling of the council in the first place. The emperor's word was not enough to stem the tide of human nature, and, not long afterwards, he wrote in a general epistle words of stunning rebuke with the refrain "According to God's law, bishops must be equal!"[350]

Campaigns and intrigue. But it was precisely because bishops were equal that the office of bishop could not solve the problem of leadership after the passing of the apostles: when equals disagree, who is to decide? Ignatius's remarkable silence on the matter of even local councils has been noted. The idea that if one can only get enough bishops to agree on a thing their opinion must be God's opinion became an obsession after Nicaea: whether 80 or 250 of 381 bishops signed a document made all the difference in the world. Number was everything—as it would not have been had the church enjoyed the leadership of a general authority. Within a province, the archbishop's word was final, but what if provinces disagreed? Who would judge among the metropolitans? Into this gap stepped the emperor—reluctantly but perforce, with no one dissenting. "When there were differences among the various provinces," says Eusebius, "acting as a common bishop appointed by God, he [the emperor] would summon synods of the ministers of God."[351] God had

---

349. Θεοῦ γὰρ εἶναι τὸ κριτήριον τῶν ἀληθεῖ λόγῳ κρειττώνων καὶ τοῖς ἀσθενεστέροις δὲ δεῖν ὑποκατακλίνεσθαι λόγῳ συγγνώμης . . . ὡς ἂν μὴ πρὸς ἀλλήλους στασιαζόντων. Eusebius, *Vita Constantini* 3.21, in *PG* 20:1081.

350. Eusebius, *Vita Constantini* 3.60, in *PG* 20:1131–32.

351. διαφερομένων τινῶν πρὸς ἀλλήλους κατὰ διφόρους χώρας, οἷά τις κοινὸς ἐπίσκοπος ἐκ θεοῦ καθεσταμένος, συνόδους τῶν τοῦ θεοῦ λειτουργῶν συνεκρότει. Eusebius, *Vita Constantini* 1.44, in *PG* 20:957–60.

appointed bishops, and he had also appointed a common bishop over them all—where was he now, if the emperor had to take his place? "He [the emperor] did not disdain to sit in the midst of such assemblies," Eusebius continues, "and share their deliberations, being the common arbiter of their episcopal affairs. . . . He sat in their midst as one of their number, entirely without armed retainers."[352] So at last the church had a general authority. Of all the men who ever lived, only Constantine was qualified, it is Eusebius's firm conviction, to call the great general Council of Nicaea—the first general conference of the church to be held in over 250 years—and that during a time when such a general council was desperately needed! "Quite rightly he observed once at a meeting of bishops that he too was a bishop. . . . As I remember it, he said, 'As you being set over the internal affairs of the church, so I as having been set by God over its external affairs, may well be called *episcopus*.' And indeed he was a true *episcopus* to all his subjects."[353] Recently, Roman Catholic scholars, aware of the grave implications of such a statement, have attempted to give it a special interpretation, but from the preceding passages the interpretation is only too obvious.

Shortly after, Hilary, writing to fellow bishops in Gaul, uses language that completely confirms the obvious meaning of Eusebius's account. Seeing the state of things, Hilary

---

352. ἐν μέσῃ δὲ τῇ τούτων διατριβῇ οὐκ ἀπαξιῶν παρεῖναί τε καὶ συνιζάνειν, κοινωνὸς τῶν ἐπισκοπουμένων ἐγίνετο. . . . καθῆστό τε καὶ μέσος. ὡσεὶ καὶ τῶν πολλῶν εἷς, δορυφόρους μὲν καὶ ὁπλίτας καὶ πᾶν τῶν σωματοφυλάκων γένος ἀποσεισάμενος. Eusebius, *Vita Constantini* 1.44, in PG 20:957–60.

353. ἔνθεν εἰκότως αὐτὸς ἐν ἑστιάσει ποτὲ δεξιούμενος ἐπισκόπους, λόγον ἀφῆκεν, ὡς ἄρα εἴη καὶ αὐτὸς ἐπίσκοπος, ὧδέ πῃ αὐτοῖς εἰπὼν ῥήμασιν ἐφ᾽ ἡμετέραις ἀκοαῖς, 'Ἀλλ᾽ ὑμεῖς μὲν τῶν εἴσω τῆς Ἐκκλησίας, ἐγὼ δὲ τὸν ἐκτὸς ὑπὸ θεοῦ καθεσταμένος, ἐπίσκοπος ἂν εἴην. ἀκόλουθα δ᾽ οὖν τῷ λόγῳ διανοούμενος, τοὺς ἀρχομένους ἅπαντας ἐπεσκόπει, προὔτρεπέ τε, ὅσπερ ὂν ἡ δύναμις. Eusebius, *Vita Constantini* 4.24, in PG 20:1172.

says that he, like the apostolic fathers of old, "cannot keep silence." "But it is necessary for me and religiously proper, I believe, to act as if I were a bishop of bishops sending out letters" to all who have written to me, asking me questions though I am most unlearned and inexperienced.[354] But he knows of no higher head to pass the letters on to, and so, like Constantine, reluctantly tries to fill the place of a general authority that no longer exists. It is interesting that Roman Catholic authorities, resting their whole claim on what they loudly describe as an unbroken chain of authority, when confronted with no end of missing links, rotten links, and rival links in the chain, blandly and piously announce that it makes no difference how broken the chain or dubious the record, since "the office always remained."[355] Their proof of the divinity of the office is an unbroken chain; their only proof of the unbroken chain is the divinity of the office. By the closest possible translation, Constantine says to the bishops: "But you over the internal affairs of the church, I over the external by God have been installed may be considered a bishop."[356] There is no doubt that the external affairs of the church are the proper sphere for the general authorities. "Every orthodox writer was fiercely conscious of the need for the unity of all Christians in the Church universal," writes John Morris of the second century, "however bitterly he might resist the claims of ... any ... given centre to exercise the authority of that universal Church."[357] All recognized that the church should have general authorities, but nobody knew for sure where to find them.

---

354. *Necessarium mihi ac religiosum intellexi, ut nunc quasi episcopus episcopis mecum in Christo communicantibus salutaris ac fidelis sermonis colloquia transmitterem.* Hilary, *De Synodis* 2, in *PL* 10:481.

355. Source unidentified.

356. Eusebius, *Vita Constantini* 4.24, in *PG* 20:1172.

357. John Morris, "Early Christian Orthodoxy," *Past and Present: A Journal of Scientific History* 3 (1953): 13.

THE OFFICE OF BISHOP IN THE EARLY CHRISTIAN CHURCH 107

We need not repeat here the story of the fights between the great city bishoprics, fights for power and mastery in which nothing was barred. It was this as much as anything that disgusted honest people everywhere and sent hordes of Christians to seek refuge from Christian society in monastic isolation. "Not all bishops are bishops," says Jerome in defense of the monks. "Ecclesiastic dignity does not make a Christian."[358] "Christ called fishermen and tent makers and tax collectors to this supreme authority," wrote Chrysostom, "but the present clergy simply spit on those who earn their living by daily toil; whereas if someone is devoted to worldly studies, avoids hard work, etc., they receive him with open arms and admiration. Why is it that they pass right by those who have toiled and sweated all their days for the upbuilding of the church to give all the highest church offices to somebody who had never raised a finger to do any work but wasted all his time dabbling in useless, ornamental, worldly learning?"[359] Certainly no one can accuse Chrysostom, as many have tried to accuse Tertullian, of sour grapes—for no one held a higher office in the church than he, though it kept him in an official world of constant and dangerous intrigue.

The real issue at Nicaea. The letters in *Patrologiae Latinae* 13:583–88 show that in the West and in the East the Arian controversy was merely an aspect of the great struggle for episcopal priority. It is not a contest between theologians but

---

358. *Non omnes episcopi episcopi sunt. . . . Non facit ecclesiastica dignitas Christianum.* Jerome, *Epistola* 14.9, in *PL* 22:353.

359. καὶ ὁ μὲν Χριστὸς ἁλιεῖς καὶ σκηνοποιοὺς καὶ τελώνας ἐπὶ ταύτην ἐκάλεσε τὴν ἀρχήν· οὗτοι δὲ τοὺς μὲν ἀπὸ τῆς ἐργασίας τῆς καθημερινῆς τρεφομένους διαπτύουσιν· εἰ δέ τις λόγων ἅψαιτο τῶν ἔξωθεν καὶ ἀργῶν τρέφοιτο, τοῦτον ἀποδέχονται καὶ θαυμάζουσι. τί γὰρ δήποτε τοὺς μὲν μυρίους ἀνασχομένους ἱδρῶτας εἰς τὰς τῆς ἐκκλησίας χρείας παρεῖδον· τὸν δὲ οὐδέποτε τοιούτων γευσάμενον πόνων, πᾶσαν δὲ τὴν ἡλικίαν ἐν τῇ τῶν ἔξωθεν λόγων ματαιοπονίᾳ καταναλώσαντα, ἐξαίφνης εἰς ταύτην εἵλκυσαν τὴν τιμήν. Chrysostom, *De Sacerdotio* 2.7, in *PG* 48:639.

between bishops, and the issue is not doctrine but power. It is only proper that in every case it is the emperor alone who is responsible for the final decision and solution, and that bishop is strongest who has the emperor's ear. St. Basil was saddened to see the great bishops fighting fiercely among themselves: "Without any cause at all the greatest of the churches have fallen out of their ancient bonds of brotherhood."[360] For all of Basil's "without cause," there nevertheless had to be a cause, an obvious cause, for the rivalry among the bishops. It is plain from his remark that the cause was not an open and admitted one (such characteristic naïveté). The cause was not doctrine, but it was not and is not hard to find: jealousy and ambition. It fairly shrieks at one in almost every episcopal cause, though no bishop could afford to admit it, yet all betray it in almost every letter they write. Was the nature of the Trinity the real issue at Nicaea? Not for a moment! This is a very trivial technical question, the emperor wrote; no one understands it, and it contributes nothing to the salvation of men. It may be a good thing for the experts to sharpen their wits by discussing such exquisitely refined and impractical things, but they should keep their discussions closely confined to their own company. When they get out into the public they only cause trouble, and what the experts themselves fight about because they cannot understand can only be a double perplexity to the laymen, who moreover welcome a good pretext for taking sides and stirring up trouble. The philosophers talk on and on about such things in their endless disputations, but they at least quarrel like gentlemen and get along with each other very well for all their technical differences. But you who call yourselves ministers of God and a holy brotherhood act like spiteful and vicious children; these recondite and unsearchable matters are nothing but a pretext

---

360. αἰτίας οὐκ οὔσης, αἱ μέγισται τῶν Ἐκκλησιῶν, καὶ ἐκ παλαιοῦ πρὸς ἀλλήλας ἀδελφῶν τάξιν ἐπέχουσαι, αὗται νῦν διεστήκασι. Basil, *Epistola* 204, in *PG* 32:756.

THE OFFICE OF BISHOP IN THE EARLY CHRISTIAN CHURCH   109

for venting your spite against each other.[361] So wrote the emperor, and the words and behavior of the churchmen support his charge to the fullest.

"This Alexander," Bishop Eusebius of Nicodemia wrote to as many bishops as would read and subscribe to his letter, "thinks the whole world depends on his nod. The nature of the Godhead is for him merely a pretext to gain power—he has been working against us for years. Don't have anything to do with him. If you meet any of his supporters in the street, look the other way—do not defile yourselves by wishing them a good day."[362] In reply to such sentiments, Alexander spills the beans: "This Eusebius is all ambition. When he saw an opening in Nicodemia he pulled wires until he long suffered his insolent attacks and diplomatic intrigues against us in silence. This is the last straw. We anathemize anyone who has anything to do with him."[363] At the opening session of the Nicene Council, while all were waiting for latecomers the emperor presided at the burning of a mountain of letters that had been submitted to him by the clergy from all over the world during the days when the council was being prepared. This huge pile of documents consisted almost entirely of charges by various churchmen against each other.[364]

At Nicaea the emperor assigned all seats, and there was no funny business. The precaution was a necessary one, for when the bishops came together at later synods, the more ambitious ones insisted on taking higher places than the others. Basil reports that the Oriental bishops complained "because the Roman bishops took exalted seats in the presence of their legates"—the master whose example they were

---

361. Eusebius, *Vita Constantini* 2.71, in *PG* 20:1044–45.
362. Source unidentified.
363. Source unidentified.
364. Sozomen, *Historia Ecclesiastica* 1.17, in *PG* 67:913.

following was a *cosmocrator* whom no one could ever accuse of being meek and lowly.[365]

Resultant pride. The growing arrogance of the clergy throughout the early centuries is only too well documented. The fifty years of peace between the Decian and Diocletian persecutions fostered the worst vices in the church, vices which the brief (two-year) Decian persecution had only interrupted. "Not even in particular instances," writes Milman, "can we discover, during the same interval, much of any very lively Christianity."[366] The corruption was general and universal. Again the Diocletian persecution did not eradicate but only arrested the evil for a short time. On the eve of that persecution when the church was blossoming under imperial favor, Eusebius tells how "some that appeared to be our pastors, deserting the law of piety, were inflamed against each other with mutual strifes, only accumulating quarrels and threats, rivalry, hostility, and hatred to each other, only anxious to assert the government as a kind of sovereignty for themselves."[367] Even during the brief pause in the midst of the Diocletian persecution, the clergy showed that they had learned nothing and forgotten nothing:

> But the events that occurred in the intermediate time, besides those already related, I have thought proper to pass by; I mean particularly the circumstances of the different heads of the churches, who from being shepherds of the reasonable flocks of Christ . . . did not govern in a lawful

---

365. Source unidentified.
366. Source unidentified.
367. Eusebius, *The Ecclesiastical History of Eusebius Pamphilus, Bishop of Caesarea, in Palestine,* trans. Christian F. Crusé, 9th ed. (New York: Stanford and Swords, 1850), 318; οἵ τε δοκοῦντες ἡμῶν ποιμένες τὸν τῆς δεοσεβείας θεσμὸν παρωσάμενοι ταῖς πρὸς ἀλλήλους ἀνεφλέγοντο φιλονεικίαις, αὐτὰ δὴ ταῦτα μόνα, τὰς ἔριδας καὶ τὰς ἀπειλὰς τόν τε ζῆλον καὶ τὸ πρὸς ἀλλήλους ἔχθος τε καὶ μῖσος ἐπαύξοντες οἷά τε τυραννίδας τὰς φιλαρχίας ἐκθύμως διεκδικοῦντες. Eusebius, *Historia Ecclesiastica* 8.1.8, in *PG* 20:741.

and becoming manner. . . . [There were] ambitious aspirings of many to office, . . . great schisms and difficulties industriously fomented by the factions among the new members, against the relics of the church, devising one innovation after another.[368]

But it was in the warm sun of imperial favor that all the worst that envy and ambition could contrive came to the fore. Many a father has commented on this phenomenon as a truism of church history: prosperity means ruin for the church. Less familiar to students than the arrogant claims and charges of the bishops of the fourth and fifth centuries are those official pronouncements of successive synods in which the bishops proclaim themselves to be above all human laws and from that thesis develop corollary powers whose arrogance knows no bounds.

The Glories (and Duties?) of a Bishop

We have seen the apostolic fathers casting about for a formula to fix the authority and tenure of bishops—and not finding it. They describe a complete breakdown of respect for authority in the churches, brought about by fights between factions and individuals trying for the office of bishop. All they can do is to insist over and over again that obedience to the bishop and presbyters is the duty of the members, appealing to them in the name of *sophia* [wisdom] and good sense to forget their squabbles. They did not forget them, and insistence on obedience to the bishop became a familiar refrain capable of many variations. And whereas the apostolic fathers emphasized the obligations and duties of bishops, priests, and deacons toward each other and the community with only incidental mention of the obligations and duties of the congregations as a whole, succeeding churchmen emphasized more and more the duties of the people to the clergy,

---

368. Eusebius, *Ecclesiastical History* 374–75; Eusebius, *De Martyribus Palaestinae* 12, in *PG* 20:1511–14.

especially the bishop, and less and less the clergy's, and particularly the bishop's, duties to others.

From duty to privilege. In the *127 Canons* we still meet the old spirit: the bishop, priest, or deacon guilty of fornication, false oath, or theft shall be deposed, but not excommunicated, since the scripture says "Do not punish twice for the same offense."[369] A neat bit of sophistry in favor of the clergy—but at least they have some responsibilities. Further, any bishop, priest, or deacon who strikes or curses an unbeliever or a guilty believer with the intent of inspiring fear thereby shall be deposed. "For nowhere did the Lord teach us to act thus; on the contrary, he supported blows with patience."[370] Such a rule is unthinkable in later centuries. But among the clergy, the bishop had all priority, and "any cleric who opposes a bishop in anything must be deposed with all his followers, as having attempted to seize power: he is a rebel. All the laymen who follow him must be excommunicated."[371] This clearly reflects the great fear of independent movements which has always haunted a church unsure of its authority.

Among the many rules on dispossessed clergy (especially bishops) collected in the tenth volume of *Patrologiae Graecae* are many old ones. From the frequent mention of dispossession of bishops, conspiracy against bishops, and revolts and accusations against bishops, one feels the insecurity of an elected office under the control of city mobs. To this day the pope may not excommunicate the citizens of the city of Rome—for they gave him his office: by virtue of them he is bishop, and by virtue of being bishop of that city he is pope. The advice to bishops in case of deposition, loss of property, or expulsion is significant: "Blessed are they who suffer persecution for the sake of justice."[372]

---

369. *127 Canons of the Apostles* 2.16, in *PO* 8:671.
370. *127 Canons of the Apostles* 2.18, in *PO* 8:671–72.
371. *127 Canons of the Apostles* 2.22, in *PO* 8:673.
372. *Beati qui persecutionem patiuntur propter justitiam.* Zephyrinus, *Epistola* 2.1, in *PG* 10:45.

THE OFFICE OF BISHOP IN THE EARLY CHRISTIAN CHURCH 113

In the third century magnificent bishops begin to assert themselves. Paul of Samosata[373] was not condemned by his fellow bishops for his theatrical throne, his host of concubines, his hired claque, his wholesale bribery, his scarlet robes, etc., but only for a technical point of doctrine. When Origen discoursed before a number of bishops gathered for a conference in Jerusalem, the cry went up. "Such a thing has never been heard of, that laymen should give a speech in the presence of a bishop!"[374] The widening gap between the ideal and the fact is plain in Origen's enthusiastic comparison of the Christian way with the pagan way: "We do not accept or tolerate those ambitious for power, who would force those who do not want to receive the common opinion of the church. Our good leaders are under the sway of the king, who we believe is the Son of God," and everyone willingly does his share in the church for the salvation of mankind. Thus they are ruled by the word of God, and thus they achieve perfect unity, wisdom, truth, and justice.[375] Such was the ideal—by the fourth century the church was so afflicted by those vices of which Origen declared it to be free in his day that by the testimony of all Christian writers of the time, her condition was far worse than that of the pagans. What was missing more than anything else was humility.

Authority as a shield. Nothing could have been easier or more inevitable than to apply the supernatural claims for the *source* of a bishop's authority to every expression of that authority. The heathen Romans had long drilled the world in

---

373. Eusebius, *Historia Ecclesiastica* 7.30, in *PG* 20:709–20.
374. τοῦτο οὐδέποτε ἠκούσθη . . . παρόντων ἐπισκόπων λαϊκοὺς ὁμιλεῖν. Eusebius, *Historia Ecclesiastica* 6.19.17, in *PG* 20:569.
375. οὐκ ἀποδεχόμενοι μὲν τοὺς φιλάρχους, βιαζόμενοι δὲ τοὺς διὰ πολλὴν μετριότητα τὴν κοινὴν φροντίδα τῆς ἐκκλησίας τοῦ θεοῦ μὴ βουλομένους προπετῶς ἀναδέξασθαι. καὶ οἱ καλῶς ἄρχοντες ἡμῶν βιασθέντες ὑπάρχουσι, τοῦ μεγάλου βασιλέως ἀναγκάζοντος, οὐ πεπείσμεθα εἶναι Υἱὸν Θεοῦ, Λόγον Θεοῦ. Origen, *Contra Celsum* 8.75, in *PG* 11:1629–32.

the useful equations: victory = superior power, superior power = divine power, divine power = divine authority, divine authority = divine office, divine office = divine officer; opposition to such can only be opposition to God, blasphemy, the sum and epitome of all that is vicious, depraved, and deserving of no other fate than extermination. With these convenient formulas constantly before them in the symbolism and the standards of the empire, it would be strange if Christian Romans did not assume the divine calling of the bishop to mean divine power and authority in all that he did. The ultimate in extravagant drawing out of this super-syllogism was to become the reasoning, already refuted by Tertullian,[376] that because Christ gave a promise to Peter, the bishop (an office not mentioned) of a city not mentioned holds all the power in the world! This is a triumph of Roman thought—of the imperial age.

"The bishop possesses the highest authority on earth," says the *Apostolic Constitutions*, "representing the type of God among men, holding the rule of all men, priests, kings, princes, fathers, sons, teachers, and of all subjects alike." The proof? "Because to you he said 'what you bind on earth shall be bound in heaven.'"[377] Who then shall judge a bishop if he does wrong? None but the bishop himself; let him follow the admonition to "Know thyself."[378] What greater sin can there be than to say anything against a bishop "through whom the Lord has given the Holy Spirit through the laying on of hands: through whom you have learned the holy doctrine; through whom you know God; through whom you have believed on Christ; . . . by whom you have been sealed with the

---

376. Tertullian, *De Pudicitia* 21, in *PL* 2:1077–80.

377. ὡς θεοῦ τύπον ἔχων ἐν ἀνθρώποις τῷ πάντων ἄρχειν ἀνθρώπων, ἱερέων, βασιλέων, ἀρχόντων, πατέρων, υἱῶν, διδασκάλων καὶ πάντων ὁμοῦ τῶν ὑπηκόων. . . . ὅτι ὑμῖν τοῖς ἐπισκόποις εἴρηται· Ὁ ἐὰν δήσητε ἐπὶ τῆς γῆς ἔσται δεδεμένον ἐν τῷ οὐρανῷ. *Constitutiones Apostolicae* 2.11.1–2, in *PG* 1:612–13.

378. γνώριζε σεαυτόν. *Constitutiones Apostolicae* 2.18.3, in *PG* 1:629.

oil of exultation and the salve of intelligence; through whom you have become sons of light"; through whom you have been baptized and God has adopted you? "Cherish the one who is your father next to God and reverence him."[379] The author here lists all the spiritual functions of a bishop that he can think of, generously expanding the list with rhetorical padding. The actual functions of a bishop boil down to baptizing and the laying on of hands. But according to modern Catholic doctrine, anyone can baptize. What does that leave the bishop? The Christians must turn over their money to the bishop, says the same source, and never question what he does with it. He is answerable to God alone. "Judge not the bishop nor the lay congregation."[380] The injunction to "judge not" is soon to be confined to judgments against clergy—a very convenient specialization. The *Apostolic Constitutions* make sharp distinctions between crimes deserving of crucifixion, stoning, fines, whipping, etc., and between crimes against kings, rulers, and equals, and finally the worst of all, crimes against God, priest, and temple. "It is not allowed to expose either a king or a priest. . . . He who affronts kings is worthy of punishment, even though it be a son or a friend; of how much greater punishment is he deserving who affronts priests?"[381] If sedition in the state is bad, how much worse is sedition in the church? This "how-much-more" device is a

---

379. δι' οὗ τὸ ἅγιον πνεῦμα ἐν ὑμῖν ὁ κύριος ἔδωκεν ἐν τῇ χειροθεσίᾳ, δι' οὗ ἅγια δόγματα μεμαθήκατε καὶ θεὸν ἐγνώκατε καὶ εἰς Χριστὸν πεπιστεύκατε, δι' οὗ ἐγνώσθητε ὑπὸ θεοῦ, δι' οὗ ἐσφραγίσθητε ἐλαίῳ ἀγαλλιάσεως καὶ μύρῳ συνέσεως, δι' οὗ υἱοὶ φωτὸς ἀνεδείχθητε . . . διὰ τοῦ ἐπισκόπου σου ὁ θεὸς υἱοποιεῖταί σε . . . στέργε, καὶ τὸν μετὰ θεὸν γενόμενόν σου πατέρα σέβου. *Constitutiones Apostolicae* 2.32.3–2.33.1, in *PG* 1:680.
380. μὴ κρῖνε τὸν ἐπίσκοπόν σου ἢ τὸν συλλαϊκόν. *Constitutiones Apostolicae* 2.36.9, in *PG* 1:688.
381. ὅτι οὔτε βασιλεία, οὔτε ἱερωσύνη θεμιτὸν ἐπανίστασθαι. . . . εἰ γὰρ ὁ βασιλεῦσιν ἐπεγειρόμενος, κολάσεως ἄξιος, κἂν υἱὸς ᾖ, κἂν φίλος· πόσῳ μᾶλλον ὁ ἱερεῦσιν ἐπανιστάμενος. *Constitutiones Apostolicae* 6.2, in *PG* 1:912.

well-worn and surefire rhetorical trick by which any merit or offense can be magnified or minimized by any desired degree. It is a favorite implement for exalting the priesthood and the teaching profession. If one loves one's physical parents, *how much more* should one love one's spiritual parents? If it is a crime to abuse one's father, how much greater a crime to affront one's heavenly father? It is effective even when used in utterly meaningless contexts: If one should be praised for singing, how much more should one be praised for dancing? If bank robbery is reprehensible, how much more reprehensible should ice skating be?

Declarations attributed to early bishops of Rome that strengthened the hand of the pope all follow the same pattern. "Bishops are to be judged by God," not by men. They are above all human law.[382] "Laymen are not to be heard if they bring charges [against bishops]."[383] The bishop has the deacons to act as his eyes and ears, spying out any cases of defection or seditious talk against him—they are his personal agents to keep an eye on his personal enemies. "No bishop may be refuted or accused of anything by the people or by vulgar persons."[384] "Anyone who says a word against [a bishop], the eyes of the Lord, is guilty of the crime of *lèse-majesté*. . . . Those who accuse bishops are slain not by human but by divine agency."[385] "There is no worse crime than to bring a charge against a priest. The priest may be guilty, but even so, he must be left entirely to the judgment of God. For if all crimes are to be punished in this world, there will

---

382. *Episcopi autem a Deo sunt judicandi.* Pius I, *Epistola* 1.2, in *PG* 5:1121.

383. *Et sicut laici et saeculare homines nolunt eos recipere in accusationibus et infamationibus suis.* Telesphorus, *Epistola ad Omnes Universaliter Christi Fideles* 1, in *PG* 5:1082.

384. *Non est itaque a plebe aut vulgaribus hominibus arguendus vel accusandus episcopus.* Evaristus, *Epistola* 2, in *PG* 5:1053.

385. *Qui [episcopos] devorant qui oculi Domini dicuntur . . . esset reus criminiis majestatis. . . . [Qui] accusandi episcopos . . . quos non humanis, sed divinis actibus mortuos esse scimus.* Alexander I, *Epistola* 1.1, in *PG* 5:1060.

be nothing left for the exercise of divine judgment!"[386] This shocking bit of sophistry, it will be noted, guarantees the immunity of priests only—to others it does not apply.

All charges against a bishop should be kept secret and referred to the same bishop. No matter what his final decision is, the business should go no further.[387] Even the basic rule *nemo de se ipso judicet* [no one should judge concerning himself] is abrogated in the need for endowing the bishop with divine authority. "[The bishops] who with their own mouths confect the body of the Lord are to be heard, obeyed, and feared by all."[388] "The populace is to be taught and dominated by [the bishop], not [he] by it."[389] It is equally wicked to speak against a bishop or to allow another to do so. . . . It is not only against divine laws but against human, which also prohibit a master.[390] "The populace shall not reprimand its pastor. Bishops are to be judged only by God, who had chosen them as his eyes."[391] At this point the text negates the report that the church is full of contentions and *aemilationes* [flatteries] and that the saints of God who are to judge the world are full of evil: "Anyone who kills his wife," a letter of Pius I avers, "and does so entirely without reason must do public penance; but if he is disobedient toward a bishop, let

---

386. *Pejus malum fore non aestimo quam Christianos suis invidere sacerdotibus. . . . Non potest autem humano condemnari examine, quem Deus suo reservavit judicio. Si omnia namque in hoc saeculo vindicata essent, locam divina non haberent judicia.* Alexander I, *Epistola* 1.2, in *PG* 5:1063.

387. Alexander I, *Epistola* 1.3, in *PG* 5:1063–64.

388. *[Episcopi] enim qui proprio ore corpus Domini conficiunt, ab omnibus sunt audiendi, obediendi, atque timendi.* Telesphorus, *Epistola ad Omnes Universaliter Christi Fideles* 3, in *PG* 5:1084.

389. *Populus enim ab [episcopis] docendus est . . . non ipsi ab eo.* Telesphorus, *Epistola ad Omnes Universaliter Christi Fideles* 3, in *PG* 5:1085.

390. Telesphorus, *Epistola ad Omnes Universaliter Christi Fideles* 3, in *PG* 5:1085.

391. *Oves enim pastorem suum non reprehendant. Plebs vero episcopum non accuset. . . . Episcopi autem a Deo sunt judicandi, qui eos sibi oculos elegit.* Pius I, *Epistola* 1.2, in *PG* 5:1121.

him be anathemized."[392] "The king received his title of Rex not from *regno*, 'rule,'" says the haughty Eleutherius to one "Lucius King of Britain," "but from *regendo*—'to be ruled,'" namely, by the clergy.[393]

From immunity to power. "Priesthood is to be more held in awe today than in the days of the ancient law," says Chrysostom. "Our power and dignity is simply overwhelming."[394] It is a power so great that there is danger in possessing it; it is such a power as can only be exercised by wise men. Wisely, he pleads for an awakening sense of responsibility among the priesthood, and to ensure its proper exercise he recommends thorough training in oratory and dialectic![395] "The minister of holy things must be just and pure as if he were acting amidst such powers and standing in heaven itself."[396] The claims to possession of boundless power, glory, and sanctity which Chrysostom puts forth are gladly accepted by the priests of all ages—the accompanying responsibility is rejected out of hand by arguments of simple sophistry.

"I am called a tyrant and worse than a tyrant,"[397] says Ambrose, who ruled the church with a power never exercised by any Roman bishop of his century, but he will not tolerate criticism from the emperor: "When did you ever hear, most gentle emperor, of laymen passing judgment on a bishop in a cause *fidei* [of faith]? ... If a bishop is to be

---

392. *Quicunque propriam uxorem ... sine causa ... interfecti ... publicam agat poenitentiam. Et si ... episcopo suo inobediens exctiterit, anathematizetur.* Pius I, *Etis*, in PG 5:1127.

393. *Rex dicitur a regendo, non a regno.* Eleutherius, *Epistola* 2, in PL 5:1144.

394. ὅτι φρικτὸν ἡ ἱερωσύνη, καὶ πολὺ τῆς παλαιᾶς λατρείας ἡ καινὴ φρικωδεστέρα. ... ὅτι πολλὴ τῶν ἱερέων ἡ ἐξουσία καὶ ἡ τιμή. Chrysostom, *De Sacerdotio* 3.4–5, in PG 48:642–44.

395. Chrysostom, *De Sacerdotio* 3.4–6, in PG 48:642–44.

396. διὸ χρὴ τὸν ἱερωμένον ὥσπερ ἐν αὐτοῖς ἑστῶτα τοῖς οὐρανοῖς μεταξὺ τῶν δυνάμεων ἐκείνων οὕτως εἶναι καθαρόν. Chrysostom, *De Sacerdotio* 3.4, in PG 48:642.

397. *Ego tyrannus appellor, et plus etiam quam tyrannus.* Ambrose, *Epistola* 20.27, in PL 16:1044.

taught by a layman, what will be the end of it? Let the layman dispute and the bishop listen—a bishop taught by a layman!!"[398] "Who would not deny that in matters of the faith bishops should be judged by emperors, and not emperors by bishops?"[399] "Your father, an older man than you, said, 'It is not for me to judge among bishops,' but you say 'I must judge.'"[400] "People say, 'Ambrose wants to have more power than the emperor.'"[401] They must have had a reason. "The emperor," Ambrose insists, "is in the church, not over the church."[402] Who is then? Accordingly, "the monarch was seated below the rails of the sanctuary and confounded with the rest of the faithful multitude" in the church, while Ambrose sat on the throne. It had been just the opposite under Constantine, where all the bishops of united Christendom were pleased to remain standing until the emperor, himself sitting, nodded for them to be seated. This was a personal campaign undertaken by Ambrose—who admitted that it had all tongues wagging. At the very same time, for example, the African bishops insisted that Macarius, the emperor's military prefect, be allowed to sit in church apart from the multitude and on a level with the bishop. Speaking of the trial and deposition of a lapsed bishop, Optatus writes: "This is a supreme sacrilege. God reserves the right

---

398. *Quando audisti, clementissime imperator, in causa fidei laicos de episcopo judicasse? . . . Si docendus est episcopus a laico, quid sequetur? Laicus ergo disputet, et episcopus audiat: episcopus discat a laico.* Ambrose, *Epistola* 21.4, in *PL* 16:1046.

399. *Quis est qui abnuat in causa fidei, in causa, inquam, fidei episcopos solere de imperatoribus Christianis, non imperatores de episcopis judicare?* Ambrose, *Epistola* 21.4, in *PL* 16:1046.

400. *Pater tuus . . . vir maturioris aevi, dicebat: Non est meum judicare inter episcopos; tua nunc dicit clementia: Ego debeo judicare.* Ambrose, *Epistola* 21.5, in *PL* 16:1046.

401. *[Populi] aiunt: . . . vult Ambrosius posse, quam imperator.* Ambrose, *Epistola* 21.30, in *PL* 16:1059.

402. *Imperator enim intra Ecclesiam, non supra Ecclesiam est.* Ambrose, *Epistola* 21.36, in *PL* 16:1061.

to judge his own, yet you insist on rushing in everywhere into things that are not your business, spoiling all pleasure. For what greater ruin of pleasure could there be for priests of God than to live as less than they were?"[403] Even if it is their fault, their office should now put them above all examination. It is a priest speaking. Of the great massacres of Donatists, he writes: We are not responsible for the way the military broke up the Donatists, urging all to unity. True, it was armed with special letters from the bishops that the commander Taurinus carried out great slaughter, but what do you do against a lot of fanatics? They had actually made the roads unsafe for bishops' carriages.[404] To the emperor, Lucifer writes: "What power have you, a profane person, over the priestly authority of the Highest God?" (Again the convenient identification of the source of the power with its extent—as if a second lieutenant, being commissioned by the president of the United States, could thereby claim all the powers of the president.)[405] "How can you dare to say that you can pass judgment on bishops, when by disobeying them you incur the death penalty as having insulted God himself?"[406] "Who are you," cries Lucifer, "to usurp this authority, which God did not give you?"[407] And even if he did give it, it was only on condition that you belong to the right church. In the rivalry between civil and eccle-

---

403. *Judicio suo Deus servavit rem suam, et tamen vos passim irruistis in alienam, corrumpentes omnium felicitatem. Nam quae major felicitas, quam Dei sacerdotes vivere, nec esse quod fuerant.* Optatus, *De Schismate Donatistorum* 2.25, in *PL* 11:984.

404. Optatus, *De Schismate Donatistorum* 3.4, in *PL* 11:1006–13.

405. *Cum haec ita sint, tu qui es profanus, ad Dei domesticos, quare istam sumis in Dei sacerdotem auctoritatem?* Lucifer, *Pro Sancto Athanasio* 1, in *PL* 13:826.

406. *Quomodo dicere poteris, judicare te posse de episcopis, quibus nisi obedieris, jam, quantum apud Deum, mortis poena fueris multatus?* Lucifer, *Pro Sancto Athanasio* 1, in *PL* 13:826.

407. *Quis es tu, inquam, qui tibi usurpasti hunc auctoritatem, quam tibi Deus non tradidit?* Lucifer, *Pro Sancto Athanasio* 1, in *PL* 13:827.

siastical power the priests are the only proper judges—are they not appointed by God? And they award the crown to themselves—are they not appointed by God? And any who withhold complete, unquestioning, and absolute submission are antichrist—for are they not appointed by God? But who says they are appointed by God? Who else has the right to say it but they themselves—for are they not appointed by God? The circular argument is the essence of sectarian authority. "How could any man who writes against the Christians do anything but lie?" says Origen,[408] using an argument that had been employed long before by Cicero, an argument to which there is but one answer: "If I bear witness of myself, my witness is not true" (John 5:31). "Prove that you have been made judge over us, however necessary such a judge may be. . . . You cannot prove not only that you have the right to rule bishops, but you cannot prove that bishops are not supposed to rule you, nay, and that if you disobey them you are not thereby judged worthy of death!"[409]

As might be expected, the same charges were brought against Lucifer as against Ambrose: Why do you call me arrogant, he asks, why do you call me proud, contumelious? Did not the ancient prophets denounce wickedness? In the end his authority is the Old Testament, but anyone can use that. Lucifer keeps asking: if the ancient prophets and patriarchs could speak and act thus freely, why should not we?[410] The answer is easy: *They* were prophets and patriarchs, the kind that God chooses when he will, and they are rare indeed; but priests appear in every age in droves and in armies—a totally different type of being, falling back for the justification of all

---

408. [ἔψευδε] δὲ σαφῶς (τί γὰρ οὐκ ἔμελλεν ὁ κατὰ Χριστιανῶν). Eusebius, *Historia Ecclesiastica* 6.19.9, in *PG* 20:568.

409. *Proba te super nos factum judicem . . . cum probare non possis quia praeceptum sit tibi, non solum non dominari episcopis, sed et ita eorum obedire statutis, ut si subvertere eorum decreta tentaveris, si fueris in superbia comprehensus, morte mori jussus sis.* Lucifer, *Pro Sancto Athanasio* 1, in *PL* 13:826.

410. Lucifer, *De non Parcendo in Deum Delinquentibus* 1, in *PL* 13:939.

their plans and ambitions on their own private interpretations of the scriptures, which they categorically forbid others to interpret without their aid. Lucifer, for example, loves to compare himself with the apostles,[411] though he was no more able to pass the test than were the priests of Rome whom Tertullian denounced.[412] Ambrose calls Lucifer the most inspired voice of his time, and Optatus was for the Oxford movement the most authoritative statement of the claims of the priesthood. Down through the centuries bishops continued to lecture emperors on authority. The patriarch, says the pious Constantine Porphyrogentius to his son, "is an emperor [*basileus*], who must provide peace and prosperity just like the emperor himself."[413]

A saga of struggle over control and conformity. When bishops insisted on ordaining clergies to dioceses other than their own, as if they were general authorities, they were soundly rebuked: "Who hath enjoined this upon them, or from what scripture have they been taught this?"[414] To which they might have rejoined, "from what scripture do we learn of metropolitans and archbishops? Who has enjoined them upon the church?" Once Raoul, archbishop of Canterbury, having begun Mass and perceiving the king seated on his throne with the crown on his head, quitted the altar and advanced to demand from him the crown on his head, which he made him take off; but the barons by their exertions compelled him to replace it. It was a rare archbishop who was satisfied with spiritual supremacy alone.

The aspirations of bishops to temporal power can be clearly traced through the synods they held from time to time. The Council of Cirta in 305 had to decide what should be done about those bishops who had been traditores (Chris-

---

411. See *PL* 13:826.
412. Tertullian, *De Pudicitia* 21, in *PL* 2:1077–80.
413. Source unidentified.
414. Source unidentified.

tians who gave officers of the law scriptures and other sacred items) during the persecutions. The president of the council was Bishop Secundus of Tigisium "because he was the oldest of the eleven bishops present."[415] All the bishops confessed to having given up their copies of the scriptures when Diocletian's agents asked for them, each excusing himself on one ground or another. When Purpurius, bishop of Limata, pointedly asked Secundus: "What did you do when the curstor [inquisitor] asked for your books?"[416] the good bishop turned to the assembly for advice. It was proposed thereupon that "every man be accountable to God only for his conduct in this matter (whether or not they gave up their copies of the scriptures)."[417] This convenient solution was passed unanimously with cries of *Deo Gratias*.

In 314 the Council of Arles passed a rule that "no bishop should annoy another bishop."[418] This followed hard upon the Council of Ancyra (held in 314 to heal the troubles attendant upon the persecutions—especially the problem of the *lapsi* [lapsed members]) where it was decreed that *"chorepiskopoi* [priestly assistants to the bishop] might not ordain presbyters and deacons nor city presbyters without permission of the bishop of the *hetera paroikia* [persons under the jurisdiction of another bishop] in writing."[419] Church property

---

415. ". . . le plus ancien des onze évêques présents." Hefele, *Histoire des Conciles d'Après les Documents Originaux*, 1:209.

416. "Qu'as-tu donc fait toi-même lorsque le curateur t'a demandé de livres les saintes Écritures?" Hefele, *Histoire des Conciles d'Après les Documents Originaux*, 1:210.

417. "Ils lui persuadèrunt [le président] de décider «que chacun rendrait compte à Dieu de sa conduite dans cette affaire» (s'il avait, oui ou non, livré les Écritures)." Hefele, *Histoire des Conciles d'Après les Documents Originaux*, 1:210.

418. *Ut nullus episcopus alium episcopum inculcet.* Council of Arles, Canon 17, in Hefele, *Histoire des Conciles d'Après les Documents Originaux*, 1:547.

419. χωρεπισκόπους μὴ ἐξεῖναι πρεσβυτέρους ἢ διακόνους χειροτονεῖν, ἀλλά, μηδὲ πρεσβυτέρους πόλεως, χωρὶς τοῦ ἐπιτραπῆναι ὑπὸ τοῦ ἐπισκόπου, μετὰ γραμμάτων ἐν ἑτέρᾳ παροικίᾳ. Council of Ancyra, Canon 13, in Hefele, *Histoire des Conciles d'Après les Documents Originaux*, 1:314.

sold during an episcopal vacancy must be sold back again if the bishop demands it.[420] Bishops not accepted by the *paroikias* to which they have been ordained will be cut off if they try to push out another bishop either in their old *paroikia* or in some other by stirring up trouble.[421] Later ecclesiastical councils determined further canons of church law and procedure in a series of efforts to regulate the powers of the bishops:

Neocaesarea, A.D. 314–325

Canon 14. The *chorepiskopoi* are the type of the seventy, but in view of the good work they do for the poor, they may have the honor of administering the sacrament.[422]

Council of Nicaea, A.D. 325

Canon 4. A bishop must be installed by all the bishops of his province; if that is not possible, by at least three bishops, with written permission from all the others, and in every case under the supervision of the metropolitan of the eparchy.[423]

Canon 5. A person excluded from a church by the personal rancor of the bishop may appeal his case before a provincial synod to be held in every province for this specific purpose twice a year, at Easter and in autumn.[424]

Canon 15. Because of great disorder and rioting it will be necessary to abolish the old custom of allowing a bishop, priest, or deacon to move from one city to another. If any

---

420. Council of Ancyra, Canon 15, in Hefele, *Histoire des Conciles d'Après les Documents Originaux*, 1:316–17.

421. Council of Arles, Canon 18, in Hefele, *Histoire des Conciles d'Après les Documents Originaux*, 1:320.

422. οἱ δὲ χωρεπίσκοπος εἰσὶ μὲν εἰς τύπον τῶν ἑβδομήκοντα· ὡς δὲ συλλειτουργοὶ διὰ τὴν σπουδὴν (τὴν) εἰς τοὺς πτωχοὺς προσφέρουσι τιμώμενοι. Hefele, *Histoire des Conciles d'Après les Documents Originaux*, 1:334.

423. Hefele, *Histoire des Conciles d'Après les Documents Originaux*, 1:547.

424. Hefele, *Histoire des Conciles d'Après les Documents Originaux*, 1:550.

presumes to do this, he shall be sent back to the city in which he was ordained.[425]

Canon 16. Priests, deacons, or others living under the canon who frivolously and irresponsibly leave their churches will be forced to return to them by all possible means. If they refuse to return they shall be deposed. If anyone steals a cleric against a bishop's will and ordains him to serve in his own church, the ordination shall be void.[426]

Encaeniis (Antioch), A.D. 341

Canon 3. A priest or deacon who moves permanently to another place and ignores his bishop's appeals to return must lose the right to all office; if he goes to work for another bishop he must be punished to the bargain for breaking church law.[427]

Canon 9. Bishops in every province must understand that the bishop in the metropolis has charge of the whole province because all who have business to transact come from all directions to the metropolis.[428]

Canon 11. Any bishop, priest, or any churchman at all who dares to go to the emperor without a letter from his metropolitan shall be ejected utterly, not only from his church, but from his priesthood. . . . If he must go to the emperor it must be with the okay of the metropolitan of the eparchy or the bishops of the same, and he must bear letters from them.[429] (Add this authority to the metropolitan.)

Canon 16. When a bishop seizes a vacant seat without the okay of a full synod, he must be deposed, even though the people have elected him.[430] (The synod becomes more powerful; popular election is going out.)

---

425. Hefele, *Histoire des Conciles d'Après les Documents Originaux*, 1:600.
426. Hefele, *Histoire des Conciles d'Après les Documents Originaux*, 1:604.
427. Hefele, *Histoire des Conciles d'Après les Documents Originaux*, 1:715.
428. Hefele, *Histoire des Conciles d'Après les Documents Originaux*, 1:717.
429. Hefele, *Histoire des Conciles d'Après les Documents Originaux*, 1:717–18.
430. Hefele, *Histoire des Conciles d'Après les Documents Originaux*, 1:719.

Canon 18. A bishop who cannot take over a church because the congregation will not have him must remain in honor and office but may not meddle in the affairs of the church where he is forced to remain.[431]

Canon 21. No matter what happens, a bishop must remain forever in the church to which God has chosen him.[432] (Church control over the bishop tightens.)

Sardika, A.D. 347

Canon 1. No bishop ever moves from a larger to a smaller city but only in the other direction.[433] (Ambition and domination are being measured always and only by the size of a city.)

Canon 2. If it can be proven that a man has bribed parties to stir up a clamor for him as bishop, "so to make it seem that the people are actually asking him to be their bishop," he shall be excommunicated.[434]

Canon 6. It is not permitted to ordain a bishop for a small place. It must be *populosa . . . quae mereatur habere episcopum* [populous in order to be worthy of having a bishop].[435]

Epaon, A.D. 517

Canon 3. If the king acts against us, all bishops will withdraw to monasteries, and no bishop shall stir out again until the king has given peace to each and all bishops alike.[436]

Orleans, A.D. 541

Canon 3. Nobles may not celebrate Easter at their own oratories but must come to the episcopal city for the yearly rites.[437]

---

431. Hefele, *Histoire des Conciles d'Après les Documents Originaux*, 1:719–20.
432. Hefele, *Histoire des Conciles d'Après les Documents Originaux*, 1:720–21.
433. Hefele, *Histoire des Conciles d'Après les Documents Originaux*, 1:760–61.
434. Hefele, *Histoire des Conciles d'Après les Documents Originaux*, 1:761–62.
435. Hefele, *Histoire des Conciles d'Après les Documents Originaux*, 1:777–78.
436. Hefele, *Histoire des Conciles d'Après les Documents Originaux*, 2:1045.
437. Hefele, *Histoire des Conciles d'Après les Documents Originaux*, 2:1166.

Canon 20. No layman may arrest, question, or punish a cleric without okay of the church. When a cleric appears in court, it must be with okay of his bishop, and no sentence may be passed without the presence of his spiritual superior.[438]

Canon 32. Descendants of church slaves who have found their way back to the original place of their ancestors must be brought back to the church slavery, no matter how long or for how many generations they have been free.[439]

Paris, A.D. 557

Canon 1. No one may hold that church property changes political dominations: no one can claim that church property ever passes under another ruler "since the dominion of God knows no geographical boundaries." No one may claim that he holds as a gift from the king property that once belonged to the church. All property given by King Chlodwig of blessed memory and handed down as an inheritance must now be given back to the church.[440]

Tours, A.D. 567

Canon 14. All priests and monks must sleep in dormitories. Two or three men must remain constantly awake, spelling each other by turns.[441]

Canon 15. Whoever enters a monastery may never leave it to marry. If he does, any judge who refuses to excommunicate him will be himself excommunicated. Anyone who defends a monk guilty of such defilement will be excommunicated until the monk returns to his monastery.[442]

---

438. Hefele, *Histoire des Conciles d'Après les Documents Originaux*, 2:1168.
439. Hefele, *Histoire des Conciles d'Après les Documents Originaux*, 2:1170–73.
440. Hefele, *Histoire des Conciles d'Après les Documents Originaux*, 3:170–72.
441. Hefele, *Histoire des Conciles d'Après les Documents Originaux*, 3:187.
442. Hefele, *Histoire des Conciles d'Après les Documents Originaux*, 3:187–88.

Macon, A.D. 585

Canon 15. Whenever a layman meets a higher cleric, he must bow to him. If both are mounted, the layman must remove his hat. If the layman alone is mounted, he must dismount to greet the cleric.[443]

Auxerre, A.D. 585

Canon 44. A layman who disregards the admonition of an archpresbyter must be shut out of the church and punished in accordance with royal decrees.[444]

Canon 45. Anyone who is lax in observing this rule or does not report an infraction of it to the bishop is excluded from Christian communion for one year.[445]

Toledo, A.D. 589

Canon 20. Many bishops burden their clerics with intolerable compulsory services and contributions. Clerics thus cruelly oppressed may complain to the metropolitan.[446]

Canon 21. Judges and secular officials who assign slaves of the church and the clergy to public or private tasks will be excommunicated.[447]

Narbonne, A.D. 589

Canon 1. No cleric may wear purple. It is for princes and not becoming in churchmen.[448]

Canon 13. Subdeacons must hold curtains and doors open for superior clergy. If they refuse to do so they must pay a fine; lower clergy who refuse must be beaten.[449]

---

443. Hefele, *Histoire des Conciles d'Après les Documents Originaux*, 3:211.
444. Hefele, *Histoire des Conciles d'Après les Documents Originaux*, 3:220.
445. Hefele, *Histoire des Conciles d'Après les Documents Originaux*, 3:221.
446. Hefele, *Histoire des Conciles d'Après les Documents Originaux*, 3:228.
447. Hefele, *Histoire des Conciles d'Après les Documents Originaux*, 3:228.
448. Hefele, *Histoire des Conciles d'Après les Documents Originaux*, 3:229.
449. Hefele, *Histoire des Conciles d'Après les Documents Originaux*, 3:230.

Paris, A.D. 614

Canon 9. Any state official who touches church property or the property of a bishop after his death is cut off from communion as an assassin of the poor.[450]

Canon 14. Whoever deserts a monastery is excommunicated to the end of his life.[451]

Reims, A.D. 624–625

Canon 13. No one, not even a bishop, may ever sell the property or slaves of the church.[452] (The church can gain property; it can never lose it.)

Toledo, A.D. 633

Canon 53. Religious persons who are neither clerics nor monks must be taken before the bishop of any area in which they are found at large, given correction, and enrolled in the clergy or assigned to a monastery.[453]

Canon 67. Bishops may not free slaves of the church unless they reimburse the church out of their private fortunes, and the bishop's successors can reclaim any thus freed.

Canon 68. A bishop who frees a slave of the church without reserving the *patrocinium* [financial holdings] for the church must give the church two slaves in his place. If the person freed makes *any* complaint about the way he was treated while he was a slave, he must again become a church slave.[454]

Toledo, A.D. 638

Canon 3. Thank God for the edict of King Chintila banishing all Jews from Spain, with the order that "only Catholics may live in the land. . . . Resolved that any future king

---

450. Hefele, *Histoire des Conciles d'Après les Documents Originaux*, 3:252–53.
451. Hefele, *Histoire des Conciles d'Après les Documents Originaux*, 3:253.
452. Hefele, *Histoire des Conciles d'Après les Documents Originaux*, 3:262.
453. Hefele, *Histoire des Conciles d'Après les Documents Originaux*, 3:273.
454. Hefele, *Histoire des Conciles d'Après les Documents Originaux*, 3:275.

before mounting the throne should swear an oath not to tolerate the Jewish *Unglauben* [unbelief]. . . . If he breaks this oath, let him be anathema and *maranatha* [excommunicated] before God and food for the eternal fire."[455]

Toledo, A.D. 646

Canon 5. Entirely abolishes the monasterial rights of the *vagi* [*les vagabonds,* wandering heretics].[456]

Toledo, A.D. 656

Canon 6. Children over ten years of age may dedicate themselves to the religious life without consulting their parents. When smaller children are tonsured or given the religious garment, unless their parents lodge immediate protest, they are bound to the religious discipline for life.[457]

Emerita, A.D. 666

Canon 15. It *often* happens that priests who fall sick blame church slaves for their condition and torture them out of revenge. This must cease.[458]

Canon 16. Bishops must stop taking more than their *third*. They must not take from the church's third for their private use.[459]

Toledo, A.D. 694

Canon 8. Jews must be denied all religious practice. Their children must be taken from them at seven years and must marry Christians.[460]

---

455. "Pour qu'il n'y ait plus dans le pays que des catholiques. D'accord avec le roi et les grands, on prescript qu'à l'avenir tout roi qui montera sur le trône devra, sans compter ses autres serments, prêter celui de ne pas souffrir l'impiéte juive. . . . S'il ne tient pas ce serment, qu'il soit anathème et *Maran-Atha* devant Dieu et qu'il soit la proie du feu éternel." Hefele, *Histoire des Conciles d'Après les Documents Originaux,* 3:279.
456. Hefele, *Histoire des Conciles d'Après les Documents Originaux,* 3:287.
457. Hefele, *Histoire des Conciles d'Après les Documents Originaux,* 3:295.
458. Hefele, *Histoire des Conciles d'Après les Documents Originaux,* 3:305.
459. Hefele, *Histoire des Conciles d'Après les Documents Originaux,* 3:306.
460. Hefele, *Histoire des Conciles d'Après les Documents Originaux,* 3:587.

Berghampstead, A.D. 697

Canons 26–28. *All* unattached persons are to be treated as thieves. All thieves may be killed (by the king) or sold over the sea.[461]

Rome, A.D. 743

Canon 3. Clerics may never wear worldly clothing.[462]

Boniface, A.D. 745

Statute 13. Pasquil [jokes about the authorities] must be severely punished, even with exile.[463]

Paderborn, A.D. 785

Canon 21. Anyone engaging in pagan rites must pay a heavy fine. If he cannot pay, no matter what his station, he becomes a slave of the church until he has paid up.[464]

Canon 23. Soothsayers and fortune-tellers shall be given to churches and priests as slaves.[465]

Canon 34. No public assemblies of the Saxon are permitted without special royal permission. The priests shall keep watch that this is carried out.[466]

Aix-la-Chapelle, A.D. 789

Canon 77. False writing, such as those claimed to have fallen last year from heaven, must not be read but must be burnt.[467]

Clermont, A.D. 1095

Canon 1. Monks, clerics, women, and their escorts shall enjoy the peace of God every day. Others may be attacked

---

461. Hefele, *Histoire des Conciles d'Après les Documents Originaux*, 3:589.
462. Hefele, *Histoire des Conciles d'Après les Documents Originaux*, 3:852.
463. Hefele, *Histoire des Conciles d'Après les Documents Originaux*, 3:927.
464. Hefele, *Histoire des Conciles d'Après les Documents Originaux*, 3:994.
465. Hefele, *Histoire des Conciles d'Après les Documents Originaux*, 3:994.
466. Hefele, *Histoire des Conciles d'Après les Documents Originaux*, 3:994.
467. Hefele, *Histoire des Conciles d'Après les Documents Originaux*, 3:1033.

without breaking the peace Monday through Wednesday. Full immunity for farmers and merchants is to be effective three years "because of the present food shortage."[468]

Lateran IV, A.D. 1215

Canon 3. All condemned heretics *must* be turned over to the secular authorities for punishment. . . . Their property must be confiscated by the church. Those who have not been able to clear themselves of charges of heresy are excommunicated and must be avoided by all. If they remain a year under the ban, they must be condemned as heretics. All civil officers must take a public oath to defend the faith and expel from their territories all heretics. Whoever, when ordered to do so by the church, does not purify his district or domain of heretics will be put under the ban. If he does not give satisfaction within a year, he must be reported to the pope, who will absolve his vassals from all duty to him and declare his lands open to legitimate conquest by Catholics: those who participate in the attack will receive the same privileges as regular crusaders. All who help, protect, or believe heretics are excommunicated, and if they do not give satisfaction within a year will lose all legal rights (a horrible list follows); all who associate with them will suffer the same. Anyone who preaches without the authorization of a bishop is excommunicated. . . . A bishop must inspect his diocese. His officers are authorized to have all inhabitants swear an oath to expose to the bishop all sectarians that can be discovered. . . . Anyone who refuses to take the oath automatically makes himself a traitor. Also any bishop who is lax in these things is to be deposed.[469]

In all this the tendency to compel and control is clear, and in our day familiar. The missionaries in central and

---

468. Hefele, *Histoire des Conciles d'Après les Documents Originaux*, 5:400–401.

469. Hefele, *Histoire des Conciles d'Après les Documents Originaux*, 5:1329–33.

northern Europe appear as the advance guard of an army of occupation. The clergy asserts complete control of civil government, private life, and family. The third canon of the Council of the Lateran is pure McCarthyism without the crippling fifth amendment that McCarthy finds so frustrating. There is the guilt by association which makes all nonconformity equally criminal. If the clergy was increasingly presumptuous and tyrannous, the clergy itself became more and more the victim of its own paralyzing limitations. No one trusts anyone anymore; there is no release in being a clergyman—all are being watched. As in the empire, where all things were solved by absolute subservience to one man, so in the church—with the paradoxical result that the one man in whom all the power and authority on earth resided was the most pitiful and insecure object imaginable. The hysterical insistence on complete submission and the pathological fear of conformity are the fruits of a thousand years of Christian rule. Nothing could be feebler than the stock explanations of "barbaric Europe" refusing to be measured by the civilizing offices of the church. The church itself was the mother and teacher of barbarism. The passion to possess and control, the insane jealousy of all that lies beyond complete domination, are the hallmarks of the great khans of Asia (who were the contemporaries of Innocent III) and the very essence of barbarism. One sees in the domination of Europe what Richard Coudenhove-Kalergi, the leader of Roman Catholic intellectuals on the continent between the two world wars, meant in his repeated declaration that "Fascism is Catholicism in action."[470]

Are the Council and the Synod the Apostolic Voice?

Almost any clergyman, if asked where the ultimate authority of the Christian church resides, will say in the universal

---

470. Source unidentified.

councils of the church. In 782, the Council of Seville condemned Migetius for the absurd doctrine "that only in Rome is divine power exercised, that only the Roman Church is the Catholic Church, that everything is holy and spotless at Rome and that the words 'Thou art Peter, etc.,' apply only to the Roman Church instead of the whole church." To show the place of the bishop of Rome, the council recalls that the Pope Liberius was condemned for heresy.[471]

In calling the first ecumenical council, the emperor was aware, says Eusebius, that "it is not possible to reach correct decisions in important matters except in synods."[472] "We should not judge each other as individuals," says Basil, "but only in general assemblies of large numbers of bishops."[473] A catholic church with a single direction "is impossible," Constantine writes in his summons to Nicaea, "unless all or at least the greater part of the bishops meet together."[474] And he states more than once the principle, "Whatever is done in the holy synods of the bishops has the force of the divine will itself."[475]

"The church teaches and is infallible," writes the ever-confident Batiffol. "The teaching office, which belonged to the

---

471. "D'après Migetius, le pouvoir divin ne se trouvait qu'à Rome, seule d'Église romaine était l'*Ecclesia catholica*. Là tout était saint, tout était sans tache, à elle seule s'appliquent les paroles: «Tu es Pierre, et sur cette pierre, etc. . . .» Elipand croit au contraire que le Christ dit cela de l'Église catholique tout entière." Council of Seville, in Hefele, *Histoire des Conciles d'Après les Documents Originaux*, 3:987–88.

472. ἄλλως γὰρ οὐ δυνατὸν τὰ μεγάλα τῶν σκεμμάτων, ἢ διὰ συνόδων. Eusebius, *Vita Constantini* 1.51, in *PG* 20:965.

473. δικαιότερον δὲ τὰ καθ' ἡμᾶς δρίνεσθαι μὴ ἐξ ἑνὸς ἢ δευτέρου τῶν μὴ ὀρθοποδούντων πρὸς τὴν ἀλήθειαν, ἀλλ' ἐκ τοῦ πλήθους τῶν κατὰ τὴν οἰκουμένην ἐπισκόπων συνημμένων. Basil, *Epistola* 204.7, in *PG* 32:753.

474. οὐχ οἷόν τ' ἦν . . . εἰ μὴ εἰς ταὐτὸ πάντων ὁμοῦ, ἢ τῶν γοῦν πλειόνων ἐπισκόπων συνελθόντων. Eusebius, *Vita Constantini* 3.17, in *PG* 20:1073.

475. πᾶν γάρ, εἴ τι δ' ἂν ἐν τοῖς ἁγίοις τῶν ἐπισκόπων συνεδρίοις πράττεται, τοῦτο πρὸς τὴν θείαν βούλησιν ἔχει τὴν ἀναφοράν. Eusebius, *Vita Constantini* 3.20, in *PG* 20:1080.

apostles, passed to the bishops taken in their totality or assembled in universal council. Its object is the continuation of the revelation or deposit of the faith and has to do with things necessary for the conservation of the deposit of the faith."[476] And yet there was no universal meeting of bishops—the supposed sole expression of apostolic instruction—for almost three hundred years after the apostles, at which time the emperor, entirely on his own authority, commanded wildly disagreeing bishops to come together in his presence. Under his eye and with his constant threats and proddings, they brought forth that creed, which is now accepted as the official statement of the Christian faith. Ignatius knows of no councils of bishops at all—even local ones. And as soon as we have the bishops meeting, those meetings are careful imitations not of the apostles, but of the Roman Senate. Batiffol himself was one of the first to point this out, though it is extremely obvious from the minutes of the meetings.

Batiffol notes first of all that the name synod (*concilium*), as used by Clement of Alexandria, is not a religious term.[477] In the time of Augustine, bishops were convoked by whichever bishop in the province had held that office for the longest time. He, regardless of his city, was the *primas* [first].[478] The expression for calling a synod, *cogere concilium*, was taken from the Roman *cogere senatum*, to call the senate; the expression to hold a council (*concilium habere*) was taken from the Roman *senatum habere*.[479] The opening words of the Council of

---

476. Source unidentified.
477. Batiffol, "Le Réglement des Premiers Conciles Africains et le Réglement du Sénat Romain," *Bulletin d'Ancienne Littérature et d'Archéologie Chrétiennes* (1913): 3.
478. Batiffol, "Le Réglement des Premiers Conciles Africains," 4.
479. "Convoquer le concile se dit *cogere concilium*, qui rappelle l'expression *cogere senatum*, convoquer le sénat. Et de même que *senatum habere* désigne l'action de tenir séance du sénat, ainsi tenir séance du concile se dit *concilium habere*." Batiffol, "Le Réglement des Premiers Conciles Africains," 6.

Carthage in 256 are "an imitation of the protocol of the *proces-verbaux* [record] of the sessions of the Roman Senate."[480] Even more significant, the meetings of the councils remained public at all times, though only bishops were allowed actually to participate. Contrast this with the secrecy of the meetings of the Lord with his apostles, of the apostles among themselves and of the *earliest* Christians, which is perhaps the best-known aspect of "apostolic" assemblies.

The preliminary reading of a case in the council was called a *relatio*, exactly as in the Roman Senate; the discussion was called the *verba facere;* the final motion the *sententia*, exactly as in the Senate. Voting was by *discessio*, standing on one side or the other of the hall. "Whether in Carthage in 256 or in 312," Batiffol concludes, "or in Rome in 313, one could not conceive of an assembly deliberating in any other form than that consecrated by the usage of the Senate."[481] "Consecrated" is a good word. Certainly what there was of order and discipline in the meetings was the inherited gravity and dignity of pagan Rome: as Christians, the bishops screamed and spat at each other, and most of the great councils were scenes of wild disorder.

Karl Joseph von Hefele's discussion on the nature of church councils at the beginning of his standard work on the subject should suffice to show the qualifications of synods as depositories of apostolic authority. Having noted that Acts 15 gives us, without doubt, the origin of councils, Hefele continues, "But the theologians are not in agreement as to whether the councils were established by divine or human

---

480. "Les premiers mots de ce protocole sont une imitation du protocole des procès-verbaux des séances du sénat romain." Batiffol, "Le Réglement des Premiers Conciles Africains," 6.

481. "Soit à Carthage en 256 ou en 312, soit à Rome en 313, on ne concevait pas une assemblée délibérant en forme autrement que dans la forme consacrée par l'usage du sénat." Batiffol, "Le Réglement des Premiers Conciles Africains," 18.

authority."[482] Then and there Hefele settles the question as to whether councils are apostolic or not—if they were apostolic, there could be no possible doubt of their divine origin, yet where all the historic church councils are concerned, that is a subject of grave controversy. What was done by apostles under the influence of the Holy Spirit, Hefele himself observes, must necessarily have been according to earlier instructions of the Lord.[483] Thereby he shows his entire miscomprehension of what apostolic authority is: why *earlier* instruction? Were not the apostles in a position to receive instructions from the Lord at *any* time? Not by Bishop Hefele's reckoning. As the strongest proof of the divine nature of councils, Hefele cites Cyprian's description of the Council of Carthage in 252: *placuit nobis sancto Spiritu suggerente*—"We decided, at the suggestion of the Holy Spirit."[484] This is the sort of vague and general rhetoric that flowed naturally from the mouths of bishops and schoolmen; and certainly the "suggestion" of the Holy Spirit is anything but a specific claim to literal guidance by revelation—a claim which cannot well be made while Christian churches all deny continued revelation.

Then Hefele cites Constantine's claim that the Council of Arles was a *caeleste judicium* [celestial court]. The emperor, desperately hunting for a principle of authority to which to hold his unruly bishops, says that it was a "celestial court" because "the judgment of priests must *always* be considered such."[485] In other words, a council, as such, is divinely inspired only in the sense that any priest is divinely led. Of his own Nicene Council, the emperor says, "What three hundred holy bishops accept is not to be interpreted as anything

---

482. "Mais les théologiens ne sont pas d'accord pour decider s'ils sont d'institution divine ou d'institution humaine." Hefele, *Histoire des Conciles d'Après les Documents Originaux*, 1:2.
483. Hefele, *Histoire des Conciles d'Après les Documents Originaux*, 1:2.
484. Hefele, *Histoire des Conciles d'Après les Documents Originaux*, 1:2–3.
485. *Sacerdotum judicium ita debet haberi*. Hefele, *Histoire des Conciles d'Après les Documents Originaux*, 1:3.

else but the opinion of the only Son of God."[486] The emperor here appeals to the argument of numbers: again, it is not the synod as such that is holy, but the size of the thing that gives it authority. Cicero had used the very same argument to prove the divinity of senatorial decrees.

In the third century we read of a "council held by the Greeks in certain places, meetings of all the churches in which were discussed the more important common problems, and a representation of the whole Christian Society [literally, name] was celebrated with great veneration."[487] Yet as late as 220, councils were still unknown in Africa, and Tertullian, in the above passage, refers to the Greek custom as a peculiar thing in the church. Later attempts are made to describe councils being held by bishops in the days of the apostles. It is not inconceivable that quarterly conferences were held in the primitive church as they are in the restored church, but nothing is more certain than that such conferences were not the origin of the episcopal synods of conventional church history. These synods are an attempt to fill a gap: "It is not possible to settle controversies on matters of major import except through synods."[488] "Whatsoever is done in the holy synods of the bishops must be attributed to the divine will."[489] "For whatever such a large *number* of bishops agrees on must be taken as arrived at, not auto-

---

486. *Quod trecentis sanctis episcopis visum est not est aliud putandum, quam solius Filii Dei sententia.* Hefele, *Histoire des Conciles d'Après les Documents Originaux,* 1:3.

487. *Agunutr praeterea per Graecias illa certis in locis concilia ex universiis ecclesiis per quae et altiora quaeque in commune tractantur, et ipsa repraesentio totius nominis Christiani magna veneratione celebratur.* Tertullian, *De Ieiuniis* 13, in *PL* 2:1023.

488. ἄλλως γὰρ οὐ δυνατὸν τὰ μεγάλα τῶν σκεμμάτων, ἢ διὰ συνόδων κατορθώσασθαι. Eusebius, *Vita Constantini* 1.51, in *PG* 20:965.

489. πᾶν γάρ, εἴ τι δ' ἂν ἐν τοῖς ἁγίοις τῶν ἐπισκόπων συνεδρίοις πράττεται, τοῦτο πρὸς τὴν θείαν βούλησιν ἔχει τὴν ἀναφοράν. Eusebius, *Vita Constantini* 3.20, in *PG* 20:1080.

THE OFFICE OF BISHOP IN THE EARLY CHRISTIAN CHURCH   139

matically, but by God's suggestion" (literally, at a nod from God).[490] The expression "at a nod from God," became a popular device to "prove" divine authority—it was an old trick of the *cratores* [power brokers] to give superhuman power to the emperor—a noncommittal sort of thing, but full of implications. Thus Leo describes the besting of a rival in a riot: "Flavian, though he stirred up a tumult, was ejected by the churches at a nod from God."[491]

The full and vivid minutes of the Synod of Carthage in A.D. 411 plainly show it to be just a copy of the local ãvil *comitia* [local assemblies], Marcellinus, *vir clarissimus tribunarius et notarius* [a distinguished and notable man], presiding. Though the accounts of the Nicene and other great councils are often full and pious, no ritual detail being omitted, it is significant that we never read of any of the councils being either opened or closed with prayer. And it was not until the twelfth century that *any* ecumenical council was held in a church! The meeting was always in a palace or other government building.

It may seem strange that an institution so clearly designated as the highest depository of divine authority in the church should stand from the first completely under the command of the emperor. That is true not only of all the ecumenical councils until the twelfth century, but of important local councils as well. Thus Hefele points out that the Council of Arles in 314 was *angeordnet* [decreed] by Constantine the Great, the ecumenical council of bishops in 381 by Theodosius, the Synod of Orléans in 533 by King Childebert, and the Synod of Frankfort in 794 by Charlemagne; even a number of *orthodox* synods were held in Rome (early sixth century) under the direction of Theodoric the Great,

---

490. οὐδὲ γὰρ ταὐτομάτου, ἀλλὰ θείῳ νεύματι, ὁ τῶν τοσούτων ἀριθμὸς ἐπισκόπων συνεκροτήθη. Socrates Scholasticus, *Historia Ecclesiastica* 4.12, in *PG* 67:492.

491. Source unidentified.

who was an Arian.[492] He is careful not to mention Nicaea, at which the role of the emperor is fully described—for to admit the unchallenged power of secular rules in the matter of councils is to rob the Christian church of its one claim to apostolic direction. In the letter he sent to all those not present at Nicaea, Constantine gives the official account:

> Having by grace of God assumed responsibility for the common peace of the empire, I considered my foremost duty to be to devise means of guaranteeing peace and love to the most blessed multitudes [*plethe*] of the universal church. But since it was not possible to establish a firm and reliable order except by having all or at least the greater part of the bishops come together at a single place, . . . I myself, [have] brought you together, and [sit] in your midst as one of your number. (For I do not deny, but rather rejoice, to have become a fellow servant with you.) I resolved that the whole thing should be discussed until a common agreement was reached, so that not the slightest possible point of disagreement should remain to cause future difficulties.[493]

This was not a case of the emperor making use of an ongoing tradition. Contemporaries all marvel at the originality and ingenuity of his idea: the first general council of the church since the days of the apostles! "No mortal man could dis-

---

492. Hefele, *Histoire des Conciles d'Après les Documents Originaux*, 1:10–11.
493. πεῖραν λαβὼν ἐκ τῆς τῶν κοινῶν εἰπραξίας, ὅση τῆς θείας δυνάμεως πέφυκε χάρις, τοῦτον πρό γε πάντων ἔκρινα εἶναί μοι προσήκειν σκοπόν, ὅπως παρὰ τοῖς μακαριωτάτοις τῆς καθολικῆς Ἐκκλησίας πλήθεσι πίστις μία καὶ εἰλικρινὴς ἀγάπη, ὁμογνώμων τε περὶ τὸν παγκρατῆ θεὸν εὐσέβεια τηρῆται. ἀλλ' ἐπειδὴ τοῦτ' οὐχ οἷόν τ' ἦν ἀκλινῆ καὶ βεβαίαν τάξιν λαβεῖν, εἰ μὴ εἰς ταὐτὸ πάντων ὁμοῦ . . . αὐτὸς δὲ καθάπερ εἷς ἐξ ὑμῶν ἐτύγχανον συμπαρών (οὐ γὰρ ἀρνησαίμην ἄν, ἐφ' ᾧ μάλιστα χαίρω, συνθεράπων ὑμέτερος πεφυκέναι), ἄχρι τοσούτου ἅπαντα τῆς προσηκούσης τετύχηκεν ἐξετάσεως, ἄχρις οὗ ἡ τῷ πάντων ἐφόρῳ θεῷ ἀρέσκουσα γνώμη, πρὸς τὴν τῆς ἑνότητος συμφωνίαν εἰς φῶς προῆλθη, ὡς μηδὲν ἔτι πρὸς διχόνοιαν ἢ πίστεως ἀμφισβήτησιν ὑπολείπεσθαι. Eusebius, *Vita Constantini* 3.17, in *PG* 20:1073.

cover a remedy to the ill," writes Eusebius, "the resources of the contestants being equally matched. Almighty God alone could cure this too with ease and in all the world but one man, Constantine alone, appeared fitting to be his agent in this. Who, when he had considered the whole cause . . . *himself* bestirred *his own* mind and concluded that it would be necessary to make war on the adversary who disturbed the peace of the church."[494]

Constantine himself, however, leaves us in no doubt as to where he got the idea: we learn that he had just removed the last enemies to civil peace by bringing the Senate together at Rome to acclaim his policies and support his lone rule of the world. There, but a few weeks before, a great and magnificent triumph had been held over the enemy of the human race, enormous canvases had been hoisted in the capital showing Constantine treading upon the serpent, the evil one, his bitter political and military rival, the Christian Licinius. Just as he had triumphed over the enemy of peace within the state, the emperor announces in speeches and letters, so now he would triumph over the enemy of peace in the church—the unrest which has thrown the empire into civil turmoil from end to end. And he would do it the same way: by issuing his orders, calling his solemn assembly, announcing his will, and sealing all with a solemn and magnificent triumph to celebrate the establishment of the heavenly rule upon earth.

The Council of Nicaea simply repeated a few weeks later the senatorial sessions that had been held in Rome. The

---

494. οὐδεὶς οἷός τε ἦν ἀνθρώπων θεραπείαν εὕρασθαι τοῦ κακοῦ, ἰσοστασίου τῆς ἔριδος τοῖς διεστῶσιν ὑπαρχούσης· μόνῳ δ' ἄρα τῷ παντοδυνάμῳ θεῷ καὶ ταῦτ' ἰᾶσθαι ῥᾴδιον ἦν, ἀγαθῶν δ' ὑπηρέτης αὐτῷ μόνος τῶν ἐπὶ γῆς κατεφαίνετο Κωνσταντῖνος· ὃς ἐπειδὴ τὴν τῶν λεχθέντων διέγνω ἀκοήν . . . τότε αὐτὸς ἑαυτοῦ τὴν διάνοιαν ἀνανικήσας, ἄλλον τουτονὶ καταγωνιεῖσθαι δεῖν ἔφη τὸν κατὰ τοῦ ταράττοντος τὴν Ἐκκλησίαν ἀφανοῦς ἐχθροῦ πόλεμον. Eusebius, *Vita Constantini* 3.5, in *PG* 20:1060, emphasis added.

identical forms and rituals were observed. The great central room of the palace was the place. Benches were placed in order, filling up the space on either side of the hall. All invited were admitted by ticket, and each took an assigned seat. When all the synod was seated and in decent order, the whole body sat in dead silence, in expectation of the *emperor's* entrance. This was dramatically staged: first came one of the emperor's attendants, then another, and then a third. Still more high officials filed in, not the usual hoplites and spearmen, but only trusted friends of the emperor. Then at a given signal announcing his approach, all arose to their feet, and at length he appeared, "like unto some heavenly angel of God, wrapped as it were in brilliant light as he cast about him the luster of pearls, gleaming in the flash of his brilliant scarlet robe and adorned with the sparkle and glitter of gold and precious stones."[495] At last a substitute had been found for the glories of Pentecost and the burning bush: Hollywood can do *anything!*

In his opening speech, the emperor left no one in any doubt as to why he had called the meeting and what he expected of it: an end to Christian rioting. He was out to get a signed agreement that would bring unity into the church forevermore. He attended the key discussions with great interest, and one thing only interested him—getting an agreement. The actual doctrinal issues at stake, he said again and again, neither interested nor concerned him, and in the closing speech of the mighty council he recommended to all a word which he had been persuaded to adopt in committee as the solution to all problems, *homoousios* [one substance], while frankly admitting that he had not the vaguest idea what it meant. But he did get his universal agreement—only

---

[495]. οἷα Θεοῦ τις οὐράνιος ἄγγελος, λαμπρὰν μὲν ὥσπερ φωτὸς μαρμαρυγαῖς ἐξαστράπτων περιβολήν ἁλουργίδος πυρωποῖς καταλαμπόμενος ἀκτῖσι, χρυσοῦ τε καὶ λίθων πολυτελῶν διαυγέσι κοσμούμενος. Eusebius, *Vita Constantini* 3.10, in *PG* 20:1065.

seventeen bishops refused to sign the final formula, and he made it so hot for them that all but two quickly changed their minds; the two were banished.

How was it possible to arrive at this marvelous consensus in so short a time? This "heavenly" unity was forever after put forward as the sure proof that the Holy Ghost had ruled the decisions of the first and greatest of the councils. Yet all our sources describe the workings of a far more tangible persuasion among the holy bishops. As soon as the emperor saw a majority favoring one side or the other of an issue, he would instantly throw his weight behind that side, "praising those who spoke in its favor or turning with withering frowns or even sharp rebukes toward those who spoke against it."[496] In this way the most God-beloved emperor gently prodded the bishops into this or that decision, until in a marvelously short time there was hardly a dissenting voice in the house. Constantine knew his human nature and declared in the closing oration that "real friends of truth are few and hard to find": what nearly everybody is interested in is a career.[497] So he found no trouble in "prescribing to the bishops those things which would be of the greatest benefit to their churches."[498] It was indeed a rare soul who held out for principles, and, while Constantine frankly admired the courage and independence of Bishop Acesius, who had refused to answer his summons to Nicaea, and was far easier on him than he was on many who "rushed to the capital eager to see the sites and see the emperor,"[499] he explained the difficulty of his position in a private conversation with

---

496. . . . τοὺς μὲν γοῦν πείθων, τοὺς δὲ καταδυσωπῶν τῷ λόγῳ, τοὺς δ' εὖ λεγόντας ἐπαινῶν, πάντας τ' εἰς ὁμόνοιαν ἐλαύνων. Eusebius, *Vita Constantini* 3.13, in PG 20:1069.

497. σπανίος αὖ ὁ τῆς ἀληθείας φίλος. Eusebius, *Vita Constantini* 3.21, in PG 20:1084.

498. . . . ἐν μέρει μὲν ἐπισκόποις ὑπὲρ τῶν ἐκκλησιῶν τοῦ θεοῦ τὰ πρόσφορα διαταττόμενος. Eusebius, *Vita Constantini* 3.24, in PG 20:1084.

499. Source unidentified.

Acesius, in which the monarch pointed out that there was no advantage in trying to climb all alone up his own little ladder to heaven.[500]

The Gospel of Bigness and Power

The emperor was perfectly sincere in his gospel of bigness and power, but to the true saint, as to the true philosopher, it has a cynical and despairing undertone. Yet in a frank and revealing study, Father Bligh has declared flatly for the emperor: whatever brings the greatest *number* of people under Christian influence is to be regarded as a blessing, no matter how it may corrupt and contaminate that influence. "The title of ἰσαπόστολος [equal to the apostles!] given to Constantine by the Eastern Church was not altogether undeserved, if one considers only the extent of his influence upon the expansion of Christianity."[501] What else is there to consider, if we grant Father Bligh his thesis that the importance of numbers outweighs all other considerations? Constantine actually did "convert" far more people than the apostles did, for Father Bligh and his church are quite content with that kind of conversion. There was some protest against the deifying of the emperor and the glorifying of the victory of the Pons Milvius at the time, but that protest was forgotten, and ever since then the Christian church has looked back on the fourth century as the golden age, which remained the ideal during the Middle Ages and for churchmen the perfect model of the heavenly order on earth.

The argument of numbers is actually only the argument of force—and that is where the emperor comes in. How frank is Pope Liberius when he writes to the Macedonians that since the opinion of such a large number of bishops (as at Nicaea) cannot be regarded as anything but God's doing, let us reason with them (the Arian opposition) "by persua-

---

500. Sozomen, *Historia Ecclesiastica* 1.22, in *PG* 67:925.
501. Bligh, "The 'Edict of Milan': Curse or Blessing?" 311.

THE OFFICE OF BISHOP IN THE EARLY CHRISTIAN CHURCH 145

sion, or, to speak bluntly, with worldly force."[502] The bishops have never been able to carry out their leadership for any length of time without the immediate and powerful support of the secular arm. "Except for thy mighty arm," wrote Leo to Peppin, "we have no other support save God alone,"[503] and plainly God alone is not enough, since Leo is begging for Peppin's army. But Tertullian was right: where the power is, there is the authority.[504] "From the moment [the emperors] began to be Christians," writes Socrates, "the affairs of the church began to be regulated by them, and the greatest synods were, and still are, held according to their mind and will."[505] The mighty Athanasius, the hero of the churchmen, repeatedly defied the emperor—and after a repeated battle of wills, knuckled under.

---

502. ἢ διὰ πειθοῦς τινος, ἤ, ἵνα ἀληθέστερον εἴπω, κοσμικῆς δυναστείας. Socrates Scholasticus, *Historia Ecclesiastica* 4.12, in PG 67:493.
503. Source unidentified.
504. Tertullian, *De Pudicitia* 21, in PL 2:1077–80.
505. διότι ἀφ' οὗ χριστιανίζειν ἤρξαντο, τὰ τῆς ἐκκλησίας πράγματα ἤρτητο ἐξ εὐτῶν, καὶ αἱ μέγισται σύνοδοι τῇ αὐτῶν γνώμῃ γεγόνασί τε καὶ γίνονται. Socrates Scholasticus, *Historia Ecclesiastica*, preface to 5, in PG 67:565.

2

The Office of Bishop in the Church in Rome

In Search of a Missing Link

Up until now, all discussion has been confined to the church in general, and, where the case of Rome has been cited, it has only been by way of illustration. But for reasons that need no explaining, it is well to give some special attention to a particular bishopric whose claims were pushed with ever-increasing insistence. Once there was a man who boasted of being a direct descendant of Abraham Lincoln. To prove his claim he would quote the Gettysburg address with the flaming challenge: "Deny if you can that Lincoln wrote *that!*" No one wants to deny it, we would tell such an one, but what has that got to do with your claims? The Roman Catholics quote certain words of the Lord to Peter, indicating that Peter was to become president of the church, and think thereby that they have demonstrated not only Peter's claim on the Lord, but through some mysterious logic their claim on Peter, though the Lord said not a word about his successors, let alone about the city of Rome. The most undeniable proof that it is raining does not prove that it is Tuesday. What the Roman Catholics have to prove is not that the Savior bestowed office on Peter, but that Peter bestowed office on them; to date they have thought to settle the whole question by endless repetition of the irrelevant "thou art Peter."

Of course, intelligent Catholics recognize the true issue. The greatest of all their scholars in modern times, Louis Duchesne, devoted his whole life to seeking for some definite tie between Peter and his church—and failed to find it. Nevertheless, we are assured, if Peter was to be head of a church, there surely was to *be* a church, and what more likely candidate than ours? Again they make their point by assuming a thing that is not said or even hinted at in the scripture: that there would be a permanent church. Irenaeus cites the case of Rome to prove that doctrinal teachings (nothing is said about authority) were handed down from the apostles, and he gives as the first bishops Linus, Anacletus, and Clement, upon which the learned editor (Masseutus) comments: "It is not our business to unravel the difficulties with which the problem of Peter's successors fairly swarms, both with regard to succession and chronology."[1] Now, we can overlook mountains of swarming difficulties in Catholic doctrine, liturgy, and priesthood once a fair case has been made for the beginning of the church. But if there is any area in which no difficulty or contradiction may exist, in which, in fact, the slightest shadow or suspicion of a difficulty is enough to throw all final judgments into a state of permanent suspension, it is the crucial moment on which all depends—the fatal moment of transmission, *not* from Christ to Peter, but from Peter to his successor. And that is precisely the moment that "swarms" with difficulties! No other moment is so laden with the future as that moment; no other moment interests us quite so much. The Romans are voluble enough in telling us what happened before that moment—a

---

1. *Difficultates, quibus scatet primorum Petri successorum tum chronologia, tum successio evolvere nostri non est institati.* Domnus Renatus Masseutus, in J.-P. Migne, ed., *Patrologiae Cursus Completus . . . Series Graeca*, 161 vols. (Paris: Migne, 1857–66), 7:849 n. 63 (hereafter *PG*).

promise given to Peter—and what happened after that moment—a proud line of succession—but on what happened *at* that moment they not only preserve silence, but forbid investigation.

We have said that the investigation of that moment was considered by Monsignor Duchesne to be the special calling of his life, yet his biographer Henri Leclercq assures us that, after a certain time of his life, that was the one subject on which he would tolerate no investigation and no discussion.[2] In 1952 the Knights of Columbus Foundation for the Preservation of Historical Documents in the Vatican Library invited the world to study its holdings from all periods of its magnificent history collection—except the fatal period of the beginning: "The documents the Church has been collecting for nearly twenty centuries include, of course, the ecclesiastical records from the earliest Christian era. These are housed separately in the Vatican archives and are not to be microfilmed."[3] Why not? What is wrong? If they supported Catholic claims, we would long since have seen these documents splashed on the covers of *Life* and *Time*—but they are not even being microfilmed. The official reason given is painfully transparent: "They are not of general interest to scholars."[4] A few minutes spent in the religious sections of the card catalogs of any of our great libraries will show that it is precisely "the earliest Christian era" that is of overwhelming interest to scholars and the general public alike. Books in that limited area far outnumber those in all the other fields and periods put together. Obviously, the disinterest of scholars is not the true reason for keeping the documents of the early church undercover, while just

---

2. Henri Leclercq, "Historiens du Christianisme: XXXVII. Monsignor Duchesne," *Dictionaire d'Archéologie Chrétienne et de Liturgie*, 6.2.2697–98.
3. Source unidentified.
4. Source unidentified.

as obviously the true reason is that their release would be quite retrograde to Catholic interests.

Duchesne was not the first Catholic to recognize that all depends on the great moment of transmission of Peter's power to his successor. The importance of that moment is dramatically pointed out in the significant collection of letters attributed to Clement in which he describes the breathtaking event of the transmission of world power in detail. The fact that these letters are obvious forgeries and are yet quite old and numerous shows that churchmen fully recognized the need for establishing historically the all-important drama of the transmission.

The most serious attempt to explain how the keys got from Peter to the next man—a thing for which no provision is made in the scriptures or anywhere else—is in the famous *Liber Pontificalis.* The study of this source was the first great work of the celebrated Duchesne, and he was still engaged in its study when he died. According to Leclercq, when friends asked Duchesne why he did not renounce the Catholic Church as a result of his studies, he explained: "I have a mother in Brittany who is 102 years old with whom I make a retreat for two months every summer. I would not sacrifice the company of her and her friends for the satisfaction of being true to myself."[5]

A passage from Duchesne's edition of the *Liber Pontificalis* reads:

---

5. "En 1888, à un de ses amis ayant perdu la foi, il écrivait: «N'ayez pas peur que je succombe à la tentation. . . . Tous les ans je fais une retraite de deux mois sous la direction de ma mère, qui a lâge du siècle, et d'une foule degens respectables, prêtres et laïces, dont aucun ne se doute du bien qu'il me fait. Je ne lâcherai pas ce paradis pour le plaisir d'être d'accord sur tous les points avec moi-même. Cependant je constate qu'on n'a pas tout à fait raison de se faire socinien. Ni la Trinité, ni l'Incarnation ne me choquent. Si j'hésitais, ce serait plutôt devant le Dieu personnel et créateur.»" Leclercq, "Historiens du Christianisme," 6.2.2696.

> The blessed Peter ... first sat on the throne of the bishopric of Antioch for seven years. This Peter having gone to Rome when Nero was emperor there sat on the throne of the bishopric for twenty-five years, two months, and three days.... He ordained two bishops, Linus and Cletus, who in his lifetime performed all the tasks of the ministry in the City of Rome, ... leaving Peter free to pray and preach and teach the people.... He consecrated the blessed Clement as bishop and committed to him the throne or rule of all the church, saying: "Just as the power of governing, binding, and loosing was given me by the Lord Jesus Christ, so I commit it to you.... Do not be concerned with the things of this world, but seek to devote yourself to speaking and preaching to the people."[6]

No wonder the good Monsignor had his doubts. One hardly knows where to begin with the contradictions in the passage. Peter is bishop of Antioch *before* being bishop of Rome. His call was that of an apostle—a missionary bearing witness to all the world—yet he must stay put "sitting on the throne" in one city's bishopric for seven years and in another for twenty-five. Since the office of a bishop is not like that of an apostle at all, it is necessary to have Peter transfer *all* his episcopal duties to two other men who function as bishops while he goes about the work of an apostle. With the appointment of Clement we then have no less than four bishops active in Rome during the lifetime of Peter. We are told that Peter went to

---

6. *Beatus Petrus ... primum sedit cathedram episcopatus in Antiochia annos VII. Hic Petrus ingressus in urbe Roma, Nerone Caesare, ibique sedit cathedram episcopatus ann. XXV m. II d. III. . . . Hic ordinavit duos episcopos, Linum et Cletum, qui praesentaliter omne ministerium sacerdotale in urbe Roma . . . beatus autem Petrus ad orationem et praedicationem, populum erudiens, vacabat. . . . Hic beatum Clementem episcopum consecravit, eique cathedram vel ecclesiam omnem disponendam commisit, dicens: «Sicut mihi gubernandi tradita est a domino meo Iesu Christo potestas ligandi solvendique, ita et ego tibi committo . . . tu minime in curis saeculi deditus repperiaris; sed solummodo ad orationem et praedicare populo vacare stude.»* Louis Duchesne, *Le Liber Pontificalis: Texte, Introduction et Commentaire* (Paris: de Boccard, 1955), 118.

Rome "when Nero was emperor there," yet Peter is supposed to have been put to death under Nero. Nero was only emperor for fourteen years, yet here we are told that Peter flourished at Rome for twenty-five years, outliving by eleven years the Nero who presided at his execution. Jesus Christ gives the power of government to Peter, but not to Clement—it is Peter who does that. Here we have a principle of horizontal succession; power is passed from hand to hand, not bestowed directly on men by God, but given by one man to the next. But not only does the present pope not choose and ordain his successor, but no one is allowed to so much as even hint at a possible successor as long as a pope is still alive. Today the transmission of the office is through the college of cardinals, an institution that did not exist until the twelfth century.

Questions about the Account of the Ordination of Clement as a Bishop

There are many versions[7] of the spurious letter of Clement "To James the lord and bishop, and bishop of bishops, ruler of the holy church of Christians in Jerusalem and of the churches founded by God's foresight and will belonging to Jesus Christ everywhere."[8] In all of these letters, Clement is "the *third* after Peter to sit on the great throne of Rome."[9] "Peter, feeling the approach of death, called all the Roman brethren together and appointed Clement their head: 'I transmit to him [he says] the power to bind and loose, etc. Until that time Peter had reserved these powers to himself.'"[10] Yet we are told

---

7. PG 1:463–84, 483–90; 2:32–56, 469–604.
8. Κλήμης Ἰακώβῳ τῷ κυρίῳ, καὶ ἐπισκόπῳ, καὶ ἐπισκόπων ἐπισκόπῳ, τῷ τὴν Ἰερουσαλὴμ ἁγίαν τῶν Χριστιανῶν Ἐκκλησίαν διέποντι, καὶ τὰς πανταχῇ θεοῦ προνοίᾳ ἱδρυθείσας καλῶς Χριστοῦ τοῦ θεοῦ ἡμῶν Ἐκκλησίας. *Epitome de Gestis Sancti Petri*, prolegomena, in PG 2:469.
9. τρίτος γὰρ μετὰ Πέτρον τὸν μέγαν τὸν ὑψηλὸν τῆς ῥωμαίων Ἐκκλησίας θρόνον καθίσας. *Epitome de Gestis Sancti Petri* 149, in PG 2:580.
10. διὸ αὐτῷ μεταδίδωμι τῆς ἐξουσίας τοῦ δεσμεῖν τε καὶ λύειν. *Epitome de Gestis Sancti Petri* 145, in PG 2:577.

that Cletus and Linus had already "sat on the great throne of Rome"; did they not already have that authority? If not, the presidency of the church is something quite apart from the bishopric of Rome. Where did *it* reside? Note that Clement must write to James at Jerusalem, without whose approval his ordination is invalid. Note also that it is James who is called "the ruler of the holy church of Christians in Jerusalem *and* of the churches . . . everywhere." In every letter Peter makes Clement promise "that when I die you write a letter to James, the Lord's brother, telling him how close you have been to me. . . . Let James be assured that after my death the seat will be occupied by a man not uninstructed in nor ignorant of the doctrines and the canons of the church."[11] Could anything be further from the calling of a prophet? Clement is a good man with the proper experience—that is all. There is not a word about any manifestations or visions. In a similar crucial situation, Peter got a direct revelation from heaven (Acts 10:9–16), but with this version of the launching of the church there is nothing but a personal endorsement with the specific statement of all of Clement's qualifications, and they are qualifications such as one would ask of any administrator, no more.

"Saying these things to the multitude, Peter, in the presence of everyone, laid his hands upon my head," writes Clement, "and made me sit down in his own chair, saying to me: I charge you as soon as I die to send a letter to James, giving him your entire life history and all your experience with me right down to the present moment. . . . He will be

---

11. ταῦτα εἰπών, καὶ ἐπὶ πάντων μοι τὰς χεῖρας ἐπιθείς, εἰς τὴν αὐτοῦ με καθέδραν καθεσθῆναι πεποίηκε· καθεσθέντι δέ, τοῦτό μοι εὐθέως ἔφη· Ἀξιῶ σε ἐπὶ πάντων μου συμπαρόντων ἀδελφῶν, ὁπηνίκα τοῦ ἐνταῦθα μεταστῶ βίου . . . πάντα τῷ κυρίῳ Ἰακώβῳ τῷ ἀδελφῷ τοῦ Κυρίου μου, ἐν ἐπιτομῇ ἀναγραψάμενον διαπέμψαι . . . ὡς ἐπ᾽ ἀρχῆς μέχρι νῦν μοι συνώδευσας. . . . Μεγίστης δὲ παραμυθίας τεύξεται μαθών, ὅτι μετ᾽ ἐμὲ οὐκ ἀμαθὴς ἀνὴρ καὶ ζωοποιοὺς ἀγνοῶν λόγους, Ἐκκλησίας δὲ κανόνα εἰδὼς μάλιστα, τὴν διδάσκοντος ἐπιστεύθη καθέδραν. *Epitome de Gestis Sancti Petri* 147, in *PG* 2:580.

very pleased to learn that after me will come a man not untaught nor ignorant of the life-giving words, and especially instructed in the laws of the church, to assume the teacher's chair."[12] What an amazing transfer of supernatural power—what a Pentecost! "Tell James not to worry because a well-trained man has taken my place."[13] But why didn't Peter dictate the letter to James on the spot? It is typical of Roman Catholic claims that Clement himself is supposed to write the letter after Peter is dead, informing James that he, as a close personal friend and apprentice of the apostle, has now taken over the rule of the entire church: It is the old Roman failing of self-anointment. Peter was alive (he died a martyr, not of sickness, though the Clementine letters seem to forget that), and yet he rested the whole problem of succession on a letter that not he but Clement himself was to write after Peter's death. If Clement were to be made head of the whole church, why did not Peter personally consult with or at least inform James and John, both of whom were still alive? He wants James "to be assured." Why, then, doesn't he write James himself? Why wait until he is dead to notify the other apostles and make the explanations that he does not hesitate to give to the multitude at Rome?

The ordination of Clement as described in the records is, to say the least, highly irregular. It was always the rule that a bishop should only be ordained by at least three other

---

12. ταῦτα εἰπών, καὶ ἐπὶ πάντων μοι τὰς χεῖρας ἐπιθείς, εἰς τὴν αὐτοῦ με καθέδραν καθεσθῆναι πεποίηκε· καθεσθέντι δέ, τοῦτό μοι εὐθέως ἔφη· Ἀξιῶ σε ἐπὶ πάντων μου συμπαρόντων ἀδελφῶν, ὁπηνίκα τοῦ ἐνταῦθα μεταστῶ βίου, ὡς ἡ τοῦ θεοῦ κέκρικε πρόνοια, πάντα τῷ κυρίῳ Ἰακώβῳ τῷ ἀδελφῷ τοῦ Κυρίου μου, ἐν ἐπιτομῇ ἀναγραψάμενον διαπέμψαι, μέχρι καὶ τῶν ἐκ παιδὸς σου λογισμῶν, καὶ ὡς ἐπ' ἀρχῆς μέχρι νῦν μοι συνώδευσας.... Οὐ γὰρ αὐτὸν λυπήσει τοῦτο, εἰδότα σαφῶς ὅτι ὃ πάντως ἔδει με παθεῖν εὐσεβῶς ἀποδέδωκα. Μεγίστης δὲ παραμυθίας τεύξεται μαθών, ὅτι μετ' ἐμὲ οὐκ ἀμαθὴς ἀνὴρ καὶ ζωοποιοὺς ἀγνοῶν λόγους, Ἐκκλησίας δὲ κανόνα εἰδὼς μάλιστα, τὴν διδάσκοντος ἐπιστεύθη καθέδραν. *Epitome de Gestis Sancti Petri* 147, in *PG* 2:580.

13. Clement, *Epistola ad Jacobum* 19, in *PG* 2:56.

bishops, for "we know that the most blessed James, who was called the brother of the Lord, was ordained bishop of Jerusalem by Peter, James, and John"; therefore no bishop should claim ordination by less than three.[14] Yet the same Peter, who with James and John established this oft-repeated precedent, now ordains his "successor" without even letting his fellow apostles know what is being done. In one letter Peter says to Clement: "I know I am giving you a hard thing—bad treatment and ingratitude at the hands of the uneducated mob." Is that the way to describe the Roman Church in its purest beginning, and is that the way to describe the highest calling on earth?[15] "I need you," Peter continues, "in the time of crisis and danger." But he admonished the new bishop to have nothing at all to do with the temporal affairs of the church. Temporal affairs, he explains, are the concern of presbyters and deacons, yet, as he describes them, the qualifications for these officers are exactly identical with those of a bishop.[16] The invincible opposition between the functions of a bishop and an apostle still make trouble.

"The bishop must be the hardest-working worker on the ship," Peter continues, forgetting that he has just said the whole of Clement's work is to be teaching and prayer, joyful activities to say the least.[17] He said, "In transmitting to you this office I am doing myself a favor, not you."[18] Here the head of the church is not merely choosing one to succeed him after his death, he is actually stepping down, shifting

---

14. *Scimus enim beatissimum Jacobum, qui dicebatur Justus, que etiam secundum carnem frater Domini nuncupatus est, a Petro, Jacobo et Joanne apostolis, Hierosolymorum episcopum esse ordinatum.* Anicetus, *Epistola ad Galliae Episcopos* 1, in *PG* 5:1129–30.

15. οἶδα δὲ αὐτός, ὦ Κλήμης, λύπας καὶ ἀθυμίας καὶ κινδύνους καὶ ψόγους ἐξ ἀπαιδεύτων ὄχλων σοι δωρούμενος. Clement, *Epistola ad Jacobum* 4, in *PG* 2:37.

16. Clement, *Epistola ad Jacobum* 5–6, in *PG* 2:40–41.
17. Clement, *Epistola ad Jacobum* 14–16, in *PG* 2:49–52.
18. Clement, *Epistola ad Jacobum* 3–4, in *PG* 2:36–40.

his burden to other shoulders. "If most of the brethren hate you because of your justice, their hatred cannot hurt you."[19] The worrisome danger to the church, he continues, comes from within. What a picture of the primitive church, and in the days of Peter, no less. Of course Clement blushes in the best schoolboy manner when Peter orders him to sit on his throne, places his hands upon his head in the presence of all the people, and says to him: "I charge you in the presence of all these people that when I die you write a letter to James, the Lord's brother, telling him how close you have been to me from the very first, observing all my activities everywhere and listening to my sermons. Let James be assured that after my death the seat will be occupied by a man not uninstructed in nor ignorant of the doctrines and the canons of the church."[20] What an ordination! What language and behavior from one possessing all the keys of heaven and earth! "And may the Lord be with you now and forever, even as he said to us when he was about to be taken to his God and Father, 'Behold I am with you always until the completion of the time.'"[21] This is clearly the transmission of a blessing understood to have been given not to all the world, but explicitly to the apostles only.

But even if these letters were really primitive, which they obviously are not, since they are of the style and vo-

---

19. ἐάν σε πολλοὶ τῶν ἀδελφῶν διὰ τὴν ἄκρον δικαιοσύνην μισήσωσιν, τὸ αὐτῶν μὲν μῖσος οὐδέν σε βλάψει. Clement, *Epistola ad Jacobum* 16, in *PG* 2:40–41.

20. Ἀξιῶ σε ἐπὶ πάντων μου συμπαρόντων ἀδελφῶν, ὁπηνίκα τοῦ ἐνταῦθα μεταστῶ βίου, ὡς ἡ τοῦ θεοῦ κέκρικε πρόνοια, πάντα τῷ κυρίῳ Ἰακώβῳ τῷ ἀδελφῷ τοῦ Κυρίου μου, ἐν ἐπιτομῇ ἀναγραψάμενον διαπέμψαι, μέχρι καὶ τῶν ἐκ παιδὸς σου λογισμῶν, καὶ ὡς ἐπ' ἀρχῆς μέχρι νῦν μοι συνώδευσας. . . . Οὐ γὰρ αὐτὸν λυπήσει τοῦτο, εἰδότα σαφῶς ὅτι ὃ πάντως ἔδει με παθεῖν εὐσεβῶς ἀποδέδωκα. Μεγίστης δὲ παραμυθίας τεύξεται μαθών, ὅτι μετ' ἐμὲ οὐκ ἀμαθὴς ἀνὴρ καὶ ζωοποιοὺς ἀγνοῶν λόγους, Ἐκκλησίας δὲ κανόνα εἰδὼς μάλιστα, τὴν διδάσκοντος ἐπιστεύθη καθέδραν. *Epitome de Gestis Sancti Petri* 147, in *PG* 2:580.

21. Source unidentified.

cabulary of the fourth century, there is a fact that invalidates any claims they might have to special and unique authority by Clement's successors: The Clement story duplicates in every detail the earlier and much better authenticated story written by the same Clement of how Peter ordained one Zacchaeus bishop of Caesarea.²² Carl Schmidt concludes his study of the subject saying: It is my firm conviction "that the homilist created this section [*Homiliae Clementinae* 3.59–62] independently in order to fill in an emerging void caused by the loss of the original, disputed material."²³ In the *Homiliae Clementinae* account,²⁴ the bishop of Caesarea (1) is ordained by Peter, (2) mounts the throne of Peter, (3) is hailed by Peter as vicar of Christ, and (4) sits on the throne of Christ, which is, according to Peter, analogous to the judgment seat of Moses.²⁵ Numerous modern scholars have maintained that the Caesarea episode was borrowed from the epistle of Clement to James, and certainly it is not likely that bishops would be ordained in such a manner by Peter.

Finding (or Not Finding) the Bishop (or Bishops) of Rome

"If we ask who were the most important people in the Christian church in the first generation, the answer undoubtedly is, the Apostles and Prophets," writes Kirsopp Lake. "If we go on farther, and ask who is the most

---

22. *Recognitiones Clementinae* 3.66, in *PG* 1:1311.
23. "[Ich bin der Meinung] daß das betreffende Stück von dem Homilisten zur Ausfüllung einer durch Versetzung von Disputationsstoffen entstandenen Lücke eigenmächtig fabriziert ist." Carl Schmidt, *Studien zu den Pseudo-Clementinen nebst einem Anhange: Die älteste römische Bischofsliste und die Pseudo-Clementinen,* Texte und Untersuchungen zur Geschichte der altchristlichen Literatur 46.1 (Leipzig: Hinrichs, 1930), 101, 332–33.
24. *Homiliae Clementinae* 3:60–72, in *PG* 2:149–57.
25. θρόνον οὖν Χριστοῦ τιμήσετε· ὅτι καὶ Μωϋσέως καθέδραν τιμᾶν ἐκελεύσθητε. *Homiliae Clementinae* 3.70, in *PG* 2:156.

important person in the church at Rome at the end of the second century, the answer unquestionably is that it was the Bishop. But the difficulty comes when we inquire how this change took place; for that is precisely the problem to which no undoubted or unquestionable answer can be given."[26] Yet that is "precisely the problem" to which an undoubted and unquestioned answer must be given if the Roman claim is to have any validity at all. (Note that Professor Lake says that the bishop of Rome enjoys supreme importance at an early date at Rome, but nowhere else.)

But the Roman bishop lists from that period are in a hopeless condition. The *Liber Pontificalis* explicitly states that Peter "ordained two bishops, Linus and Cletus, who should be present in Rome for the carrying out of all sacerdotal ministration for the benefit of the populace or any who should repair thither. But the blessed Peter himself devoted all his time to prayer, preaching, and teaching the people."[27] Here we have it: the administration of the city bishopric of Rome is a full-time job for at least two men. Even the mighty Peter cannot fill that office and at the same time perform the spiritual functions of an apostle. Linus and Cletus are both bishops with specific instruction to be present *in* Rome, for the office of bishop is that of an overseer who must remain present on the spot. That leaves Peter free to go elsewhere, which, as a general authority, he must. Next, according to the same source, Peter made Clement the bishop, though the names of Linus and Cletus appear before his "because they were ordained bishops by the prince of the apostles him-

---

26. Kirsopp Lake, "Christian Life in Rome," *Harvard Theological Review* 4 (1911): 37.
27. *Hic ordinavit duos episcopos, Linum et Cletum, qui praesentaliter omne ministerium sacerdotale in urbe Roma populo vel supervenientium exhiberent; beatus autem Petrus ad orationem et praedicationem, populum erudiens, vacabat.* Duchesne, *Le Liber Pontificalis*, 118.

THE OFFICE OF BISHOP IN ROME

self."[28] Counting Peter, that makes, as we have noted, no less than four bishops in Rome at once.

But in the *Apostolic Constitutions,* actually a much earlier text, Peter is represented as saying, "Of the church of the Romans first Linus the son of Claudius was ordained by Paul, and then after the death of Linus, Clement was ordained by me, Peter, being the second one."[29] Here we have apostles ordaining bishops in Rome as they did elsewhere, but not acting as bishops themselves at all. Certainly no one claims that Paul was bishop of Rome. Both he and Peter outlived at least one bishop of Rome, and when he was dead they appointed his successor. Here we see Clement not as the successor of Peter and Paul at all, but of Linus, who was of course no successor to the apostles, for they outlived him. Conflicting lists of early Roman bishops are given in the fifth volume of the *Patrologiae Graecae*.[30] The most recent official Roman Catholic list, as given by Heinrich Denzinger, is: Petrus Apostolus, (?)–67(?), *sub cuius nomine exstant duae epistolae canonicae*; Linus, 67(?)–79(?); (Ana)cletus, 79(?)–90(?); Clemens I, 90(?)–99(?). Then the epistle to Corinth is quoted. All succeeding bishops of Rome have question marks after their dates until Callistus I, 217–22.[31] (This is bad, and Giovanni Battista Pighi duly omits the question marks, though his dates differ from Denzinger's.)[32] In Denzinger's list, Clement succeeds to the throne

---

28. *Ideo propterea Linus et Cletus ante [Clementem] conscribuntur, eo quod ab ipso principe apostolorum ad ministerium sacerdotale exhibendum sunt episcopi ordinati.* Duchesne, *Le Liber Pontificalis,* 123.

29. τῆς δὲ Ῥωμαίων ἐκκλησίας Λίνος μὲν ὁ Κλαυδίας πρῶτος ὑπὸ Παύλου, Κλήμης δὲ μετὰ τὸν Λίνου θάνατον ὑπ' ἐμοῦ Πέτρου δεύτερος κεχειροτόνηται. *Constitutiones Apostolicae* 7.46.6, in *PG* 1:1052–53.

30. *PG* 5:1096.

31. Heinrich Denzinger, *Enchiridion Symbolorum Definitionum et Declarationum de Rebus Fidei et Morum,* 31st ed. (Rome: Herder, 1957), 2–3.

32. Optatus has his own list (J.-P. Migne, ed., *Patrologiae Cursus Completus . . . Series Latina/Rom,* 221 vols. [Paris: Migne, 1844–64], 11:947–950 [hereafter *PL*]), which omits Cletus, as do also Irenaeus (*Contra Haereses* 3.3.3., in *PG* 7:849–51), Eusebius (*Historia Ecclesiastica* 5.6, in *PG* 20:445),

about the year 90(?), with Peter about thirteen years before. By that, all our pious letters describing how Peter ordained Clement his successor when he felt the approach of death are worthless.

The oldest Roman bishop lists, according to Carl Schmidt, simply follow Irenaeus, who had no original sources to follow. The reason for the lack of documents was that "in Rome they bothered themselves very little about the past, and therefore the collection could only be a very scanty one."[33] This unconcern with the past has been noted by others, including Eusebius, and such an attitude could not possibly have been inherited from an apostolic foundation that looked forward to continued existence. Cardinal Baronius rhapsodizes over the exquisite care with which the apostolic Christians preserved such relics as the swaddling clothes of Christ for the blessing of future ages—that *should* have been the mood of the early church, but it was not. The earliest mention of Peter as bishop of Rome is in Epiphanius, *Adversus Octaginta Haereses* 41.1, who is wildly guessing, like the others, for he calls both Paul and James bishops of Rome.[34]

Of course the slipup is pardonable, for Paul came to Rome before Peter and is said to have been killed on the same day. That means that he was longer in Rome than Peter—how could he live and function there as an apostle without being bishop? Plainly there were authorities higher than bishops in the church, for Paul installed bishops everywhere. As for James, haven't we seen that he was submissively addressed by Clement of Rome as "bishop of

---

and Augustine (*Epistola* 53.2, in *PL* 33:196). Pighi, however, includes Cletus and omits Anacletus. See Giovanni Battista Pighi, *Institutiones Historiae Ecclesiasticae ad Vota Leonis XIII in Epistola "Saepenumero," 18 Augusti 1883* (Verona: Cinquetti, 1906), 9–122.

33. "Man hatte in Rome sich wenig um die eigene Vergangenheit gekümmert, deshalb konnte die Sammlung nur höchst dürftig ausfallen." Schmidt, *Studien zu den Pseudo-Clementinen nebst einem Anhange*, 387.

34. Epiphanius, *Adversus Octaginta Haereses* 41.1, in *PG* 41:692.

Rome as well as of Jerusalem."³⁵ If we accept Epiphanius along with the letter of Clement, we have no less than six bishops of Rome operating at once. This is, of course, the result of the disastrous assumption that the highest officers in the church must be bishops.

To make things more confusing, Eusebius, after a thorough search of the records, says that "Clement the third bishop of Rome was a fellow worker of Paul"³⁶ and became bishop after Anacletus had been bishop for twelve years, following Linus, who had been bishop for twelve years, also "*after* the death of Peter and Paul."³⁷ It is a relief to read Eusebius's explanation that "it is not easy to say who of these were the legitimate ones, recognized of worthy in zeal and capable of shepherding the foundations [of the apostles]; except for a few hints in Paul, we have nothing to go on. He had countless fellow workers, whose names are immortalized in the scripture."³⁸ For the rest, the records by the fourth century were already silent. From a study of all the lists of bishops (which appear first in the fourth century), Erich Caspar can maintain that "until the first third of the third century, they are typical fabrications of chronographers devoid of the slightest documentary value, and the possibility of laying down certain dates for the Roman bishops thus appears much later than even critical investigation has hitherto

---

35. Clement, *Epistola ad Jacobum*, in PG 2:32–33.

36. ὁ Κλήμης, τῆς Ῥωμαίων καὶ αὐτὸς ἐκκλησίας τρίτος ἐπίσκοπος καταστάς, Παύλου συνεργός γεγονέναι. Eusebius, *Historia Ecclesiastica* 3.4.9, in PG 20:221.

37. μετὰ τὴν Παύλου καὶ Πέτρου μαρτυρίαν. Eusebius, *Historia Ecclesiastica* 3.2, in PG 20:216.

38. ὅσοι δὲ τούτων καὶ τίνες γνήσιοι ζηλωταὶ γεγονότες τὰς πρὸς αὐτῶν ἱδρυθείσας ἱκανοὶ ποιμαίνειν ἐδοκιμάσθησαν ἐκκλησίας, οὐ ῥᾴδιον εἰπεῖν, μὴ ὅτι γε ὅσους ἄν τις ἐκ τῶν Παύλου φωνῶν ἀναλέξοιτο· τούτου γὰρ οὖν μυρίοι συνεργοὶ . . . ὧν οἱ πλείους ἀλήστου πρὸς αὐτοῦ μνήμης ἠξίωνται. Eusebius, *Historia Ecclesiastica* 3.4.3–4, in PG 2:220.

assumed."[39] The first date that can be considered nearly certain is that of Pontiarus, A.D. 235.

"If Peter ever came to Rome," writes Maurice Goguel, "which cannot be denied in view of the total ignorance of what became of him after his sojourn at Antioch, his presence there left no direct or deep memories."[40] This is a most significant fact, and its significance is only pointed up by Goguel's amusing effort to explain it:

> Whether he was there for too short a time or because the church was already too strongly organized there to have been strongly influenced by a new arrival, a generation after his death Clement of Rome has nothing precise to say on the subject, and if it was later claimed that he founded the Roman community and was its first bishop, etc., that was certainly not because other documents were discovered in the meantime which were not known to Clement. We must be content with the ideas of the simple operation of popular imagination.[41]

---

39. "Bis ins erste Drittel des dritten Jahrhunderts hinein [sind die Bischofsliste] typische Chronographenmache ohne jeden Überlieferungswert, und die Möglichkeit, bestimmte Daten für die römischen Bischöfe fortzulegen, ist somit erst viel später gegeben, als nach die kritische Forschung bisher angenommen hat." Erich Caspar, *Geschichte des Papsttums von den Anfängen bis zur Höhe der Weltherrschaft,* 2 vols. (Tübingen: Mohr, 1930), 13.

40. "Si Pierre est venu à Rome, ce qui, en tout cas, ne peut être catégoriquement nié dans l'ignorance totale où nous sommes de ce qu'il est devenu après son séjour à Antioche, sa présence n'y a pas laissé de souvenirs directs et profonds." Maurice Goguel, *Jésus et les Origines du Christianisme: L'Église Primitive* (Paris: Boulevard St. Germain, 1947), 230.

41. "Soit qu'il y ait séjourné trop peu de temps pour avoir pu y développer son influence, soit qu'il y ait trouvé une Église déjà trop fortement organisée et ayant trop sa physionomie propre pour avoir pu être fortement influencée par un nouveau venu. Une génération après la date qui serait celle de sa mort, s'il était venu à Rome, Clément Romain n'a rien de précis à dire à son sujet et si, dans la suite, on s'est cru mieux renseigné, si on a raconté qu'il avait fondé la communauté romaine et avait été son premier évêque, si on s'est cru en état de raconter son mar-

The idea of Peter's arrival occasioning no flurry at all in Rome, so well-founded was the church there, is amusing, but the complete silence of the early records regarding any activity at all of Peter in Rome is a serious thing.

After Peter leaves Antioch, the apostle drops out of sight. We all know the legend of his martyrdom at Rome, but what about the twenty-five years during which this mighty, dynamic, towering prophet and high priest is supposed to have governed the affairs of the church from Rome? The *Patrologiae Graecae* contains two stout volumes of the writing and doings of Clement,[42] who was bishop for ten years at most and who regards Peter as one infinitely above him. Clement depicts a dynamic, wise, simple, honest, world leader in Peter—a powerful and straightforward speaker, a man of action and immense popular appeal. Compared with him, Clement himself is a midget. But if we turn to the oldest traditions for Rome, it is all of Clement that we hear and never of Peter. Where are his sermons, his miracles, his intimate conversations, the delightful stories of his simple personal habits with which the Clementine writings abound *as long as Peter is in Palestine*. As soon as he leaves there, Clement too loses sight of him. That has made it possible for a number of contemporary scholars to maintain that Peter never went to Rome at all, though there is no reason for doubting it. If he did go to Rome, the silence of the record is even more significant. The record makes it plain enough that he did not govern the church from there, for he could not have done much in Rome without its being noted and remembered at least as well as were his exploits elsewhere.

---

tyre et sa sépulture, ce n'est certainement pas parce que, entre temps, on aurait découvert des documents restés inconnus à Clément et aux écrivains de la première moitié du second siècle. On ne peut se contenter de l'idée d'un simple travail de l'imagination populaire." Goguel, *Jésus et les Origines du Christianisme*, 230.

42. *PG* 1–2.

Strife over the Elections of the Bishop of Rome

The complete absence of any clear principle of succession at Rome is loudly attested by the immense strife and confusion that attended the election of bishops in that city, especially during the fourth century. About A.D. 220 the double election of Callistus and Hippolytus led to a serious schism in the city, and the trouble was not settled until 235. Next came a schism between Cornelius and Novatus. Eusebius regards it as a shocking irregularity that Novatus should insist that there should be only one bishop in Rome at a time. In 354 Liberius was ordained thirty-fourth bishop of Rome, but the emperor wanted one of his own men in the position and made it an issue of doctrine to install his friend Felix. The people had elected Liberius, however, and were so insistent that the emperor recalled him to preside in Rome as joint bishop of Rome with Felix. But popular demonstrations continued, and the circus resounded with the shout of thousands who repeatedly exclaimed, "One God, One Christ, One bishop!"[43] It was not enough for the emperor to accept the submission of Liberius and reinstall him: "His rival was expelled from the city by the permission of the emperor and the power of the opposite faction; the adherents of Felix were inhumanely murdered in the streets, in the public places, in the baths, and even in the churches; and the face of Rome, upon the return of the Christian bishop, renewed the horrid image of the massacres of Marius and the proscriptions of Sylla."[44]

Even worse trouble arose a few years later with the ordination of the next bishop of Rome, Damasus, whose election was challenged by the bishops, who elected a rival, Ursinus. The partisans of Ursinus entered a church in which "the Dam-

---

43. εἶς Θεός, εἶς Χριστός, εἶς ἐπίσκοπος. Theodoret, *Historia Ecclesiastica* 2.14, in *PG* 82:1041.

44. Source unidentified.

THE OFFICE OF BISHOP IN ROME 165

asian part of the *populus* had assembled and perpetrated the cruelest killings against those of both sexes."[45] When Damasus became bishop, writes Socrates, rioting instantly broke out all over Rome because the preceding bishop had chosen not Damasus but Ursinus to be his successor.[46] "So all the people rose in arms against each other, not because of any doctrine or heresy, but purely and simply over the issue of who was authorized to sit in the episcopal throne."[47] Plainly there was still no definite rule of succession. "From that," Socrates continues, "arose the *symplegades*"—the mighty rushing together of the mobs.[48] In the melee many were killed, and a great many of both clergy and laymen were sentenced by the Eparch Maximus so that Ursinus finally gave up and his followers quieted down. As in the preceding cases, it was the emperor's favor alone that decided the issue—a civil officer putting an end to the trouble.

The next papal election brought on another crisis, reported by a contemporary, Ammianus: Under Theodoric, "Symmachus and Laurentius being both consecrated, fought for the episcopal throne of Rome. By God's decree, Symmachus, being worthy of the office, was victorious."[49] That is a significant principle of succession, for the barbarians who were ruling at the time—and Theodoric and Ammianus were both barbarians—firmly believed in trial by duel: that the winner of a ritual combat was chosen of God. They now apply that principle to the election of the Roman bishop, though it does

---

45. Source unidentified.
46. Socrates Scholasticus, *Historia Ecclesiastica* 4.29, in PG 67:541.
47. ἐστασίαζον οὖν πρὸς ἑαυτούς, οὐ διά τινα πίστιν ἢ αἵρεσιν, ἀλλὰ περὶ τοῦ μόνον τὶς ὀφείλει τοῦ ἐπισκόπου θρόνου ἐγκρατὴς γενέσθαι. Socrates Scholasticus, *Historia Ecclesiastica* 4.29, in PG 67:541.
48. ἐντεῦθεν δὲ συμπληγαδες τῶν ὄχλων ἐγίνοντο. Socrates Scholasticus, *Historia Ecclesiastica* 4.29, in PG 67:541.
49. *Eodem tempore contentio orst est in urbe Roma inter Symmachum et Laurentiam; consecrati fuerant ambo. Ordinatio deo, qui et dignus fuit, superavit Symmachus.* Ammianus Marcellinus, *Excerpta Valesiana* 12.65.

not seem very apostolic. Later, another Symmachus, a deacon, became bishop of Rome, being "consecrated by a crowd of deacons," says Theophanes, "from which came rioting, killing, and plundering in the city, which lasted for *three years*."[50]

Before that, however, an attempt was made to establish something like a rule to go by in determining the solution to the question that had not been answered—namely, not who was Christ's successor, but who was Peter's. There was no sure way of determining. Theodosius the Great nominated Felix IV, he in turn named Boniface II to be his successor, and Boniface chose one Vigilius to follow him. But Boniface was not strong enough to get Vigilius accepted, and the result was a *Senatus consultum,* i.e., a law passed not by the apostles, but by the Roman Senate governing the election of popes. (This was followed by the Edict of Athalarich, a German prince, "on the election of Roman bishops.")[51] So Boniface petitioned the emperor for help, and in reply the emperor issued this edict: "When two bishops of Rome are elected, neither shall be bishop, but only that one shall remain on the apostolic chair whom the doom (Ordeal) of God and the Will of the Generality have chosen from among the clergy by a *new* ordination."[52] Soon after, however, the Will of the Generality discovered that Boniface had been acting treasonably with the Gothic enemy and deported him to Greece, setting up Vigilius as bishop in his stead. Then one Matalius challenged the ruling bishop and had him assassinated. In 789, the relative of the blessed Pope Madrian stirred up the people; they revolted against Pope Leo, won the victory, and blinded him.

In the Middle Ages the trouble of popes and counterpopes became really deadly. We need not retell the story of

---

50. χειροτονοῦσι Σύμμαχον ἕνα ὄντα τῶν διακόνων, ἔνθεν λοιπὸν ἀταξίαι πολλαὶ καὶ φόνοι καὶ ἁρπαγαὶ γεγόνασιν ἐπὶ τρία ἔτη. Theophanes, *Chronographia* 493, in *PG* 108:344.

51. Source unidentified.

52. Source unidentified.

the Babylonian captivity. Two less familiar accounts may serve as illustrations of what happened in a church that had been left strangely unprovided with the means of implementing that injunction which it has come to regard as the very essence of its being. On the eve of the First Crusade, Pope Urban II found his claim challenged "by a certain adversary named Guidbert," who had been elected pope by the Imperial party in 1061. Guidbert was "goaded on by pride," writes Fulcher of Chartres, a contemporary and secretary to the French king, who was supporting Urban against the emperor and his Honorius. "He addressed himself to the confusion of the populace" and got a large following,

> though the larger and holier part of the populace followed Urban, rightly elected and consecrated by cardinal bishops. But Guidbert, with the support of the aforementioned emperor and inspired by the unrighteous backing of the greater part of the citizens of Rome, as long as he could, kept Urban away from the monastery of the blessed Peter. But he being thus driven out of the church, went about in the country, holding popular meetings everywhere for God; Guidbert, however, puffed up with pride at having become the prince of the church, showed himself a pope prone to favor those who strayed ... condemning the acts of Urban as illegal. So Urban in that same year in which the Franks began to pass through Rome on their way to Jerusalem, got complete control of the apostolic power thanks to the aid of the most noble matron Matilda [this was the stepsister of the Emperor Henry III, who gave all her holdings in Lorraine and Italy as a present to the Roman church, which she was supporting against Henry IV]. Guidbert was in Germany. So now there were two popes, but a very great number of people did not know which one they should obey, or to whom they should turn for instruction in the matter, or who could cure the disease.[53]

---

53. *Sed diabolus, qui ad detrimentum hominum semper insistere nititur et veluti leo quaerit circumeundo quem devoret, huic adversarium quendam nomine Guidbertum, superbiae stimulis inritatum, ad confusionem populi concitavit. Qui*

Seven centuries before, Eusebius had used these very words to describe the state of the church when the bishops were then in a deadlock—the question is still unsolved in the eleventh century (he found the solution in the emperor). Exactly like Eusebius, Fulcher continues: "Some favored the one man, some the other. As far as human intelligence could judge, Urbanus was the juster, since he was the less given to lust for money."[54] Then he tells how Guidbert, as archbishop of Ravenna, had lost his throne through greed. He was especially in the wrong for having seized "the sceptre of God's empire, which of course is not to be taken by force but should rather be received with fear and devotion. It was no wonder that the whole world was disquieted and stirred up, since if the Roman Church, in which resides the principle for the correction of universal Christianity, is confounded by any disturbance, it instantly affects all the members subject to

---

dudum imperatoris praefate Baioariorum protervitate suffultus, dum praedecessor Gregorius, qui et Hildebrandus, in sede iure habebatur, apostolatus officium usurpare coepit, ipso Gregorio a liminibus basilicae S. Petri excluso. Et quia sic perverse egit, populus melior eum cognoscere noluit, Urbano autem iure electo et ab episcopis cardinalibus consecrato, maior et sanctior pars populi post Hildebrandi excessum oboediendo aspiravit. Guidbertus vero sustentamine imperatoris praedicti et plerorumque civium Romanorum inritamento animatus, Urbanum quamdiu potuit a monasterio beati Petri alienum fecit. Sed dum ab ecclesia sic eliminatus erat, per regiones incedens, populum in aliquantis devium Deo conciliabat. Guidbertus autem ob ecclesiae principatum turgidus papam proclivem oberrantibus se ostentabat et apostolatus officum, licet iniuste, inter consentientes exercebat et Urbani facta tamquam inrita vilipendebat. Urbanus autem eo anno, quo Franci primitus Iherusalem euntes per Romam transierunt, totam omnino potestatem apostolicam adeptus est, auxilio cuiusdam nobilissimae matronae, Mathildis nomine, quae in Romana patria potestate multa tunc vigebat. Guidbertus vero tunc in Alemmania erat. Itaque duo papae Romae praeerant; sed cui oboediretur, a quamplurimis ignorabatur, vel a quo consilium posceretur, vel quis aegrotis mederetur. alii huic, alii alteri favebant. Fulcher of Chartres, Historia Hierosolymitana 1.5.1–1.5.6.

54. *Prout intelectibus hominum patebat, Urbanus iustior erat: putandus est recte melior qui cupiditates tamquam hostes subiicit.* Fulcher, Historia Hierosolymitana 1.5.7.

her, the disease spreading from the head through the fibers to the whole organism, which becomes sick and weak. . . . And when the head is thus afflicted, then all the members suffer continually."[55] Early fathers tell us that the apostles took good provision that while the church lasted, the offices would be properly transmitted. Plainly this rickety system is something entirely different. "The head having thus been wounded, the members withered from the pain that attacked them, so that in all parts of Europe, peace, goodness, *fides* went under, both within the churches and without, by great as well as small, and suffered an eclipse. Hence it was necessary . . . to transfer against the pagans that war which they were waging against themselves."[56] And that, according to Fulcher, our best authority, is the reason for the First Crusade: A complete spiritual, economic, moral, and political collapse resulting from Roman rule, and the main cause of trouble was the lack of any rule of papal succession.

"When they got to Rome, they naturally went to the basilica of the blessed Peter."[57] Fulcher was there: "When we went in," he reports, "there before the altar we found the men of Guidbert, the silly [*stolidus*] pope standing with swords in their hands before the oblations on the altar; others crawled up along the rafters and while we were

---

55. *Sceptrum imperii Dei. Sane non est vi rapiendum, verum cum timore et devotione suscipiendum. Nec mirum si mundus inquietabatur totus et conturbabatur, quoniam si Romana ecclesia, in qua principalitas correctionis universae Christianitatis obtinetur, quolibet turbine confunditur, confestim accidit membra sibi subdita, a capitaneis fibris dolore derivante, compassibiliter debilitari. . . . Cumque caput sic tritum est, continuo membra laesa sunt.* Fulcher, *Historia Hierosolymitana* 1.5.8–1.5.10.

56. *Capite autem sic laeso, etiam membris marcescentibus dolore concepto, quia in partibus omnibus Europae pax, bonitas, fides, in ecclesias et extra, tam a maioribus quam minoribus viriliter subigebantur, necesse erat ut . . . contra paganos saltem certamina inter se dudum consueta distenderent.* Fulcher, *Historia Hierosolymitana* 1.5.11.

57. Source unidentified.

prostrate in prayer threw rocks down at us. For whenever they spotted anyone faithful to Urban, they wanted to kill him. But one of the towers of the same monastery was held by men of Lord Urban, who, faithful to him, had guarded it tenaciously, resisting all attackers to the best of their ability. We had our share of pains for getting involved in that sort of thing."[58]

The following is an excerpt from Sir John Froissart:

> About this period, he who signed himself pope Urban the sixth, came from Rome to Genoa. . . . All England was obedient to him, both church and commonalty, and now more than ever because the king of France and that country were Clementists. Urban (whom the English and several other countries obeyed), during his residence at Genoa, sought how he could obtain succors from England to annoy the king of France; and I will tell you by what means. He was to send his bulls to the archbishops and bishops of the country, to proclaim that he absolved, and would absolve, from all crime of fault, every one who would assist in the destruction of the Clementists. He had heard that his adversary Clement had resorted to this means in France, and was daily doing so; and that the French called the Urbanists, as to matters of faith, dogs, which those resorted back on the Clementists, whom Urban was very desirous of condemning to the utmost of his power, and he knew that he had no other means of hurting them but through the English. It was necessary, however, that he should have a considerable sum of ready

---

58. *Et cum in basilica beati Petri introissemus, invenimus ante altare homines Guidberti papae stolidi, qui oblationes altari superpositas, gladios suos in manibus tenentes, inique adripiebant; alii vero super trabes ipsius monasterii cursitabant et inde deorsum ubi prostrati orabamus labides iaciebant. Nam cum viderent aliquem Urbano fidelem, ilico eum trucidare volebant. In arce autem una basilicae inerant homenes domini Urbani, qui eam sollicite custodiebant in eiusdem fidelitatem, et adversantibus sibi, prout poterant, obsistebant. Proinde satis doluimus, cum tantam atrocitatem ibi fieri vidimus.* Fulcher, *Historia Hierosolymitana* 1.7.2–1.7.3.

money, if he wished to put his plans into execution; for it was well known that the nobles of England would not, for all the absolutions in the world, undertake any expedition, unless such were preceded by offers of money. Men-at-arms cannot live on pardons, nor do they pay much attention to them except at the point of death. . . . [Urban] sent upwards of thirty bulls to England, where they were received with much joy. The prelates preached up in their dioceses this expedition in the manner of a croisade; and . . . none of either sex thought they should end the year happily, nor have any chance of entering paradise, if they did not give handsomely to the expedition as pure alms. At London, and in that diocese, there was collected a large Gascony tun full of money, and he who gave most, according to the pope's bull, gained the greatest number of pardons. All who should die at this time, and who had given their money, were absolved from every fault.[59]

A churchman, Henry Spenser, bishop of Norwich, was chosen to lead the expedition; he was "young and eager, and wishing to bear arms" and was all for conquering all of Flanders, but the experienced Sir Hugh Calverly reminded him:

> Sir . . . our expedition has nothing to do with what concerns the wars of kings, but is solely pointed against the Clementists. We are the soldiers of pope Urban, who has given us absolution from all faults if we destroy the Clementists. Should we march into Flanders . . . we shall forfeit our engagement; for, I understand, that the earl of Flanders and all the Flemings are as good Urbanists as ourselves.[60]

---

59. Sir John Froissart, *Chronicles of England, France, Spain, and the Adjoining Countries: From the Latter Part of the Reign of Edward II to the Coronation of Henry IV*, trans. Thomas Johnes (New York: Green's Son, 1882), 326–27 (2:131–32).

60. Ibid., 327 (2:133).

But in a rage the good bishop overruled him that there should be good pickings in Flanders, for "in the country I have named ... they have never been harassed by the war." So the expedition went forward and, as the issue between the two popes was not settled, it continued with their successors, in whose days the Turks threatened Europe and took all the Balkans: "[The Turks] only [laughed] at the two popes, one at Rome and the other at Avignon, saying, 'The two gods of Christendom are waging war against each another, by which their government is weakened and easier to be destroyed.'"[61]

When the Christian princes asked the king of Armenia why he would willingly submit to the Turk Amurat, the king explained that the Turkish rule over subjects was far more decent, generous, and humane than anything one met with in Christian lands.[62]

> About this period, Otho of Brunswick came to pope Clement at Avignon to receive his pay for the war he had carried on for the pope and church against the Romans and Bartholomew Prignano, who styled himself pope Urban VI. ... [But as he] could not obtain one penny ... [he] left them much discontented. ... About this time, the forces subsidized by pope Clement ... had shut up pope Urban in the city of Perugia, [where] Count Conrad, a leader of a large body of Germans, would have delivered him up to pope Clement for [the sum of 20,000 crowns]. [But Clement could not raise the money so] the siege was slackened on both sides, and Urban escaped ... to Rome.[63]

Froissart here enters a discourse upon the fall of the church and the feudal nobility, whom he describes as utterly cynical and corrupt: he tells of a reforming friar who proph-

---

61. Ibid., 388 (3:23).
62. Ibid.
63. Ibid., 390 (3:25).

esied true things and was locked up for his pains and gives an amazing account of the donation of Constantine, but the burden of his story is that the church and the nobility are a single organism: clergy and aristocrats must band together against the common people, who are of another order of being.[64] Froissart keeps repeating that the nobility alone have broken their part of the contract, while the story he tells is all of how the churchmen broke theirs.

The Establishment of an Episcopal Hierarchy and College of Cardinals

What determined the papal succession for a thousand years? In whose hands did the office reside? Depending on circumstances, the office was in the hands of a French or English king, an Austrian emperor, a Milanese duke, a rich banking family, a city mob, an ambitious woman, a successful general, an intriguing churchman—who could tell? The bishops from the largest cities naturally played a leading role. They came to be known as cardinal bishops, and as such they first played an important role in public affairs in the twelfth century. This college of cardinals at that time took over the functions of the regular synods, which ceased to be held regularly. "More and more it became the custom," writes Martin Souchon, "for popes to seek the counsel of this college in matters of faith, the administration of bishoprics, monasteries, and church lands, and, finally, in questions of foreign policy; in this it became increasingly common to call upon the services of individual cardinals. By 1300 the cardinals had so firmly established their privileged positions as advisors of the pope" that they began to think of themselves as having official sanction and position.[65]

---

64. Ibid.
65. "Mehr und mehr gewöhnten sich die Päpste, in Glaubenssachen, bei Verwaltung der Bistümer, Klöster und der Kirchenländer, endlich in Fragen der äußeren Politik ihre Entscheidungen unter Zuziehung des Beirats des Kollegs herbeizuführen und sich dabei außerdem vielfach der Dienste einzelne Kardinäle zu bedienen. Um 1300 hatten die

The *Constitutio de Sede Apostolica Vacante* (24 May 1882) states that "in the course of time, it has come about that these laws concerning the election of the Roman pontiff have imperceptibly increased in number and variety ... to such an extent that it now appears no small labor to discern which rules are to be observed in electing the highest pastor. So we have sought out those rules which venerable age has sanctified, albeit some of them have suffered change."[66] The *Constitution* contains the interesting provisions that (1) "while a seat is vacant, the college of cardinals shall have absolutely no power or jurisdiction at all ... but holds all merely in reserve for the future pontiff."[67] The cardinals do not, thus, have apostolic power delegated to them, but it automatically falls on whomever they choose. (2) "The college of cardinals has no power to dispose of the laws of the apostolic chair."[68] (3) "No law passed by the popes can be corrected or changed in any way while the church is without a pope."[69] (4) But if questions persist the college has power to settle them by a majority vote.[70] Number 4 is a conces-

---

Kardinäle ihre bevorrechtigte Stellung als Berater des Papstes beriets so weit gefestigt." Martin Souchon, *Die Papstwahlen in der Zeit des Grossen Schismas: Entwicklung und Verfassungskämpfe des Kardinalates von 1378 bis 1417* (Darmstadt: Scientia Verlag Aalen, 1970), 1:3.

66. *Verum, decursu aetatum, factum est ut hae de Romano eligendo Pontifice indictae ac promulgatae leges sensim multiplici varioque numero augerentur . . . ita ut haud exigui laboris esse videatur discernere quaenam in Summo Pastore eligendo servanda sint. Nos igitur . . . omnia in unam Constitutionem digerere opportunum duximus . . . quae veneranda vetustas sanctivit, nonnullis tamen mutatis. Constitutio de Sede Apostolica Vacante.*

67. *Sedis Apostolicae vacatione durante, S. Collegium Cardinalium in iia, quae ad Pontificem Maximum dum viveret pertinebant, nullam omnino potestatem aut iurisdictionem habeat . . . sed ea omnia futuro Pontifici reservare teneatur. Constitutio de Sede Apostolica Vacante* 1.

68. *Item praecipimus, ne S. Cardinalium Collegium de iuribus Sedis Apostolicae Romanaeque Ecclesiae quomodolibet disponere valeat. Constitutio de Sede Apostolica Vacante* 2.

69. *Leges a Romanis Pontificibus latae, per coetum Cardinalium Romanae Ecclesiae, ipsa vacante, corrigi, vel immutari nullo mode possunt. Constitutio de Sede Apostolica Vacante* 3.

70. *Constitutio de Sede Apostolica Vacante* 4.

sion to hard reality that completely conceals the beautiful theory of number 3: it is the cardinals who have the power after all, though of course there is not the slightest suspicion of anything apostolic about *their* calling. (5) In an emergency, any matters can also be settled by a majority vote of the cardinals.[71] Further down the list of provisions, (12) "The highest cardinals all keep their offices when a pope dies."[72] But (23) *"all* authority of the congregations is that granted them beforehand by a living pope."[73] That is natural enough since originally the cardinals were only his personal friends and advisors.

But Christ and the apostles had the authority to bestow upon their fellow workers offices akin to those they themselves held. The cardinals receive no such office. The formula in which a cardinal casts his vote is significant, in view of the fact that he has no authority at all, save that of voting: "I testify before Christ the Lord, who has designated me, that I elect one who should by the judgment of God be elected."[74] A thousand years after Nicaea the church discovered that a one-man organization could not provide a dependable succession and hit upon the idea of a council of men. This is exactly what the primitive church had in the Twelve Apostles, but at that late date the sacred college could not and did not pretend to be apostolic in origin. What better indication that the primitive church had been taken away? For plainly, the old traveling apostolate, with prophets, teachers, etc., did not vanish because it had been found inadequate—it was far more adequate than any other system ever devised. It was not because of changing needs and conditions as the "infant church outgrew old institutions" that they were abolished—for when they left, not a stronger church,

---

71. *Constitutio de Sede Apostolica Vacante* 5.
72. *S. R. E. Camerarii et Poenitentiarii Maioris officia non cessant per obitum Pontificis. Constitutio de Sede Apostolica Vacante* 12.
73. *Constitutio de Sede Apostolica Vacante* 23.
74. *Testor Christum Dominum, qui me iudicaturus est, me eligere, quem secundum Deum iudico eligi debere. Constitutio de Sede Apostolica Vacante* 67.

but only an empty gap remained, which was quickly filled with swarms of impostors, claims and counterclaims, charges and countercharges, riots and assassination—in a word, darkness and confusion.

The establishment of an episcopal hierarchy was, as we have seen, from the bottom up, not from the top down. It was agreed that the largest cities should be the most important bishoprics and enjoy higher honor and greater glory than the others. It was claimed that the apostles, in establishing this, simply repeated what the state had done before, following, as it were, a law of nature. This argues the absence of any real ruling head in the church. The great cities who claimed first place and constantly harped upon the theme of priority and precedence would have had to buck the whole church—not just each other—had they been usurping the claims of an established head. The whole controversy never takes the form it must have taken had such a head existed from the time of the apostles. The emperor reiterated the old principle of the perfect equality of bishops in his closing speech to the Council of Nicaea when the biggest cities claimed greater authority than the others. They watched as a group with the closest jealousy lest any one of their number should think to claim for himself an office superior to the rest, for once a hierarchy of bishops was established, the principle of equality was preserved as strictly as ever *within* the hierarchy. And at the very top of the system stood the four or five biggest churches, never just one. That was a thing that no bishop would allow—unless, of course, his church was the one. But in such cases the others would promptly gang up against him in the name of Christian equality—the ambitions of any one bishop could always be countered with appeal to a principle, not the authority of the ruling bishop but the principle of episcopal equality.

The Roman Role and the Big Four

It is interesting to see the game that Rome plays in this system. When at the Council of Trent in the sixteenth

THE OFFICE OF BISHOP IN ROME   177

century, "Lainez, in the name of the whole fraternity, proclaimed ... that the government of the faithful had been committed by Christ to the pope alone, that in the pope alone all sacerdotal authority was concentrated, and that through the pope alone priests and bishops derived whatever power they possessed," the French and Spanish bishops were shocked and angered.[75] Throughout all the Middle Ages the absolute ascendancy of one bishop over the rest had never been accepted. The Romanists have attacked the problem from various angles, and their strained logic proclaims their dearth of evidence. Thus Karl Joseph von Hefele finds the one passage that definitely proves Roman priority, the statement by Socrates referring to the Synods of Antioch: Speaking of Julius of Rome, Socrates says, "nor did he send a representative, though there was an ecclesiastical canon that the churches could not pass a general order in council without consulting the opinion of the bishop of Rome."[76]

This is a passage in which much rests on translation, so we have followed Hefele's own interpretation of canonizing: "To pass a general decree through and at synods."[77] The meaning of the passage is clear: the synods, not Rome, are passing laws, and those laws which are of universal and general application must be approved by all—as long as the bishop of Rome withholds his vote, the legislation is stopped. The Roman bishop, like an obstructionist senator on a committee,

---

75. Source unidentified.

76. οὐδὲ μὴν εἰς τὸν τόπον αὐτοῦ ἀπεστάλκει τινά· καίτοι κανόνος ἐκκλησιαστικοῦ κελεύοντος, μὴ δεῖν παρὰ τὴν γνώμην τοῦ ἐπισκόπου Ῥώμης, τὰς ἐκκλησίας κανονίζειν. Socrates Scholasticus, *Historia Ecclesiastica* 2.8, in PG 67:196; see Karl Joseph von Hefele, *Histoire des Conciles d'Après les Documents Originaux*, trans. a Benedictine monk of St. Michael's Abbey in Farnborough, 10 vols. (Paris: Letouzey et Ané, 1907), 1:13.

77. "Poser en principe des ordonnances générales par et dans un synode." Hefele, *Histoire des Conciles d'Après les Documents Originaux*, 1:13, emphasis in original.

could hold up legislation indefinitely, and so, in a literal sense, the whole business waited upon his pleasure. But that does not prove, as Hefele insists, that Rome was running things: it was the meeting that was passing the laws, not Rome, and all that was needed of Rome was to send a representative—not to preside; so much Socrates states specifically.

Rome was the western representative of the Big Four, "governing a very large number of churches in the West," Duchesne surmises, "without interposition of metropolitans"—exactly, Duchesne observes, as Alexandria did in the East.[78] Rome's position is thus not unique, but certainly is very important, and if a law was to apply to the whole church, the bishop of Rome would of course have to be consulted. Many a time a single U.S. senator has for a moment held almost dictatorial power, but for one finding himself in such a position to claim that he is therefore the legitimate ruler of the land—being elected *de furia* and holding his power *de facto*—would be the height of presumption. The meeting could not pass general rules without the vote of Rome; neither could it without Alexandria or Antioch. The Roman bishop in his position of western counterweight, much farther removed from the other three than they were from each other, enjoyed a position of detachment. When the others were deadlocked, as they often were, it was for Rome to tip the scales—of course in the way that pleased Rome. Accordingly, the other three usually played up to Rome, and this enhanced the impression that Rome was really running things. Rome was no more determined nor skillful in pushing claims to priority than the others, but Rome by geographical position held a better hand.

The Roman bishop appears in the West as more imposing, aggressive, and magnificent than the others, which makes it hard for the student of Western history to doubt that here we

---

78. "Gouvernait . . . sans interposition de métropolitains, un très grand nombre d'églises." Louis Duchesne, *Origines du Culte Chrétien: Étude sur la Liturgie Latine avant Charlemagne*, 5th ed. (Paris: de Boccard, 1925), 23.

THE OFFICE OF BISHOP IN ROME

have something really and essentially out of the ordinary. But let that student turn his attention to Asia and the methods and manners of the Roman bishop immediately appear in another light—everything about him then proclaims him to be not a unique phenomenon in the world, but rather a typical member of the Big Four. It never occurred to Athanasius, Duchesne says, "that an appeal to the bishop of Rome might strengthen his fortunes" when he was cast out of his bishopric.[79] Yet it was on the strength of παρρησιαστικοῖς γράμμασιν from Julius of Rome that Athanasius and Paulus resumed their bishoprics.[80] Now *parresiatikos* means, literally, "speaking aside," or "outside"; "irregular order"; "bold," "unauthorized"; and *parresiatikos grammasin* means "on one's own authority." The bishop of Rome was simply taking a chance; as the word shows, his proposal was entirely irregular and was in fact not used again in the controversies of the fourth century. This was the last resort for Athanasius, not the first resort, as would be the case if it were a regular solution. It was also something of an innovation, since originally the idea had never occurred to Athanasius.

In the same aggressive spirit, Liberius of Rome writes to the Macedonian bishops that the Arians must be eliminated "either by persuasion or, to put it more plainly [*alethesteron*—to blurt out the truth], by temporal force."[81] It is all very well to speak of Christian principles, but the bishop of Rome knows that truth is with the big battalions. To support the historic claims of Rome, Denzinger quotes at length the claims made by the Roman bishops of the fourth century that they had their authority from Peter[82]—as if such proclamations bore any weight at all

---

79. "... qu'un appel à Rome pourrait rétablir ses affaires." Louis Duchesne, *Histoire Ancienne de l'Église*, 5th ed. (Paris: de Boccard, 1929), 2:661.
80. Socrates Scholasticus, *Historia Ecclesiastica* 2.15, in *PG* 67:212.
81. ἢ διὰ πειθοῦς τινος, ἤ, ἵνα ἀληθέστερον εἴπω, κοσμικῆς δυναστείας. Socrates Scholasticus, *Historia Ecclesiastica* 4.12, in *PG* 67:493.
82. Denzinger, *Enchiridion Symbolorum*, items 57b, 57e, 87.

where the question is not whether such claims were made as early as the fourth century but whether those claims were valid, which is another thing entirely.

It was the equality of the city bishoprics that made it necessary for the emperor to act as common umpire and made it possible for him to do so without shocking or annoying anybody and without a word of protest from any churchmen anywhere. The church agreed to this in theory as well as in fact, says Duchesne, and not a voice was raised in protest.[83] Cyril writes to the emperor Constantius, "May God strengthen thee, and the common association of the holy churches," and he illustrates the case of the Roman government, describing that monarch as "the common bond of the holy churches, the glorious guarantor of the Roman government," adorned by his acts of umpireship in major cases concerning the faith.[84] Tertullian was caustic and scathing concerning the completely unauthorized claims comparing the Roman leader to "the bishop of bishops." Cyprian was even more cutting, so much so that Catholic divines have found it convenient to declare the most unflattering letters as forgeries (though as documents they are as well attested as any of the other letters) "since it is unthinkable that anyone should use such language against the pope."[85] It is indeed unthinkable, and for that very reason it is clear that Cyprian did not for a moment consider the bishop of Rome to be the pope. To use some passages of Cyprian to support Roman claims, it is therefore necessary for Karl Adam to make of Cyprian himself "a complete *Wirrkopf* [addlepate]."[86]

Rome was able to capitalize not only on her geographical position, but also on what Andreas Alföldi calls "the in-

---

83. Duchesne, *Histoire Ancienne de l'Église*, 2:661–63.
84. ἐρρωμένον σε . . . καὶ τὴν συνήθη τῶν τε ἁγίων ἐκκλησιῶν, καὶ τῆς Ῥωμαίων ἄρχης κηδεμονίαν ἐπιδεικνύμενον. Cyril, *Epistola ad Constantium Imperatorem* 8, in *PG* 33:1173.
85. Source unidentified.
86. Source unidentified.

voluntary reverence ... for the Roman past," which gave the guardians of the great tradition other opportunities of flying the old flags before the eyes of the peoples of the empire.[87] "The development of the tradition of Peter at Rome and the importance of the conclusion based on it," writes Goguel, "ran so exactly parallel to the development of the role of the church of Rome and to the increase of its authority, that one is obliged to conclude that there was an organic relation between the two; the tradition of Peter was affirmed and developed at the same time the expression and justification of the claims of Rome developed hand in hand."[88] Professor Pierre Batiffol has labored with characteristic determination to show that the expression *prima cathedra* in Canon 58 of the Council of Elvira refers to the Roman See,[89] while Adolf Jülicher was able to point to many examples of the use of the expression in reference to other churches.[90] Batiffol would have *summan martyrii sublimitatem* in Cyprian Epistle 69:4 mean "the highest peak of martyrdom," but Hugo Koch showed its use to refer to martyrdom in general.[91]

To prove the primacy of Rome, Victor Martin asks the question, "Is there upon the earth a qualified instance of an

---

87. Andreas Alföldi, *The Conversion of Constantine and Pagan Rome*, trans. Harold Mattingly (Oxford: Clarendon, 1948), 116.

88. "Le développement de la tradition sur Pierre à Rome et, plus encore, l'importance qu'on lui a donnée et les conséquences qu'on en a tirées ont été si exactement parallèles au développement du rôle de l'Église de Rome et à la croissance de son autorité qu'on est obligé de conclure à une relation organique. C'est en tant qu'expression et en même temps que justification de la position particulière de l'Église de Rome que la tradition sur Pierre s'est affirmée et développée." Goguel, *Jésus et les Origines du Christianisme*, 231.

89. Pierre Batiffol, *Cathedra Petri: Études d'Histoire ancienne de l'Église* (Paris: de la Tour Maubourg, 1938), 105–21.

90. Adolf Jülicher, "Die Synode von Elvira als Zeuge für den römischen Primat," *Zeitschrift für Kirchengeschichte* 42 (1923): 45.

91. Hugo Koch, "Bischofsstuhl und Priesterstühle zu Canon 58 von Elvira," *Zeitschrift für Kirchengeschichte* n.s. 7 (1925): 171.

accusation against the Roman pontiff?"[92] For his answer he cites the fact that "already in 495 St. Gelasius declares that in all cases the See of Rome is qualified to pass on all cases, and that no one has the authority to modify its decisions."[93] This is the earliest instance Martin can find of such a claim—the very end of the fifth century—and it comes from the Roman bishop himself, which is not the least surprising. The fact that the claim of St. Gelasius was inserted into an imperial decree of a hundred years earlier illustrates well the methods employed to establish in retrospect the antiquity of claims that could not be proven, a system of skullduggery culminating in the False Isidorian Decretals. "The legal fiction arose," says Eduard Schwartz, "that the apostles and Paul had placed monarchical bishops in all the churches founded by them and gave them in an unbroken line of succession . . . the true apostolic doctrine. . . . Soon after this was generally accepted, the bishop lists of the large churches were composed and filled out by working backward to the apostles."[94]

Long before John Chrysostom had written, Antioch—the oldest and greatest of all the churches, the community to which the name Christian was first applied—was beyond any doubt the mother church. Chrysostom was transferred to be bishop of Constantinople and found New Rome and

---

92. "Existe-t-il, sur terre, une instance qualifiée pour connaître d'une accusation contre le Pontife romain?" Victor Martin, *Les Origines du Gallicanisme* (Paris: Bloud et Gay, 1939), 2:10.

93. "Déjà en 495, saint Gélase affirme que le siège de Rome peut se prononcer sur toutes les causes et que personne n'a qualité pour modifier ses arrêts." Martin, *Les Origines du Gallicanisme*, 2:10.

94. "Es kam die Rechtfiktion auf, daß die Urapostel und Paulus in allen von ihnen gestifteten Gemeinden monarchische Bischöfe eingesetzt und diese in ununterbrochener Reihe kraft des ihnen bei der Ordination mitgeteilten Geistes die apostolische, reine Lehre bewahrt haben. . . . Die Bischofsliste der großen Gemeinden [wurden], bald nachdem die Theorie durchgedrungen war, nach rückwärts bis zu den Aposteln ergänzt." Eduard Schwartz, *Kaiser Constantin und die Christliche Kirche* (Stuttgart: Teubner, 1969), 24.

Old Rome competing for priority of holiness. He wrote that Constantinople is greater than Rome.

> A city is not to be judged by its buildings. Don't tell me of the enormous size of the city of Rome [this obviously being the common boast], but show me rather an obedient population [Rome had an unenviable reputation of rowdyism in electing its bishops]. The angels visited Abraham in his hut rather than in the towers of Sodom. Go into the church at Constantinople and see the fine quality of the city—the prayers that never cease, day or night; the vast numbers of the poor at their devotions. Great city, indeed, but also the metropolis of the empire. How many bishops and teachers come there to be taught![95]

You cannot judge truth by numbers, cries Athanasius, as the poor, simple, ignorant apostles were the equal of ten thousand times ten thousand. "Thus the power ever resides with the truth, even though it is found among but few." It is the man who cannot give his reasons who flees to the support of numbers. "Can you overcome falsehood by a multitude, which is bought by flattery and gifts, easily impressed in its ignorance and stupidity, easily tripped up in its timidity and cowardice, which always prefers the pleasure of the moment to the enjoyment of eternal life; all these things are well enough known. The strength of

---

95. ἡ γὰρ πόλις οὐκ ἀπὸ τῶν οἰκοδομῶν, ἀλλὰ ἀπὸ τῶν ἐνοίκων θαυμάζεται. μὴ μοι λέγε, ὅτι ἡ Ῥωμαίων πόλις μεγάλη τῷ μεγέθει· ἀλλ' δεῖξόν μοι ἐκεῖ οὕτω λαὸν φιλήκοον. ἐπεὶ καὶ τὰ Σόδομα πύργους εἶχεν, ἡ δὲ καλύβη τοῦ Ἀβραάμ· ἀλλ' ἐλθόντες οἱ ἄγγελοι, τὰ μὲν Σόδομα παρέδραμον, ἐπὶ δὲ καλύβην κατήχθησαν. . . . εἴσελθε εἰς ἐκκλησίαν, καὶ βλέπε τῆς πόλεως τὴν εὐγένειαν. εἴσελθε, ἰδὲ πένητας ἐκ μεσονυκτίων μέχρι τῆς ἡμέρας παραμένοντας, βλέπε παννυχίδας ἱερὰς ἡμέρᾳ καὶ νυκτὶ συναφθείσας. . . . μεγάλη πόλις, καὶ μητρόπολις τῆς οἰκουμένης. πόσοι ἐπίσκοποι, πόσοι διδάσκαλοι ἦλθον ἐνταῦθα, καὶ παιδευθέντες παρὰ τοῦ λαοῦ ἀναχώρουσι, καὶ τὸν νόμον τὸν ἔμφυτον ἐντεῦθεν μεταφυτεῦσαι παρασκευάζονται. John Chrysostom, *In Illud, Vidi Dominum Homilia* 4.1, in *PG* 56:120.

falsehood is in a multitude."[96] It is no wonder that modern Catholic editors want to view these remarks of Athanasius as spurious.

The opposite side of this picture is the argument of John Bligh: "Although there is obvious wisdom in delaying the baptism of men whose conduct is likely to bring disgrace upon the Christian name, the Church is not the sort of society that can restrict its membership merely in order to be more select."[97] Father Bligh forgets that *ekklesia* means "select." He would be hesitant to baptize rascals only if that would hurt the reputation of the church—he shuns public disgrace, but apart from that would have no limitations at all: big membership is more important than what the membership stands for. In the end, Optatus, Lucifer, Augustine, Jerome, Ambrose—all the great ones of the fourth century—rest their final argument on the size of their church. Had Rome been an ordinary city, the claims of the bishop of Rome would be far more impressive than they are, for then they would stem from ecclesiastical office and position alone. As it is, the weight of Rome was so overwhelmingly political and especially cultural, that, in view of the close identity of a bishop's importance with that of his city, one is surprised that the Roman See was not rather far more important than it was. There is nothing the Roman bishops do or claim that one would not normally expect from the bishop of the most important city in the world. Their claims are not out of proportion to those made by bishops of other cities; bishops

---

96. οὕτως ἀεί τῆς ἀληθείας τὸ κράτος, κἂν παρ' ὀλίγοις τέως εὑρίσκηται. . . . ποῖον δέ μοι καὶ πλῆθος λέγεις; τὸ μισθωθὲν καλοκείᾳ καὶ δώροις, τὸ κλαπὲν ἀμαθείᾳ καὶ ἀγνοίᾳ, τὸ πεπτωκὸς δειλίᾳ τε καὶ φόβῳ, τὸ προτιμῆσαν πρόσκαιρον ἁμαρτίας ἀπόλαυσιν τῆς αἰωνίου ζωῆς, ἅπερ πολλοὶ φανερῶς ὡμολόγησαν· πλήθει τὸ ψεῦδος κρατύνεις. Athanasius, *Confutationes quarumdam propositionum* 1, in *PG* 28:1340–41.

97. John Bligh, "The 'Edict of Milan': Curse or Blessing?" *Church Quarterly Review* 153 (1952): 311.

of the largest cities and of the capital as a matter of course put forth identical claims, which from the third century on bear no weight at all in proving the apostolic nature of one church or another. Yet the earliest Roman claims date from the fourth century.

The Double Apostolate: Peter and Paul

When cities started appealing to their apostolic foundation as proof of superior merit, the principle of equality was surmounted by the useful fiction of the "double apostolate." All the earliest churches had been founded by apostles, so on that ground they were equal. But in an age in which numbers were everything, a neat and mechanical application of the rule of numbers to this problem was inevitable: what could be more obvious than that an office bestowed by two apostles was twice as valid as an office bestowed by one! At the Council of 381 in Constantinople appeared the doctrine of the three thrones of Peter: Rome, Alexandria, and Antioch. How then could Rome claim to be superior through Peter? In no other way but by the addition of another apostle, Paul, to establish the claim of double apostolate. Damasus explains that Alexandria has second place and Antioch third because Peter lived in those places, but Rome has undoubtedly the first place "because Peter and Paul, dying there on one and the same day equally consecrated the above said church of Rome to Christ the Lord."[98] This is speculation unlimited. It destroys the Clementine claims, and it introduces principles of authority that are nowhere mentioned in scripture or in the fathers, but that undoubtedly would give Jerusalem, with its *triple* apostolate and its consecration by the Lord's own death, overwhelming priority.

---

98. *[Petrus et Paulus], uno, eodemque die, gloriosa morte ... agonizans ... et pariter supradictam Romam Ecclesiam Christo Domino consecrarent.* Damasus, *Epistola de Explanatione Fidei*, in PL 13:374.

"I Paul and I Peter decree" is the formula in the *Apostolic Constitutions,* giving Paul first place.[99] A letter attributed to Anacletus states, "That is therefore the *prima sedes* which belongs by celestial bounty to the Roman Church, which the most blessed Peter and Paul consecrated by their *martyrium.*"[100] Where does one find a rule that the place in which a hero dies is the place in which most of his authority resides? Not in Christian thinking, certainly. It is rooted rather in the thinking of the pagan world—where a hero dies, *there* is his shrine and the place of his spiritual survival. It is the foundational theory of those earthbound cults that are the essence of Mediterranean religion. The cults of shrines and caves that abound in Pausanias dominate the Near East at all times and flourish as much as ever in the world of the Lady Aetheria, who at the end of the fourth century visits the grottoes in which Christ was born, raised, preached, held the Last Supper and was buried, resurrected, and ascended to heaven.[101] The same letter of the dubious Anacletus notes that Alexandria comes second "because Mark preached there under Peter's direction and there received his glorious martyrdom."[102] Antioch comes third because Peter there installed its bishop, Ignatius, and the name "Christian" originated there. Note how carefully the letter avoids making Peter himself bishop of either of the other two places, though there is every bit as much evidence that he was bishop in those cities as that he was bishop at Rome.

Yet the same letter says that Rome receives its *principatum* not from the apostles at all, but from the Lord himself.[103]

---

99. ἐγὼ Παῦλος καὶ Πέτρος διατασσόμεθα. *Constitutiones Apostolicae* 8.33.1, in *PG* 1:1133.

100. *Prima ergo sedes est caelesti beneficio Romanae Ecclesiae quam (ut memoratum est) beatissimi Petrus et Paulus suo martyrio consecrarunt.* Anacletus, *Epistola* 3.3, in *PG* 2:813.

101. Aetheria (Silvia), *Peregrinatio ad Loca Sancta,* 4th ed. (Heidelberg: Heraeus, 1939).

102. *Quia [Marcus] . . . directus a Petro, praedicavit, et gloriosum suscepit martyrium.* Anacletus, *Epistola* 3.3, in *PG* 2:814.

103. Anacletus, *Epistola* 3.4, in *PG* 2:815.

THE OFFICE OF BISHOP IN ROME 187

Any church founded by an apostle could make this claim with equal truth—for all the apostles were commissioned by the Lord. No matter what the Lord said to Peter, the question here is how and to whom Peter's authority was given, and in the absence of any evidence at all, it is assumed that because Peter died at Rome, more of his authority must reside there than elsewhere. Yet the argument is spoiled by giving Peter and Paul equal authority. If it can be proved that a church has a direct claim on the Lord's promise to Peter, there is no need to bring Paul's office into the picture. Indeed it only confuses the issue where a single head and a monarchical authority is insisted upon. Peter, Paul, and Ignatius died at Rome for the same purpose, says Chrysostom, which was "to extinguish idolatry with their blood," not to establish a principle of authority.[104] Bringing Ignatius into the picture weakens the double apostolate just as the figure of Paul weakens the Petrine doctrine.

"Peter and Paul preached the gospel and founded the church at Rome," writes Irenaeus, "and after they departed, Mark, the disciple and interpreter of Peter, himself gave to us in writing the things taught by Peter."[105] If one remembers that Clement was supposed to have been chosen by Peter to head the church solely because of his experiences and intimacy with Peter and his teachings, it is hard to see how Mark would not have been the better candidate. It was Mark who survived Peter as his closest disciple and personal interpreter, not Clement; it was Mark who as Peter's scribe should have written the letter to James if any was to be written. It was

---

104. διὰ τοῦτο καὶ Πέτρος καὶ Παῦλος καὶ [Ἰγνάτιος] ἐκεῖ πάντες ἐτύθησαν· τοῦτο μὲν ἵνα μολυνθεῖσαν τὴν πόλιν τοῖς τῶν εἰδώλων αἵμασι, τοῖς οἰκείοις αἵμασιν ἐκκαθάρωσι. John Chrysostom, *In Sanctam Martyrem Ignatium* 4, in *PG* 50:593.

105. τοῦ Πέτρου καὶ τοῦ Παύλου ἐν Ῥώμῃ εὐαγγελιζομένων, καὶ θεμελιούντων τὴν 'ἐκκλησίαν. μετὰ δὲ τὴν τούτων ἔξοδον, Μάρκος ὁ μαθητὴς καὶ ἑρμηνευτὴς Πέτρου, καὶ αὐτὸς τὰ ὑπὸ Πέτρου κηρυσσόμενα ἐγγράφως ἡμῖν παραδέδωκε. Irenaeus, *Contra Haereses* 3.1.1, in *PG* 7:845.

Mark who excelled in the very qualities which are supposed to have given Clement his position: yet absolutely no mention of Mark is found anywhere in the Clementine accounts.

Though Gustav Krüger expresses his personal conviction that Peter was at Rome, "since without that the history of the early church cannot be explained," he says that it "cannot be strictly proven by undoubted evidence.... I cannot prove it, and neither can anyone else."[106] If Peter was there, he says "it was as we find him in Clement, as one of those modest, unprepossessing, and very impressive missionaries of the Messiah."[107] For "he left no early impressions at all,"[108] and "nearly everything in the traditions of Peter is legend."[109] Goguel also believed Peter was in Rome, but finds it strangely obvious that he did not play an important role there and certainly did not found the church there, and, what is more, he had no influence in its development. The tradition that makes him the founder of the Roman Church and first bishop of Rome comes from the middle of the second century, according to Goguel, having its rise "in a very vague statement in Clement of Rome."[110]

---

106. "Denn ... [ich] müßte sagen, daß für mich der römische Aufenthalt des Petrus zu den Tatsachen gehört, ohne die ich mir den Verlauf der Geschichte der Alten Kirche nicht denken kann. Aber, beweisen kann ich das nicht und kann es niemand." Gustav Krüger, "Petrus in Rom," *Zeitschrift für die neutestamentliche Wissenschaft und die Kunde der älteren Kirche* 31 (1932): 301.

107. "Kleine, menschlich unscheinbare, aber gottbegeisterte Missionare ihres Messias ... um mit «Klemens» zu reden." Krüger, "Petrus in Rom," 305.

108. "[Er] hat ... keinen nachweisbaren Einfluß geübt." Gustav Krüger, *Das Papsttum: Seine Idee und ihre Träger*, Religionsgeschichtliche Volksbücher für die deutsche christliche Gegenwart 4.3–4 (Tübingen: Mohr, 1907), 5.

109. "Fast alles an der Petrusüberlieferung [ist] Legende." Krüger, "Petrus in Rom," 301.

110. "Par une phrase assez creuse de Clément Romain." Goguel, *Jésus et les Origines du Christianisme*, 231.

Clement to the Corinthians—Proof of Roman Supremacy?

In the so-called letter of Clement to the Corinthians, "nearly all modern Catholic historians see the first manifestation known to us of the special authority of the church of Rome in the universal church." At the end of the first century, "Clement of Rome writes already like a pope and intervenes with imposing authority in the internal conflicts of the church."[111] Does that make him a pope? At the same time Ignatius was intervening with far more "imposing authority" in the internal affairs of half a dozen other churches. There is not the slightest evidence that no other church but Rome intervened in the affairs at Corinth, Jacques Zeiller notes.[112] But what is more important is that Rome does not intervene at all—there is nothing in the letter but the expression of a timid opinion, given, it is clearly explained, only because and only when the Corinthians themselves asked for it (and the word translated as "asked for" implies a general request made to various quarters for information). There is no mention of the name of Clement in the letter—if he wrote it, it was as a scribe; and he speaks only in the name of "the church temporarily staying at Rome, to the church temporarily dwelling in Corinth."[113] So much for the church that was to "remain firm and steadfast until the end of the world."[114] He gives no orders, though he states that the situation is desperate and ruining the whole church; he never once mentions his office, his authority, or his name, though

---

111. Source unidentified.
112. Jacques Zeiller, "A Propos de l'Intervention de l'Église de Rome à Corinthe," *Revue d'Histoire Ecclésiastique* 31 (1935): 762.
113. ἡ ἐκκλησία τοῦ θεοῦ ἡ παροικοῦσα Ῥώμην τῇ ἐκκλησίᾳ τοῦ θεοῦ τῇ παροικούσῃ Κόρινθον. Clement, *Epistola Primera ad Corinthios* 1:1, in *PG* 1:201–4.
114. See Hugh Nibley, *Mormonism and Early Christianity*, CWHN 4 (Salt Lake City: Deseret Book and FARMS, 1987), 293.

the situation desperately calls for a strong assertion of authority. He appeals to the Corinthians only lamely "in the name of blessed Sophia," quoting very cautiously a passage from the scriptures and leaving the Corinthians to draw their own conclusions and do as they see fit. What "imposing authority."

Eusebius tells us that Dionysius, bishop of Corinth, later wrote a letter to the Romans in which he patronizingly compliments the Romans on the Roman custom of helping the needy and the mine workers by special foundation. The letter business was reciprocal. This letter, however is not written to Soter, bishop of Rome, whom it praises, but is specifically addressed to "the church of Rome," which is always addressed "you" in the plural. "Today is Sunday," says the letter, "and we are reading the letter of yours—the first one, which was written down by Clement."[115] How rude of them to forget to mention that this Clement was a bishop, let alone president of the church—while all other bishops are receiving due respect and recognition. What it does mention is that it was he who actually wrote the letter—not dictating it, as a bishop would. If Rome intervened in Corinth, Bishop Polycarp of Smyrna intervened in Roman internal affairs with far more authority, coming in person to the city, allowing Irenaeus to boast that the doctrine of the Roman Church is apostolic—because a man who had actually known an apostle had taught there.

The Catholics see proof of Roman priority in the fact that Ignatius, talking to seven churches (far more frankly, incidentally, than Clement does to Corinth), does not rebuke the Roman Church as he does the others. But he was on his way to Rome and had actually seen conditions in the other churches—he had never yet been to Rome. When he rebukes

---

115. τὴν σήμερον οὖν κυριακὴν ἁγίαν ἡμέραν διηγάγομεν, ἐν ᾗ ἀνέγνωμεν ὑμῶν τὴν ἐπιστολήν . . . τὴν προτέραν ἡμῖν διὰ Κλήμεντος γραφεῖσαν. Eusebius, *Historia Ecclesiastica* 4.23.11, in *PG* 20:388.

THE OFFICE OF BISHOP IN ROME

the other churches it is always on the basis of personal observation, and as yet he had made no personal observations in Rome. On that head he naturally preserves silence. Eusebius notes that Ignatius, "the second successor of Peter in Antioch, wrote letters to all the churches in which he had sojourned."[116] Then he lists the cities receiving such letters and adds: "Besides these he also wrote to the church of the Romans."[117] Here we see that Rome is indeed in a special category and immune to firsthand criticism—the only kind that Ignatius indulged in—because the saint had not yet visited there and not because he thought of it as particularly pure and holy.

A Dutch Benedictine, R. Van Cauwelaert, has removed the last excuse for arguing that Rome's intervention in the Corinthians' trouble is an indication, let alone proof, of her position of leadership in the whole church. For Rome had always had special and intimate ties with Corinth that did not extend to the rest of the church. Already Paul notes close ties between the two cities, independent of the churches. American excavations in Corinth have proven beyond a doubt, says Van Cauwelaert, that there were indeed very special ties between the city of Rome and the city of Corinth. "Is it not perfectly natural to assume that the relations between the two [Christian] communities were of the same nature as those relations which united the two cities?"[118] "The Christians of Rome and Corinth must have conserved their previously established social relationships, their civic spirit, their national sentiment,

---

116. Κατ' Ἀντιόχειαν Πέτρου διαδοχῆς δεύτερος τὴν ἐπισκοπὴν κεκληρομένος. Eusebius, *Historia Ecclesiastica* 3.36.2, in *PG* 20:288.

117. πρὸς ταύταις καὶ τῇ ῥωμαίων ἐκκλησίᾳ γράφει. Eusebius, *Historia Ecclesiastica* 3.36.6, in *PG* 20:288.

118. "Or, n'y a-t-il pas tout à parier que les relations des deux communautés entre elles sont de même nature que les relations qui unissaient les deux villes?" R. Van Cauwelaert, "L'Intervention de l'Église de Rome a Corinthe vers l'An 96," *Revue d'Histoire Ecclésiastique* 31 (1935): 283.

and even the pride in their cities. . . . We may accept it as certain that . . . the profane rapport [secular ties] would furnish the desired foundation for religious ties."[119]

Van Cauwelaert then reviews the history of events by which, through a special founding, Corinth became and remained a uniquely Roman community in an island of resentful Greeks. "The cult at Corinth was actually more Roman than that of Rome itself because it was less cosmopolitan."[120] "In its official life," our researcher concludes, "whether political or religious, Corinth appears before us in the first century [A.D.] as a city entirely and exclusively Roman, with an unequivocal note of puritanical Romanism."[121] The offices, customs, names, dress, manners, and tastes of the city were all aggressively Roman; words on public arts and private gadgets were all in Greek, Latin, and Latin and Roman. Such a state could have persisted, Van Cauwelaert notes, "only through the persistent influence and continual intervention of Rome itself, and an extreme docility, a veritable spirit of submission on the part of Corinth."[122] "Why then," he asks, "should not the Christians, conscious of forming a single body, remain without such connections? Arguing apart from the secular ties between Corinth and Rome, we can admit that the Chris-

---

119. "Les chrétiens de Rome et de Corinthe ont dû conserver leurs précédentes relations sociales, leur esprit civique, leur sentiment national, et même la fierté de leurs cités. . . . Nous pouvons tenir pour assuré que . . . les rapports profanes durent leur fournir l'occasion désirée de rapports religieux." Van Cauwelaert, "L'Intervention de l'Église de Rome," 283.

120. "Le culte [à Corinthe] y était, dans son ensemble, plus romain, parce que moins cosmopolite, qu'à Rome même." Van Cauwelaert, "L'Intervention de l'Église de Rome," 293.

121. "Dans sa vie officielle, tant politique que religieuse, Corinthe se présente donc, au 1er siècle, comme une ville entièrement et exclusivement romaine, avec une note non équivoque de romanisme puritain." Van Cauwelaert, "L'Intervention de l'Église de Rome," 293.

122. "Seule [pour] l'influence persistante, l'intervention continuelle de Rome, et une extrême docilité, un véritable esprit de courtisan de la part de Corinthe." Van Cauwelaert, "L'Intervention de l'Église de Rome," 302.

tians of the two cities were not less united among themselves than their heathen fellow citizens."[123] If anything, they would be more so.

Clement himself refers to the hospitality of the Corinthians and speaks to them "in the language not of a distant brother but of a recognized member of the Christian family of Corinth."[124] Socrates, giving a long list of men who have been bishops of more than one city, notes especially the Rome-Corinth connection.[125] In conclusion, Father Van Cauwelaert writes: "Consequently, the question of whether *1 Clement* is presented as an act of the Roman supremacy must receive, it appears, a negative answer. Evidently from the fact that the church of Rome did not appeal to any special rights, one would not be authorized to conclude that she was not conscious of some primacy."[126] But *1 Clement* cannot be taken as proof or even evidence for it, and, says Van Cauwelaert, "we must underline the modest style of the document as in perfect harmony with the principles which it itself announces for those who wish to instruct others."[127]

---

123. "Pourquoi les chrétiens, conscients de ne former qu'un seul corps, seraient-ils restés ici sans rapports? Arguant *a pari* des relations profanes de Corinthe avec Rome, nous pouvons admettre que les chrétiens des deux villes n'étaient pas moins unis entre eux que leurs concitoyens païens." Van Cauwelaert, "L'Intervention de l'Église de Rome," 304.

124. "Leur a tenu le langage, non d'un frére du dehors mais d'un membre reconnu de la famille chrétienne de Corinthe." Van Cauwelaert, "L'Intervention de l'Église de Rome," 305.

125. Socrates Scholasticus, *Historia Ecclesiastica* 7.36, in *PG* 67:820–21.

126. "Par conséquent, la question de savoir si la *1ª Clementis* se présente comme un acte de la primauté romaine doit recevoir, semble-t-il, une résponse négative. Évidemment, du fait que l'église de Rome ne s'y prévaut pas de droits spéciaux, on ne serait pas autorisé à conclure qu'elle n'avait pas conscience de sa primauté." Van Cauwelaert, "L'Intervention de l'Église de Rome," 305–6.

127. "Il faudra souligner que le style modeste du document est en parfaite harmonie avec le principe qu'elle énonce elle-même à l'usage de ceux qui ont la mission d'instruire les autres." Van Cauwelaert, "L'Intervention de l'Église de Rome," 306.

"The more meek and humble a man is, the greater he appears, and the proper thing is ever to seek the common advancement—not one's own."[128] Certainly the fact that Rome presumes to intervene in Corinthian affairs was anything but an indication that Rome was ruling the church.

Not only is the passage in *1 Clement* exhibit A in the claims of Roman supremacy over the church, but it is also the only evidence exhibited, and after that solitary example, one must travel for over three hundred years before coming upon another such useful reference in the literature. Heinrich Vogels's collection of *Ante-Nicene Texts Referring to the Primacy of Rome* is an extremely instructive lesson in the extent to which human ingenuity will go in trying to make ancient writers say what they have no intention of saying.[129] Not one of the passages Vogels produces even remotely suggests a reference to the primacy of Rome.

The Leading Role the Roman Church Did Not Play

The thundering silence of history regarding the primacy of Rome is most significant only when we know just what role Rome was supposed to have been playing all along. The present claim of the Roman Church is that the church is a perfect society and has an independent organization. "The church has ... the right and office of preserving and of expounding the revealed doctrine, and in that function is infallible. It preserves inviolate the deposit of the faith and explains its infallibility, being never at any time in error. ... The pope is infallible even without the consensus of the church. A general council acting in common with the pope never errs" though national synods are fallible.[130]

---

128. τοσούτῳ γὰρ μᾶλλον ταπεινοφρονεῖν ὀφείλει, ὅσῳ δοκεῖ μᾶλλον μείζων εἶναι, καὶ ζητεῖν τὸ κοινωφελὲς πᾶσιν καὶ μὴ τὸ ἑαυτοῦ. Clement, *Epistola Primera ad Corinthios* 48.6, in *PG* 1:309.

129. Heinrich Vogels, *Textus Antenicaeni ad Primatum Romanum Spectantes*, Florilegium Patristicum tam Veteris quam Medii Aevi Auctores Complectens 9, ed. Bernhard Geyer and Johannes Zellinger (Bonn: Hanstein, 1937).

130. Source unidentified.

"[The infant church]," writes Batiffol, "was a hierarchical society, a church of churches, a unity preserved by the unity of the *cathedra Petri*, and she was conscious of being all that."[131]

One of many spurious letters attributed to Anacletus, that very early pope whose name is missing entirely from many of the lists, says: "The apostles established the apostolic seat . . . so that the more important and difficult questions could always be referred to the apostolic seat."[132] Another very early pope, Evaristus, is quoted as writing to the Africans: "It is necessary to refer to the apostolic seat, as to the head, whose charge it is to take charge in doubtful matters, and does not hold its office by usurpation."[133] Evaristus is represented as writing a charge to the whole church: "If you have anything against [your bishop], . . . refer all charges to the holy seat."[134]

Here we have a clear enough statement of the things the head of the church should be and do, functions for which there was a crying need in the church from the time of the apostles until the Council of Trent, when the extent of the pope's authority was still very much in question. They are functions that remained unfulfilled for a thousand years in a church of chaos. Let us consider the argument of silence in this connection.

If the primacy of Rome had been a fact, it would have solved at a blow all the most burning controversies of the first

---

131. "[L'Église naissante] était . . . une société hiérarchisée, une église d'églises, une unité gardée par l'unité de la *cathedra Petri*, elle était consciente d'être tout cela." Batiffol, *L'Église naissante et le Catholicisme*, xii.

132. *[Apostolicam sedem] apostolic hoc statuerunt . . . ut majores et difficiliores quaestiones semper ad sedem deferantur apostolicam.* Anacletus, *Epistola* 1.4, in *PG* 2:800.

133. *Ad sedem apostolicam referre maluit, quasi ad caput, quid deberet de rebus dubiis custodire, potius quam usurpatione praesumerit.* Evaristus, *Epistola* 1, in *PG* 5:1047.

134. *Si autem adversus [vestrum episcopum] aliquam querelam habueritis . . . inquirendum erit, et auctoritate hujus sanctae sedis terminandum.* Evaristus, *Epistola* 2, in *PG* 5:1052.

four centuries. While everyone was casting about desperately for a way out, an appeal to such primacy is suggested by no one. It did not, Duchesne notes, occur to Athanasius.[135] How gladly Constantine would have availed himself of it. It was with great reluctance that he himself took over the office of "bishop of bishops." He was a Latin-speaking Westerner, and if anyone knew of the Roman claims, he should have. A nod from him was enough to sustain the authority of any bishop without limitation and without opposition, as was proven again and again. He was eagerly seeking some principle of authority, some theory of general rule for the church, and any theory became an enthusiastic practice at Constantine's word. Yet it is never hinted for a moment that in the primacy of Peter he has the obvious solution to his problem.

"Christianity was born catholic," writes the ecstatic Batiffol, referring to its unified, universal, centralized organization,[136] and he is right. But why did it not remain so? "With the passing of the earliest age, all this itinerant, ubiquitous personnel disappeared, and nothing remained but local ecclesiastical organizations."[137] Could they be trusted to follow the right path independently? Their courses promptly diverged in all directions, so that the historian Socrates can report that in his day no two churches had the same rites or doctrines[138]—a central control was badly needed, but it simply was not there.

"It was to the great Babylon of the West, so cursed by the Jewish prophets, that the role of leadership fell," says Du-

---

135. Source unidentified.

136. "La chrétienté est née catholique." Batiffol, *L'Église naissante et le Catholicisme*, xi.

137. "Les premiers temps passés, une fois disparu tout ce personnel itinerant, ubiquiste, il ne resta plus que les organizations ecclésiastiques locales." Duchesne, *Origines du Culte Chrétien*, 14.

138. Socrates Scholasticus, *Historia Ecclesiastica* 5.22, in *PG* 67:640.

chesne.[139] Why then does it not lead? It is very strange that in spite of this hierarchical preeminence, Rome was organized exactly like the church in any other city with no more and no less official machinery than was necessary to carry on the business of the local city church. Were these offices adequate to supply the central leadership which the church so badly needed? Just as a bishop and an apostle cannot, by the nature of their callings, fill each other's offices, so the episcopal organization of Rome was neither designed to be the government of the church nor equal to it. Duchesne argues elsewhere that the proof that certain offices must have existed in the primitive church lies in the fact that certain functions were carried out: without the office the function would have been impossible and inconceivable.[140] And so when we find that "no one dreams" at Rome of establishing that personnel indispensable to the functions of church government, it can only be because those functions were lacking. We can trace the periodic introduction of offices and functionaries to fill a crying need, but those offices were not original to the Roman system.

Though Paul is thought to be the real founder of world Christianity, Karl Holl can only marvel at Paul's unconcern for problems of organization:[141] it was the elders at Jerusalem who worked all that out. Paul, as we have seen, did not think of himself as establishing either a large or a permanent institution. If we are to believe the Roman claims, both Peter and Paul each spent at the very least twenty-five years in Rome, engaged in the work of organizing the church. Now, Clement really was something of an organizer, and we have volumes of stories about his activities, albeit legendary. But neither Peter nor Paul has left behind that corpus of stories, legends, and true accounts which each of these dynamic

---

139. "C'est à la grande Babylone de l'Occident, tant maudite des prophètes juifs, que ce role était échu." Duchesne, *Origines du Culte Chrétien*, 14.

140. Duchesne, *Origines du Culte Chrétien*, 8–11.

141. Source unidentified.

men most assuredly must have if the Roman claim is valid. We have noted Ignatius's complete silence on the apostolicity of the episcopal office, though his purpose in writing was to build up the prestige of that office; we have noted his distress at the condition in which he finds the church, how he takes it upon himself to write disciplinary letters "because his love will not be silent,"[142] though no one has ordered him to do so. He knows of no general authority to whom he can appeal for orders to the churches; he himself has received no authorization from such. Ignatius refuses to name the troublemakers, exactly as Clement will not name them at Corinth. Why not? Paul is quite specific in naming the ringleaders in that same church. Why doesn't Clement follow his example?

As we have seen, in the days of the apostolic fathers everyone was writing letters to everyone else. These letters were sent directly, copied, and spread among the churches to provide general edification and instruction. Thus on the death of Polycarp, the church of Smyrna sends out an epistle "to the church of God in Philomelium and to all the churches throughout the entire world."[143] There are numbers of well-attested instances of this sort of thing (e.g., Ignatius to Polycarp, Papias, Barnabas, later Irenaeus to Rome, etc.), but there is no central clearinghouse in action. Remembering that these letters are official and addressed to the whole church and that the writers justify themselves by feelings of love and urgency while admitting that they are not authorized to give orders to other churches—one must accept this as evidence that there is no central authority in the church. When a serious question arose, to whom

---

142. . . . ἀγαπῶν ὑμᾶς. Ignatius, *Epistola ad Trallianos* 3, in *PG* 1:780.

143. τῇ ἐκκλησίᾳ τοῦ θεοῦ, τῇ παροικούσῃ ἐν Φιλομηλίῳ καὶ πάσαις ταῖς κατὰ πάντα τόπον τῆς . . . ἐκκλησίας παροικίαις. *Martyrdom of Polycarp* 1, in *PG* 5:1029.

should it be referred? We have quoted the claim of Anacletus that it was the very purpose of the Roman See to handle just such cases[144]—that is logical and sound, and it shows us thereby that a head of the church did not exist, for in that case all these questions of doctrine and authority would have been referred to it; bishops would not have attempted to correct widespread troubles in other churches by direct letter but would have referred matters of rioting and insubordination to the head, and from that head we would have a stream of letters and directives, to be copied and quoted everywhere. This is recognized by the Romans themselves in their numerous attempts to forge such letters. But there is neither direct nor indirect evidence that the churches were being governed from Italy, and there is a good deal of evidence that they were not.

Irenaeus says that after the persecutions in which Peter and Paul lost their lives, John returned from Patmos "and continued to govern the churches," as he had authority to do.[145] With the Easter controversy, a rush of epistle writing and exchange of visits broke out again, as the only means of reaching general agreement. Irenaeus, bishop of Lyons, says that he has written "various letters" refuting a false conception of Easter that has become popular at Rome. "The elders before us, and those who lived with the apostles never handed down such teachings to you," he says, rebuking Victor, bishop of Rome.[146] Who ordered Irenaeus to write letters of instruction to Rome, let alone to administer a rebuke? He

---

144. Anacletus, *Epistola* 1.4, in *PG* 2:800.

145. ἐπειδὴ γὰρ τοῦ τυράννου τελευτήσαντος ἀπὸ τῆς Πάτμου τῆς νήσου μετῆλθεν ἐπὶ τὴν Ἔφεσον, ἀπῄει παρακαλούμενος καὶ ἐπὶ τὰ πλησιόχωρα τῶν ἐθνῶν, ὅπου μὲν ἐπισκόπους καταστήσων, ὅπου δὲ ὅλας ἐκκλησίας ἁρμόσων, ὅπου δὲ κλῆρον ἕνα γέ τινα κληρώσων τῶν ὑπὸ τοῦ πνεύματος σημαινομένων. Eusebius, *Historia Ecclesiastica* 3.23.6, in *PG* 20:257.

146. ταῦτα τὰ δόγματα οἱ πρὸ ἡμῶν πρεσβύτεροι, οἱ καὶ τοῖς ἀποστόλοις συμφοιτήσαντες, οὐ παρέδωκαν σοι. Irenaeus, fragment 2, in *PG* 7:1228.

tells us who. He says it was his own idea because he felt the church needed a defender and it should be he. "Let a bishop be judged by a bishop, a layman by a layman, and a prince by a prince," says the *Apostolic Constitutions*.[147] And he continues: "The sheep are [answerable as] rational beings [for their own behavior]. Hence they should flee from pernicious pastors."[148] But where is the head? "A bishop be judged by a bishop"—not the later rule that the bishop of bishops judges a bishop.[149]

Again, the well-known rule is that a bishop must be ordained by at least three or, at the very least, by two other bishops. What about his being ordained by the pope? Is not Peter supposed to have single-handedly ordained his successor? In all the epistles of the earliest "popes," none refers to himself as anything but "Archbishop of the Roman Church."[150] Sixtus I, according to our Catholic editor, is the first one to use the title *universalis apostolicae Ecclesiae episcopus*.[151] But if ever there was a well-defined title, it is that of archbishop, a term so specialized that its use here is the equivalent of calling the king of England lord mayor of London—an honorable title, indeed, but one that excludes him from the throne by impli-

---

147. τουτέστιν, ἐπίσκοπον πρὸς ἐπίσκοπον κρινῶ, καὶ λαϊκὸν πρὸς λαϊκόν, καὶ ἄρχοντα πρὸς ἄρχοντα. *Constitutiones Apostolicae* 2.19.1, in *PG* 1:633.

148. λογικὰ γάρ τὰ πρόβατα. . . . διὸ φευκτέον ἀπὸ τῶν φθορέων ποιμένον. *Constitutiones Apostolicae* 2.19.3, in *PG* 1:633.

149. Source unidentified.

150. The following are the earliest bishops of Rome with their self-proclaimed titles: Linus, Cletus, Clement, Evaristus (*episcopus, Epistola* 2, in *PG* 5:1051); Alexander (*episcopus, Epistola* 1, in *PG* 5:1057; *Epistola* 2, in *PG* 5:1069); Sixtus I (*archepiscopus, Epistola* 1, in *PG* 5:1073; *episcopus, Epistola* 2, in *PG* 5:1077); Telesphorus (*archepiscopus, Epistola ad Omnes Universaliter Christi Fideles*, in *PG* 5:1081); Hyginius (*episcopus, Epistola* 1, in *PG* 5:1087; *papa, Epistola* 2, in *PG* 5:1091); Pius I (*archepiscopus, Epistola* 1, in *PG* 5:1119; *Epistola* 2, in *PG* 5:1122); Soter (*archepiscopus, Epistola* 1, in *PG* 5:1133; *papa, Epistola* 2, in *PG* 5:1136); Eleutherius (*episcopus, Epistola* 1, in *PG* 5:1139).

151. J.-P. Migne, note 15 on Sixtus I, *Epistola* 2, *PG* 5:1077.

cation. If the bishop of Rome were really the president of the church from the beginning and were recognized as such, he would have had a special and fitting designation and would not always be referred to, as he is, merely as bishop or archbishop. This again is recognized by those Catholic divines who faithfully, but inaccurately, translate the word *episcopus* as "pope" when the bishop in question happens to be bishop of Rome, but simply as "bishop" when he is any other *episcopus*. One learned Romanist in his enthusiasm even translates *episcopus* as "pontiff" whenever it applies to the bishop of Rome even when mentioned by Eusebius—though Eusebius died years before anybody but the Roman emperor was allowed to bear the august title of pontiff. On the other hand, with admirable consistency and determination, the same scholars—when they find African bishops such as Cyprian or the bishop of Alexandria called "pope" long before the title is applied to anybody at Rome—mechanically translate the word as "bishop." So *episcopus* is to be read "pope" when it applies to the bishop of Rome, and "pope" is to be read *episcopus*, or "bishop," whenever it applies to anybody else. By such methods it is possible to make out in translation a pretty good case for Rome—but only by such methods.

Who shall judge a bishop when he does wrong? asks the *Apostolic Constitutions*. Naturally, the bishop's superior. But the *Apostolic Constitutions* knows of no such superior. The bishop must judge himself; there is no higher authority. He must follow the admonition of the Delphic oracle: "Know thyself."[152] It is indeed a sore absence of authority that leads Christian bishops to seek their ultimate appeal for authority in the judgment of holy Apollo.

In the *Contendings of the Apostles* we read: "And when I Clement met my master Peter, he appointed me to be the Archbishop of the city of Rome, and he made me chief of the congregation; and he appointed Euodius . . .

---

152. γνώριζε σεαυτόν. *Constitutiones Apostolicae* 2.18.3, in *PG* 1:629.

to be the Archbishop of the city of Antioch; and Paul appointed Mark, the son of Aresto to be Archbishop of the city of Alexandria," etc.[153]

"God has long ago removed all external danger from the church," writes Origen. "But I do not believe this security ... in this life can last long. Already the troublemakers are stirring up stasis inside the multitude of the believers, and they are not being opposed by the leaders, as they were in ancient times."[154] This is the very situation described by Hegesippus with the passing of the last apostle: "As soon as the apostles and those who knew them firsthand had all passed, those who had been lurking in dark corners came out openly, threw off the disguise, and began to preach their false doctrines with utter impunity, there being no more apostles around to put them in their place."[155] They sprang up, says Irenaeus, in the absence of apostolic authority. Had the apostles actually chosen and fully authorized successors and had the nature and location of that authority been clearly declared to all the church, the passing of the apostles would of course only have been an episode and not the complete disaster it was. Those who had been intimidated by the presence of genuine apostles and elders would have continued to stand in awe of their genuine successors. But such was not the case.

Celsus sneers at the way the Christians, a united body in the early days, had finally broken up into innumerable

---

153. E. A. Wallis Budge, *The Contendings of the Apostles* (London: Oxford University Press, 1935), 421.

154. Source unidentified.

155. ὡς δ' ὁ ἱερὸς τῶν 'ἀποστόλων χορὸς διάφορον εἰλήφει τοῦ βίου τέλος, παρεληλύθει τε ἡ γενεὰ ἐκείνη τῶν αὐταῖς ἀκοαῖς τῆς ἐνθέου σοφίας ἐπακοῦσαι κατηξιωμένην, τηνικαῦτα τῆς ἀθέου πλάνης τὴν ἀρχὴν ἐλάμβανεν ἡ σύστασις, διὰ τῆς τῶν ἑτεροδιδασκάλων ἀπάτης· οἳ καὶ ἅτε μηδενὸς ἔτι τῶν ἀποστόλων λειπομένου, γυμνῇ λοιπὸν ἤδη τῇ κεφαλῇ, τῷ τῆς ἀληθείας κηρύγματι τὴν ψευδώνυμον γνῶσιν ἀντικηρύττειν ἐπεχείρουν. Eusebius, *Historia Ecclesiastica* 3.32.8, in *PG* 20:284.

wrangling sects—and Origen must admit the charge, justifying that state of things by a feeble comparison with the wholesomeness of differing opinions among philosophers and scientists. But his answer is beside the point: philosophers and medics may quarrel no end about their theories, but the revealed word of God should not be the subject of bickering, and we have seen that the Romans claim the Holy See was established from the very beginning to preserve unity and perfect agreement. Why doesn't Origen, the most learned Christian of his time, know about that? Clement of Alexandria observes with sorrow that there are people everywhere who say they cannot join the Christian church because it is a hotbed of warring sects. His answer is the same as Origen's: the Greeks and Jews are just as bad! Forced himself to choose among the sects, Clement bases his choice wholly on the argument of numbers: the biggest sect must be the true one, an argument on which Athanasius pours withering scorn.[156] The largest consensus-group must be the true preservers of the tradition, and the others must be the strays, Clement concludes. What an argument for divine authority! But what we wish to note here is that the existence of a clearly recognized head in the church somewhere would have immediately solved Clement's problem: the only possible norm would be to follow the teachings of the established head, no matter which sect was biggest, if only such a head existed. But Clement knew of none.

That the fourth-century idea of mother church comes from the idea of mother city is clear from the earlier Corinthian concept of a spiritual mother. When the Judge Hieraz, an early Christian martyr, was asked who his parents were, he replied: "Our father is Christ, and our mother our belief in him."[157] And Eusebius tells how under Constantine all the human race was in a holy family "having one father, God,

---

156. Athanasius, *Doctrina ad Antiocham Ducem*, question 43, in *PG* 28:625.
157. Source unidentified.

and one mother, true piety."¹⁵⁸ The religious role of Constantine and the instantaneous and ecstatic acclaim he received from the churchmen would have been out of the question had the church possessed a single leader anywhere—even as a faintly remembered tradition. But for three hundred years there had been no general conference, simply, we are told, because there had been no one with the authority to call such a conference until the appearance of Constantine. "He was common with all men; when the various provinces of the church differed among themselves, he, as a common bishop established by God, would summon synods of God's ministers. And he would sit in their midst, not ashamed to be one of their number, becoming the common bishop, acting as umpire for all in matters of God's peace."¹⁵⁹ This is the office that Rome should have been performing, yet there was no protest from Rome, whose aged bishop sent ambassadors, and we are told in no uncertain terms that since the days of the apostles no one else had done anything like what Constantine was doing. Yet Constantine did what he did reluctantly; he begged the bishops to settle their affairs among themselves. "Since you will fight about trifles," he wrote to all the bishops, "I have been forced to write this letter, finding it necessary to come forward as a guardian of the peace. I am forced to set myself up as a moderator among you."¹⁶⁰

---

158. αὐτίκα γοῦν ὥσπερ ἐξ ἑνὸς φύντες πατρὸς, ἑνός τε θεοῦ οἷα παῖδες, καὶ μητρὸς μιᾶς τῆς ἀληθοῦς εὐσεβείας. Eusebius, *De Laudibus Constantini Oratio* 16.7, in *PG* 20:142.

159. διαφερομένων τινῶν πρὸς ἀλλήλους κατὰ διφόρους χώρας, οἷά τις κοινὸς ἐπίσκοπος ἐκ θεοῦ καθεσταμένος, συνόδους τῶν τοῦ θεοῦ λειτουργῶν συνεκρότει. ἐν μέσῃ δὲ τῇ τούτων διατριβῇ οὐκ ἀπαξιῶν παρεῖναί τε καὶ συνιζάνειν, κοινωνὸς τῶν ἐπισκοπουμένων ἐγίνετο, τὰ τῆς εἰρήνης τοῦ θεοῦ βραβεύων τοῖς πᾶσι· καθῆστό τε καὶ μέσος. ὡσεὶ καὶ τῶν πολλῶν εἶς. Eusebius, *Vita Constantini* 1.44, in *PG* 20:957–60.

160. μοι ... ἄγαν εὐτελὴς καὶ οὐδαμῶς ἀξία τῆς τοσαύτης φιλονεικίας ἡ πρόφασις ἐφωράθη. διόπερ ἐπὶ τὴν τῆς ἐπιστολῆς ταύτης ἀνάγκην ἐπειχθείς, καὶ πρὸς τὴν ὁμόψυχον ὑμῶν ἀγχίνοιαι γράφων ... οἷον εἰρήνης πρύτανιν ἐμαυτὸν προσάγω εἰκότως. Eusebius, *Vita Constantini* 2.68, in *PG* 20:1040–41.

As a peace officer, it is his duty to intervene and bring peace into the church, and to do that he uses the civil techniques: "Being desirous of bringing this plague to a halt, I could find no other means of cure or of casting out the common evil, than to send abroad my messengers."[161]

At the council, Julius is described as "Leader of the Ruling City"—that is, the most important thing that can be said about him is that his city is imperial.[162] Had it been the case, this would have been the time to say that he was the ruling bishop, the head of the church, the one and only successor to the apostles, etc., and not just bishop of what everybody knew was the imperial city. The priests he sent took orders from him, but no one else did. Since the primary question at Nicaea concerned who was to rule the church—the doctrinal issue, as has been said above, was merely a tool of power groups—now of all times was the time for Rome to assert her claim, this being the first and holiest of all the general synods. But instead, "since the beginning of the world only one man, the Emperor Constantine, having woven a crown of peace in the bond of Christ, offered to his Savior a godly thanksgiving offering for victory over his public and private enemies, having brought to pass as it were a likeness of the assembly of the ancient apostles in our own time."[163] A miracle and a wonder—the first general assembly since the days of the apostles—and only one man was able to bring it about!

---

161. ταύτην ἐγὼ τὴν νόσον κατασεῖλαι βουληθείς, οὐδεμίαν ἑτέραν ἄρκουσαν τῷ πράγματι θεραπείαν εὕρισκον ἐξελών . . . ἐνίους ὑμῶν πρὸς τὴν τῶν πρὸς ἀλλήλους διχονοούντων ὁμόνοιαν βοηθοὺς ἀποστείλαιμι. Eusebius, *Vita Constantini* 2.66, in *PG* 20:1037–40.

162. τῆς δέ γε βασιλευούσης πόλεως ὁ μὲν προεστὼς ὑστέρει διὰ γῆρας. Eusebius, *Vita Constantini* 3.7, in *PG* 20:1061.

163. τοιοῦτον μόνον ἐξ αἰῶνος, εἷς βασιλεὺς Κωνσταντῖνος, Χριστῷ στέφανον δεσμῷ συνάψας εἰρήνης, τῷ αὐτοῦ Σωτῆρι τῆς κατ' ἐχθρῶν καὶ πολεμίων νίκης θεοπρεπὲς ἀνετίθη χαριστήριον, εἰκόνα χορείας ἀποστολικῆς ταύτην καθ' ἡμᾶς συστησάμενος. Socrates Scholasticus, *Historia Ecclesiastica* 1.8, in *PG* 67:61.

Calling it a miracle is no exaggeration. Bishops came from all over the world to the meeting wearing strange dresses, speaking strange languages, teaching strange doctrines, practicing strange rites. Socrates says no two churches had the same liturgy, viewing each other as strangers from other planets[164]—what better demonstration of the effect of centuries of isolation during which no single center gave them instruction or ever brought them together? Constantine's opponent, the Christian Licinius, was for the churchmen "a wild beast," and the worst thing he ever did, according to them, was to forbid the holding of synods, "the only way in which the church could be governed."[165]

When just after the Nicene Council Julius of Rome wrote a triumphant letter to Alexandria on behalf of Athanasius, glorifying the successes of the West, he made no mention of the primacy of Rome.[166] At the same time we find Hilary of Poitiers writing in his own name letters to his "brothers and cobishops in Germany, Belgium, Lyons, Aquitaine, Narbonne, Tolosay and Britain," that is, the whole Western church except Italy, giving doctrinal instructions and an official report on events in the East.[167] "Though you are firm in the faith," he writes, "still there are some of you who have forwarded to me letters asking for communications from me: I will therefore, inexperienced and untaught as I am, undertake the heavy task of clarifying things."[168] How dare

---

164. Socrates Scholasticus, *Historia Ecclesiastica* 5.22, in *PG* 67:640.
165. ἄλλως γὰρ οὐ δυνατὸν τὰ μεγάλα τῶν σκεμμάτων, ἢ διὰ συνόδων. Eusebius, *Vita Constantini* 1.51, in *PG* 20:965.
166. Socrates Scholasticus, *Historia Ecclesiastica* 2.23, in *PG* 67:252–57.
167. *Dilectissimis et beatissimis Fratribus et coepiscopis provinciae Germaniae primae, et Germania secundae, et primae Belgicae, et Belgicae secundae, et Lugdunensi primae, et Ludgunensi secundae, et provinciae Aquitanicae, et provinciae Novempopulanae, et ex Narbonensi plebibus et clericis Tolosanis, et provinciarum Britanniarum episcopis, Hilarius servus Christi, in Deo et Domino nostro aeternam salutem.* Hilary, *De Synodis* 1, in *PL* 10:479.
168. *Tamen etiam in eo ferventis spiritus ardorem probates, quod nonnulli ex vobis, quorum ad me potuerunt scripta deferri, quae exinde Orientales in fidei*

he! Was not the apostolic seat established for that very purpose? Hilary protests that he is reluctant and poorly qualified—why then does he not "forward" to the head of the church the difficult doctrinal questions that have been "forwarded" to him, not from this or that small suffragan church of his own French diocese, but from all over Europe? This is double outrage! Are not both these functions—(1) the official reporting of acts and decisions and (2) the judgment of their orthodoxy—the exclusive and proper business of Rome? The Romanists later claim so, but Hilary knows of no such claim.

The terrible rioting, charges, and countercharges that resulted from parties competing for the office of bishop in the church in the days of the apostolic fathers continued unabated. We have read vivid descriptions of all these riots: "some are actually filling the churches with murder, leading whole cities to riot and revolt, all because they are fighting [to be elected bishops]."[169] If Clement, viewing this very situation three hundred years before, intervened "with opposing authority," as the Catholics say, to put an end to it, why did it continue to grow constantly worse? Why did not somebody now intervene? Somebody did—and it was always the emperor. But the point is that a central authority in the church would have quickly worked out a way of dealing with these local uprisings if that central authority had only existed. Later on, when there was such a central authority in Rome, the rioting at episcopal elections, the commonest cause of unrest in the church, ceased.

---

professionibus gerant et gesserunt, significari vobis humilitatis meae litteris desiderastis: etiam hoc mihi onus imperitissimo atque indoctissimo omnium ex affectu charitatis addentes, ut quid ipse super omnibus dictis eorum sentiam indecim. Hilary, *De Synodis* 5, in *PL* 10:483–84.

169. ὅτι γὰρ καὶ φόνων τὰς ἐκκλησίας ἐνέπλησάν τινες, καὶ πόλεις ἀναστάτους ἐποίησαν ὑπὲρ ταύτης μαχόμενοι τῆς ἀρχῆς. John Chrysostom, *De Sacerdotio* 3.10, in *PG* 48:647.

The apostles knew, writes Clement, that there would be trouble about this office of bishop, and so they made an *epinome* (i.e., a bylaw or special order) to take care of it.[170] The apostles also knew, writes Socrates, that there would be trouble about doctrine, so they also wrote down an official statement of doctrine—"but this letter was held as a thing of naught," and so the problem was not solved.[171] In these cases we are told how the apostles "transmitted their authority," and it is not through the person of a chosen successor. From the first, the sorest spot in the church, the episcopal election, was to have come under special surveillance: yet nothing is more evident than that after the passing of the apostles there is no such general surveillance over the elections. "I charge you by the fathers," writes Basil to the people of Neocaesarea, whose bishop has died, "and by the true faith, [each man must seek to do good in electing a new bishop]."[172] "Inasmuch as the infirmity of the churches is becoming greater," writes Basil to Athanasius, the bishop of Alexandria, "more and more we must look to thy perfection . . . to deliver us from this terrible tempest [wintertime]."[173] When a church elected a new bishop without consulting Basil, he could only wring his hands in protest and cry, "There is no stability in this sort of thing!"[174] How true. Does he not know where there is stability? Is the man to whom all must turn in the general shipwreck of the church Athanasius and no other? Where is the imposing authority of Rome?

---

170. *1 Clement* 44.2.
171. παρ' οὐδὲν δὲ τὴν τῶν ἀποστόλων νομοθεσίαν τιθέμενοι. Socrates Scholasticus, *Historia Ecclesiastica* 5.22, in *PG* 67:641–44.
172. ἀλλ' ἐπισκήπτω ὑμῖν πρὸς τῶν πατέρων, πρὸς τῆς ὀρθῆς πίστεως. . . . Basil, *Epistola* 28.3, in *PG* 32:309.
173. ὅσον τῶν ἐκκλησιῶν τὰ ἀρρωστήματα ἐπὶ τὸ μεῖζον πρόεισι, τοσοῦτον πάντες ἐπὶ τὴν σὴν ἐπιστρεφόμεθα τελειότητα . . . διασώσασθαι ἡμᾶς ἐκ τοῦ φοβεροῦ τούτου χειμῶνος. Basil, *Epistola* 80.1, in *PG* 32:456.
174. Basil, *Epistola* 54, in *PG* 32:400–401.

THE OFFICE OF BISHOP IN ROME

Cyril, Basil's contemporary, always calls the church leaderless. He argues that Manes cannot be the Paraclete [Holy Spirit], as his followers claim he is, because he came two hundred years after the death of the apostles, while the Paraclete came only in the time of the apostles.[175] Where has it been in the meantime? "There are three periods in the history of the church," writes Cyril, "that of Christ, that of the apostles and"—we wait in eager anticipation for the successor in the leadership, but in vain—"those times which have passed since the apostles."[176] What a strange way to designate the third period of the church. It is as disappointing as Clement's announcement that Christ gave the gnosis to Peter, James, and John; they "passed it on" to the rest of the Twelve; and they in turn "passed it on to the Seventy."[177] Since the discussion is of the transmission of the key—the knowledge of the gospel—we wait for the next link in the chain, but there is none.

Even so the apostolic fathers assure us that God the Father gave his authority to the Son and that Christ gave the same authority to the apostles, but they refuse to say that that authority was passed on to bishops.[178] Instead we are told that in the places where they preached, the apostles chose firstfruits in the faith and made provision that when these fell asleep, others not unworthy should succeed them.[179] Here is definite mention of succession, but pointedly not of succession from the apostles to the bishops. The fathers scrupulously avoid defining the succession, which

---

175. Cyril, *Catechesis* 16.9, in *PG* 33:929.
176. *In ecclesia tempora tria, Christi, apostolorum et illud quod in sequentes aetates excurit.* Cyril, in *PG* 33:1666; see also *PG* 33:930 n. 6.
177. Ἰακώβῳ τῷ Δικαίῳ καὶ Ἰωάννῃ καὶ Πέτρῳ μετὰ τὴν ἀνάστασιν παρέδωκε τὴν γνῶσιν ὁ Κύριος. οὗτοι τοῖς λοιποῖς ἀποστόλος παρέδωκαν. οἱ δὲ λοιποὶ ἀπόστολοι τοῖς ἑβδομήκοντα. Eusebius, *Historia Ecclesiastica* 2.1.4, in *PG* 20:136.
178. *1 Clement* 42.1.
179. *1 Clement* 42.4, 44.2.

they must if the Roman claim is true. "When you are visiting a strange city," Cyril advises his Alexandrian congregation, "never ask simply, 'Where is the church?' for every vile sect calls its meeting place by the good name of the Lord; neither ask simply, 'Where is the *ekklesia*?' but say rather, 'Where is the catholic church?' for this name happens to be holy even as the mother of all of us."[180] This still preserves the old original sense of "catholic," namely, the general society as opposed to the individual communities. Thus we have very early letters addressed to individual churches by name and still others addressed to "the general church." That is the meaning of the word *catholic*—it does not mean universal. But its very early use in letters shows it to go back to a time when there were actually general authorities. The secondary meaning is given it by Cyril: "It is called the catholic church because it is found throughout all the inhabited world, because it is the complete preaching of every wholesome doctrine, because the whole human race is disciplined for piety, because it is a whole cure for every appearance of sin, and because it contains every concept of what is called virtue."[181] This is an obvious rhetorical etymologizing, but note how completely silent Cyril is on the subject of a single head.

"Your father said," writes Ambrose to Constantius, "'it is not my business to judge between bishops,' but you say, 'I must do

---

180. κἄν ποτε ἐπιδημῇς ἐν πόλεσι, μὴ ἁπλῶς ἐξέταζε, ποῦ τὸ κυριακοῦ ἐστι (καὶ γὰρ αἱ λοιποὶ τῶν ἀσεβῶν αἱρέσεις κυριακὰ τὰ ἑαυτῶν σπήλαια καλεῖν ἐπιχειροῦσι)· μηδέ, ποῦ ἔστιν ἁπλῶς ἡ ἐκκλησία· ἀλλά, ποῦ ἔστιν ἡ καθολικὴ ἐκκλησία. τοῦτο γὰρ ἰδικὸν ὄνομα τυγχάνει τῆς ἁγίας ταύτης, καὶ μητρὸς ἡμῶν ἁπάντων. Cyril, *Catechesis* 18.26, in *PG* 33:1048.

181. καθολικὴ μὲν οὖν καλεῖται, διὰ τὸ κατὰ πάσης εἶναι τῆς οἰκουμένης . . . καὶ διὰ τὸ διδάσκειν καθολικῶς καὶ ἀνελλειπῶς ἅπαντα τὰ εἰς γνῶσιν ἀνθρώπων ἐλθεῖν ὀφείλοντα δόγματα . . . καὶ διὰ τὸ πᾶν γένος ἀνθρώπων εἰς εὐσέβεια ὑποτάσσειν . . . καὶ διὰ τὸ καθολικῶς ἰατρύειν μὲν καὶ θεραπεύειν ἅπαν τὸ τῶν ἁμαρτιῶν εἶδος . . . κεκτῆσθαι δὲ ἐν αὐτῇ πᾶσαν ἰδέαν ὀνομαζομένης ἀρετῆς. Cyril, *Catechesis* 18.23, in *PG* 33:1044.

THE OFFICE OF BISHOP IN ROME

the judging.'"[182] What Constantine did say was that it is nobody's business to judge between bishops. As a matter of fact, Ambrose has taken that function upon himself, so that people say, he notes, "that Ambrose wants to have more authority than the emperor."[183] But where does this discussion leave Rome? Who is to judge between bishops? On that head, Rome and Ambrose played a rough game against each other.

Why does even the devoted Optatus, a Roman by birth and living not far off, use such restrained language when he writes: "[The line of popes ends with] Siricius, who today is our associate, along with whom all the rest of us they make a common society of all the world, in the concord of a single society."[184] No mention is made of subordination but only of agreement. "Should people be baptized again in the name of Trinity?"[185] he asks. Since no one is "qualified to judge these things on earth, no judge is to be found, and so we must look to the judge in heaven."[186] But why ask heaven when we already have heaven's answer? Why indeed? Because it was the interpretation of the New Testament that they were fighting about in the first place. What a gross insult to Rome, if Rome had anything like the authority she is now assumed to have had! Optatus continues: But why is even the New Testament necessary? "As long as the Father is present, . . . testament [i.e., a witness of him in his absence] is not necessary. Christ told the apostles all that was necessary. The one of whom the Testament bears witness is actually alive in

---

182. *Pater tuus . . . vir maturioris aevi, dicebat: Non est meum judicare inter episcopos; tua nunc dicit clementia: Ego debeo judicare.* Ambrose, *Epistola* 21.5, in *PL* 16:1046.

183. *[Populi] aiunt: . . . vult Ambrosius posse, quam imperator.* Ambrose, *Epistola* 21.30, in *PL* 16:1059.

184. *Siricius, hodie qui noster est socius: cum quo nobiscum totus orbis commercio formatarum, in una communionis societate concordat.* Optatus, *De Schismate Donatistorum* 2.3, in *PL* 11:949.

185. Source unidentified.

186. *. . . ergo in terris de hac re nullum poterit reperiri judicium; de coelo quaerendus est judex.* Optatus, *De Schismate Donatistorum* 5.3, in *PL* 11:1048.

heaven: therefore his will is to be required in the gospels as if in a will." The answer to rebaptize is therefore Matthew 28:29, plus John 13:10.[187] In the end Optatus falls back, as do all sectarians, on the scriptures, but he comes very near the answer when he points out that God is still alive and falls into the inevitable conclusion: why not ask him, then, directly? In the nick of time he catches himself by falling back again on the scriptures, the very subject of dispute! But throughout the whole discourse this loyal Italian preserves a total and very significant silence regarding the proper function of the Holy See—a few miles away.

A few years later in 416, a bishop of Rome writes to the bishop of Gubbio, within his own metropolitan district, deploring the fact that the ritual and liturgy of that church is not and never has been that practiced at Rome.[188] Where is the Roman control? Rome is supposed to be guiding the church, and the soul of the church is the mass. Yet in the ninth century, liturgy had entirely died out at Rome, and it was necessary for the Frankish church, aided by the reform of the Cluniac monks, to save it for Rome and the world! "[These]," says Gerhart Ladner, "compelled the papacy by main force to return to the path of leadership of the general church."[189]

Is there one who has not merely transmitted the teaching of the church to others, but has taught the church itself, and whose doctrine has consequently been generally followed and authorized by the church? But would this not be a usur-

---

187. *Quamdiu pater praesens est, ipse imperat singulis; non est adhuc necessarium testamentum: sic et Christus . . . pro tempore quidquid necessarium erat Apostolis imperavit . . . vivus, cuius est testamentum, in coelo est: ergo voluntas ejus, velut in testamento, sic in Evangelio requiratur.* Optatus, *De Schismate Donatistorum* 5.3, in *PL* 11:1049–50.

188. Innocent I, *Epistola*, in *PL* 20:551–52; Duchesne, *Origines du Culte Chrétien*, 89–91.

189. "[Diese] zwingen das Papsttum gewaltsam in die Bahn universaler Kirchenführung zurück." Gerhart Ladner, "Das Heilige Reich des Mittelalterlichen Westens," *Die Welt als Geschichte: Eine Zeitschrift für Universalgeschichte* 11 (1951): 146.

pation of the authority of the apostolic see? The earliest instance of such teaching would seem to be that of Hermas. "In those days," says a letter attributed to Pius I, "Hermas, doctor of the faith and scripture, scintillated among us. An angel of the Lord appeared to the same Hermas dressed as a shepherd and told him that Easter should be on Sunday. Hence we are able to teach this by apostolic authority."[190] This must have been written long after Hermas, for the writer does not even know that it is just an allegory. But it is very significant that Pius I rests his authority in this decision not on Peter, but rather on the claim of a man who was not a bishop that an angel had appeared to him. Therefore, he says amazingly, we know that his doctrine is apostolic. For the same doctrine of Easter as taught in Rome, Irenaeus gives a wholly different authority[191]—he had never heard of the angel, a later invention. He says the Roman version is apostolic because Polycarp, bishop of Smyrna, actually went to Rome in person and put the bishop of Rome on the right track—and Polycarp, he reminds us, has actually known John.[192] He gives this as the best proof he knows that Rome teaches apostolic doctrine. But how insulting to the Petrine claims! Polycarp and Hermas should be taking instruction from the head of the church—not giving it.

The introduction to Origen's great *Peri Archón* is a most significant document.[193] Next to Augustine, Origen was most important. In the establishing of Christian theology, he kept seven secretaries busy night and day answering the questions of doctrine and authority that poured in to him from all parts of the church. In the *First Principles* he announces

---

190. *Istis ergo temporibus Hermes doctor fidei et scripturarum effulsit inter nos. Et . . . eidem Hermae angelus Domini in habitu pastoris apparuit, et praecepit ei, ut Pascha die Dominico ab omnibus celebraretur. Unde et vos apostolica auctoritate instruimus.* Pius I, *Epistola* 1.1, in *PG* 5:1120.
191. Eusebius, *Historia Ecclesiastica* 5.24, in *PG* 20:493–508.
192. Eusebius, *Historia Ecclesiastica* 5.24, in *PG* 20:493–508.
193. Origen, *Peri Archón* introduction, in *PG* 11:111–14.

his intention to deal not with trivial and technical details of doctrine, but with the great first principles on which the whole thing is founded. Christians disagree, he announces at the outset, not only on minor but on major matters, on the very fundamentals.[194] They agree, for example, that the Holy Ghost comes next in honor to God and Jesus Christ, "but it is *not* stated clearly whether the Holy Ghost was begotten or not—that we must find out from the scripture to the best of our ability by a sagacious inquisition."[195] It is agreed that "the devil and his angels exist, but why or how or what they are has not been clearly enough set forth."[196] It is agreed "that the world was created ... but what comes before or after ... is not evident in the teachings of the church";[197] we know that there are angels, but what, how, and when they are "is not sufficiently manifest";[198] the word that best describes God is *asomaton*—bodiless—yet that word is unused and unknown in the scriptures.[199] And so on. Origen announces that he must to the best of *his* ability seek a solution to such problems in philosophy because the church has not given an answer to them and he knows not to whom he can turn for information.

Have we not been told that the very purpose of the Holy See was to answer such questions and that it alone has the authority to do so? Everyone has his own ideas; all claim to be

---

194. Origen, *Peri Archón* 1.2, in *PG* 11:115–16.
195. *In hoc non jam manifeste discernitur, utrum natus an innatus. . . . Sed inquirenda jam ista pro viribus sunt de sacra scriptura, et sagaci perquistition investiganda.* Origen, *Peri Archón* 1.4, in *PG* 11:117–18.
196. *[Diabolus et angeli ejus] sunt . . . [sed] quae autem sint, aut quomodo sint, non satis clare exposuit.* Origen, *Peri Archón* 1.6, in *PG* 11:119.
197. *. . . quod mundus iste factus sit. . . . Quid tamen ante hunc mundum fuerit, aut quid post mundum erit . . . non . . . evidens . . . in ecclesiastica praedicatione.* Origen, *Peri Archón* 1.7, in *PG* 11:119.
198. *. . . non satis in manifesto designatur.* Origen, *Peri Archón* 1.10, in *PG* 11:120–21.
199. Origen, *Peri Archón* 1.9, in *PG* 11:120; *Contra Celsum* 7.27, in *PG* 11:1460.

THE OFFICE OF BISHOP IN ROME

followers of Christ, Origen announces, and yet they disagree about everything. He says he will follow "the ecclesiastical preaching through order of succession handed down from the apostles and remaining until the present in the churches,"[200] but he knows of no authoritative head to which he can turn and says that basic doctrines "are not manifestly set forth in our preaching."[201] Something had to be done about it—but was it his calling, who was not even a bishop, to become the great authority? How can heretic groups be distinguished from the followers of the true apostolic teaching, which all of them pretend to be following? Aside from the lame argument of number, Clement of Alexandria introduces another test: "They can be distinguished by interpreting the law of clean and unclean animals in a mystical sense."[202] But "a mystical sense" covers anything, and Clement is perfectly aware that one group is just as able to turn the scriptures against its enemies as another. Yet he knows of nothing better than this—no general doctrinal head to appeal to. "It is foolish," he says, "to turn down Christianity because it is divided into many sects. We must by demonstration and hard study show from the scriptures that only in the true and ancient church are the most holy gnosis and the best choice of things. There are many who appear wise and who really believe they have found the truth and who are followed by large congregations . . . but as a matter of fact they only obscure the truth by their clever manipulations."[203] Here Clement recommends his brand of Christianity as the best heresy—that is, the best

---

200. *Ecclesiastica praedicatio per successionis ordinem ab apostolis tradita, et usque ad praesens in ecclesiis permanens.* Origen, *Peri Archón* 1.2, in *PG* 11:116.

201. *. . . in praedicatione nostra manifeste non designatur.* Origen, *Peri Archón* 1.10, in *PG* 11:120.

202. περί τε Ἰουδαίων τῶν χυδαίων, περί τε τῶν αἱρέσεων μυστικῶς διακρινομένων, ὡς ἀκαθάρτων ἀπὸ τῆς περὶ καθαρῶν καὶ ἀκαθάρτων ζώων θείας ἐκκλησίας. Clement of Alexandria, *Stromata* 7.18, in *PG* 9:553.

203. Source unidentified.

choice among many. Where are the pure teachings and imposing authority of Rome? At the end of every major discussion, Origen can only invite "the reader to decide for himself."[204] Yet Clement and Origen were the greatest theologians of their times.

The situation in the fourth century is neatly stated by Lactantius: "Only the catholic church, therefore, retains the true cult [the word *retains* is significant, suggesting that the others once had it but lost it, thus admitting the awareness as well as the possibility of loss]. But since, however," he continues, "separate groups of heretics insist that they are the true Christians and firmly believe that they are the catholic church, we must identify the true church as the one which salubriously cures sins and wounds. To do this we must fight more wholly and devotedly against all the sects of liars."[205] Still nobody thinks of the See of Peter! Nobody thought of it when upon the death of the last apostle, the heretics, seeing that there were no longer any apostles, were free to cast off their long disguises.

There was a Bishop Nepos in Egypt, greatly admired for his noble character and his great gift for hymn writing, who tried to revive the old doctrine of the millennium, using Revelation as a text. One of his warmest admirers, Bishop Dionysius of Alexandria, protested against this dangerous literalism but observed, "If Christ and the apostles were still

---

204. *Unusquisque legentium . . . judicet.* Origen, *Peri Archón* 2.7, in *PG* 11:197.

205. *Sola igitur catholica Ecclesia est, quae verum cultum retinet. . . . Sed tamen quia singuli quique coetus haereticorum se potissimum Christianos, et suam esse Catholicam Ecclesiam putant, sciendum est illam esse veram, in qua est confessio et poenitentia, quae peccata et vulnera, quibus subjecta est imbecillitas carnis, salubriter curat.* Lactantius, *Divinarum Institutionum* 4.30, in *PL* 6:542–44. Cyril had advised those of his group to use the word *catholic* since all the sects were calling themselves Christians, but now that is no longer a touchstone since all the sects now call themselves catholic! Cyril, *Catechesis* 18.26, in *PG* 33:1048.

here we could ask them about such things. As it is, we had best content ourselves with a 'spiritual' interpretation of the scriptures."[206] Here we see that the scriptures are at best a poor substitute for direct revelation. But again we ask the question, If Christ and the apostles could tell about such things, then why not their successors? Bishop Dionysius was not impressed by the authority, in doctrinal matters, of himself or any other man upon the earth, including the bishop of Rome.

"When can we convince ignorant and uneducated people that among all the heresies, the Catholic Church has the correct faith and does not make mistakes?" asks Athanasius, aware that scriptural demonstrations, especially of the "spiritual" sort recommended by Bishop Dionysius, are not too convincing for the masses.[207] Now would be the time for Athanasius, one of the very greatest heroes of the Roman clergy, to come out with "thou art Peter." But he does nothing of the sort. Instead, he gives an astonishingly weak form of orthodoxy: The best way to convince the people of the preeminence of the Catholic Church is through teaching them about the holy places, where Christ did this or that. The holders of the holy places must be the true sect, says Athanasius, since God would not allow those places to fall into the hands of heretics.[208] What a last-resort argument! Another writing attributed to Athanasius opposes those who teach that things they are told should be believed outright on authority, without checking whether they are proper or improper.[209] But where is authority when he can talk like that?

---

206. Source unidentified.
207. ποίῳ δὲ τρόπῳ πείσομεν τὸν ἰδιώτην καὶ βάρβαρον, ὅτι ὑπὲρ πάσας τὰς αἱρέσεις ἡ καθολικὴ ἐκκλησία τὴν ὀρθὴν πίστιν ἔχει, καὶ οὐ σφάλλεται. Athanasius, *Doctrina ad Antiocham Ducem*, question 44, in *PG* 28:625.
208. Athanasius, *Doctrina ad Antiocham Ducem*, question 44, in *PG* 28:625.
209. Source unidentified.

In writing his famous report on the synods to the Western bishops in the middle of the fourth century, Hilary, bishop of Poitiers, justifies the liberty he takes by the great demands that have been made of him and by his inability in a crisis to keep silence: "I think it is [a] necessary and religious act for me to forward these colloquia to you as a bishop to bishops."[210] Great numbers of letters have been written to him by bishops asking for his report, and though he is "very unexpert and untaught," he acts boldly on his own authority to answer them.[211] Hilary uses a neat rhetorical device for discovering which of the more than seventy-two warring sects is the true one: They all fight against each other, he says, accusing each other of being heretics and thus mutually canceling each other out. But in one thing they agree—they all make war together against our church, and, since their mutual disagreements show them to be false, the common object of their opposition must be the true church. The problem with this argument, as a little reflection will show, is that it can be applied with equal validity by any sect. For if the churches are all fighting each other, then any one of them can say with perfect truth that all the others have the one thing in common—namely, that they are fighting it and that therefore it stands alone against them all and can be the only pure and undefiled one of the lot.[212]

Yielding to the urging that comes from bishops all over Europe, Hilary discloses that he has frequently sent them important doctrines, reports, and interpretations, without dreaming of consulting Rome.

> Fearing lest I be guilty, among such and so many bishops, of disastrous impiety or in peril of error: For as

---

210. *Necessarium mihi ac religiosum intellexi, at nunc quasi episcopus episcopis mecum in Christo communicantibus salutaris ac fidelis sermonis colloquia transmitterem.* Hilary, De Synodis 2, in PL 10:481.
211. Hilary, *De Synodis* 5, in *PL* 10:483.
212. Hilary, *De Synodis*, in *PL* 10:479–546.

THE OFFICE OF BISHOP IN ROME

> I have frequently signified to you in most of the cities of the Roman provinces what is being considered by our religious brethren the bishops of the East ... fearing lest either amidst the disastrous impiety of the larger number of bishops, or in the danger of error, assuming that your own silence came from the despair born of the awareness of pollution and impiety, I decided that I too should preserve silence before you (for I cannot deny that you have often been admonished to silence).[213]

He thinks it *necessarium* and *religiosum* to transmit the latest information to the bishops of the West, "as a bishop to a bishop." This is surely a most remarkable situation. This man is the main intermediary between the vast empires of the church in the East and West: all write to him directly for communication, and whether he communicates or not, what he says and how he says it is entirely his own decision. Whatever control there is of this vital intercourse lies entirely with Hilary, the bishop of Poitiers—not the bishop of Rome, who is not consulted one way or the other. In exactly the same spirit, in 375 some Cyprian monks wrote to Epiphanius, who was then a bishop in Cyprus, begging him to write against all the heresies. "Since not only these, but a great many others were appealing to him, as it were, forcing him to comply,"[214] Epiphanius was willing to make

---

213. *Constitutum mecum habebam, Fratres carissimi, in tanto silentii vestri tempore nullas ad vos ecclesiastici sermonis litteras mittere. Nam cum frequenter vobis ex plurimis Romanarum provinciarum urbibus significassem, quid cum religiosis fratribus nostris Orientis episcopis fidei studiique esset . . . ; verens ne in tanto ac tam plurium episcoporum calamitosae impietatis vel erroris periculo, taciturnitas vestra de pollutae atque impiatae conscientiae esset desperatione suscepta (nam ignorare vobis frequenter admonitis non licebat).* Hilary, *De Synodis* 1, in *PL* 10:480.

214. . . . περὶ τοῦ κατὰ αἱρέσεων πασῶν γράψαι· οὐ μὴν ἀλλὰ καὶ πολλῶν προτρεψαμένων, καὶ, ὡς εἰπεῖν, ἀναγκασάντων αὐτὸν εἰς τοῦτο ἥκειν. Acacius et Paulus, *Epistola ad Epiphanium*, in *PG* 41:156.

use of learned men's services and would commission them to write. If there were a head of the church somewhere, he would have entreated him. That is the way it would be done if there were a head of the church, but that is never the way it was done.

Hilary is in exactly the same position as the apostolic fathers and their successors—all of whom taught because they could not restrain themselves and not by any special commission. But who gives such a commission? "The aging Bishop Augustine," wrote Hans von Campenhausen, "became for the Latin world the authority—all churches and theologians of the West turn to him for information and advice. The question of freedom and grace was his special interest, but he died before he solved it."[215] Had Augustine been commissioned by God rather than chosen by men to solve the deep and distressing doctrinal questions of the church, he could not possibly have died before he solved the four gravest and most burning questions. In fact, he would not have "solved" them at all—that, says Justin, is the method of philosophers, but the church's questions are solved by prophets, who operate in an entirely different manner.[216]

Again we return to the claims of the Roman Church—that one see alone was established for the specific purpose that men might appeal to it with "the more important and difficult problems of doctrine."[217] Why didn't people turn to Rome then? Why didn't Augustine himself? Why did he

---

215. "Der alternde Bischof Augustin ist für die lateinische Welt die Autorität geworden—alle Kirchen und Theologen des Abendlandes wenden sich an ihn um Auskunft und Rat. Doch diese eine Frage nach Freiheit und Gnade ist in der letzten Epoche seines Lebens für ihn selbst schlechterdings die entscheidende Frage geworden." Hans von Campenhausen, "Augustin als Kind und Überwinder seiner Zeit," *Die Welt als Geschichte: Eine Zeitschrift für Universalgeschichte* 13 (1953): 9.

216. Justin Martyr, *Cohortatio ad Graecos* 8, in *PG* 6:256–57.

217. Von Campenhausen, "Augustin als Kind und Überwinder seiner Zeit," 9.

not refer his questioners to Rome? On occasion he did send them on a pilgrimage to the tomb of St. Felix near Milan.[218] He knew all about Rome—it was his old stamping grounds, but in his mighty wrestling with the great problems of theology to which his personal solutions were to remain the authoritative ones for all time, it never occurred to him that there he might find his answer. When during many years he sought desperately for someone—anyone—who would give him an authoritative and convincing exposition of Christian doctrine, he never thought of going to what is now put forth as the fountainhead, as he certainly would have done had that fountainhead existed in his day. It also did not occur to Augustine's great contemporary, Jerome, who knew of no ultimate authority on the question of doctrines: "I know that the most learned men have disputed this question from various sides, and each one has declared what he has thought correct according to his lights and understanding. Since therefore it is a dangerous thing to judge among the opinions of the teachers of the church, and to prefer one to another, I will report what each one says and leave it to the judgment of the reader which opinion should be followed."[219] Another double insult to Rome, and this time by the author of the Vulgate: (1) In all the church there is no authority whose opinion is to be preferred to another's, and so (2) the individual reader is free to decide for himself.

Socrates tells how "the apostles had many differences of doctrine to deal with in their own times, and since they knew these would be the cause of great disturbances among the gentiles, they all came together and formulated the holy

---

218. Augustine, *Epistola* 78.3, in *PL* 33:268–69.
219. *Scio de hac quaestione ab eruditissimis viris variae disputatum, et unumquemque pro captu ingenii sui dixisse quod senserat. Quia igitur periculosum est de magistrorum Ecclesiae judicare sententiis, et alterum praeferre alteri, dicam unusquisque senserit, lectoris abritrio derelinquens, cuius expositionem sequi debent.* Jerome, *Commentariorum in Danielam Liber 9*, in *PL* 25:542.

law.... But the teachings of this letter were distorted and the injunctions of the apostles held as a thing of naught."²²⁰ As a result, he says, there are hardly two churches in the world today who have the same rites, observances, and doctrine. Here he claims that the apostles confided all their doctrinal instructions and authority not to a personal successor, but to a letter, and that when the letter failed to work, the result was chaos. This completely rules out any awareness on the part of Socrates, a major historian, that the apostles left any special successor to control such matters. In preserving doctrine, Jonkers notes, the church tries to follow Paul's directions, but by 585 Paulus Relagius can write: "And though many instructions are taught by the authority of subtlety, still the defect of our times, in which not only the merits but the very bodies of men are failing, does not allow censure of this limitation in all things."²²¹

Establishing a Connection with Peter— A Return to Matthew 16:18

In the Vatican excavations of recent years, the announced intent of discovering definite ties with Peter has something of a last-ditch determination about it. This air of finality is matched by the distressing finality of the results. "It appears," writes Paul Lemerle, summing up the evidence, "that there is no chance of possessing a tomb or any *authentiques reliques* of Peter. The Vatican excavations ... might well have established whether there was a tomb and relics, authentic or not."²²²

---

220. ἐπεὶ γὰρ ἔγνωσαν οἱ ἀπόστολοι ταραχὴν ἐκ τῆς διαφωνίας τῶν ἐθνῶν κινουμένην τοῖς πιστεύουσι, πάντες ἅμα γενόμενοι θεῖον νόμον ἐθέσπισαν.... ἀντιστρέψαντες μὲν τὰ τοῦ θεοῦ παραγγέλματα ... παρ' οὐδὲν δὲ τὴν τῶν ἀποστόλων νομοθεσίαν τιθέμενοι. Socrates Scholasticus, *Historia Ecclesiastica* 5.22, in *PG* 67:641–44.

221. Source unidentified.

222. "Il semblait ... que nous n'avions aucune chance de posséder un tombeau ou des reliques authentiques de Pierre. Les fouilles du Vatican

The world is never allowed to forget that the foundation and stay of the whole Roman position is that verse of scripture that adorns the highest circle of the interior of the dome of St. Peter's in a convenient mistranslation and in letters of heroic size. In the nineteenth century, the Protestant attacks on Matthew 16:18 were all aimed at showing that those words were very probably never spoken by Christ. The most powerful argument in favor of that theory is Adolf von Harnack's observation that until the middle of the third century no one ever quotes that all-important verse. Yet it is precisely because Christ did speak those words that the silence of the early centuries is so thunderous. The fact that no one thinks to cite Matthew 16:18 through three long centuries of ferocious controversy on the subject of authority does not prove that those words were not available to the early fathers, but it does most emphatically prove that those fathers did not see in those words the organic franchise of an established church. That high and holy matters are under discussion in this important conversation, of which we have only a few broken fragments in Matthew 16, is apparent to all; that the three gospels have no intention of revealing to the world what these matters were should be equally apparent—if only from the strict injunction to silence placed upon the apostles at the time.

From the Christian point of view, Protestant as well as Catholic, the important passage is not "thou art Peter," but "the gates of hell shall not prevail." For while no one has been able to establish historical connection with Peter, the statement about the gates of hell seems a general and unequivocal promise that the church will go forth invulnerable, from which we cannot avoid the conclusion that the church is not only to continue "firm and steadfast until the end of the world,"[223] but that it actually has in the end nothing to

---

... pourraient bien avoir établi qu'il n'y a ni tombeau ni reliques, authentiques ou non." Paul Lemerle, "Les fouilles de Saint-Pierre de Rome," *La Nouvelle Clio* 2 (1950): 411.

223. See Nibley, *Mormonism and Early Christianity*, 293.

fear. "The gates of hell" is quoted as often and as fervidly by Baptists as by the Catholics themselves, and that to prove that their church, marked by its "trail of blood," must have persisted through the ages from the time of Christ. But does the magnificent assurance of the "gates of hell" hint at anything as poor as an intermittent trail of blood? Just what is meant by the peculiar expression, "the gates of hell shall not prevail against it"? That is the all-important question for both Catholics and Protestants—a question which they never examine.

Once the meaning of the phrase "gates of hell" is clear, it is equally clear why no one in the first centuries of the church ever referred to that verse to prove that the church would survive or to show where its head would be. It has nothing to do with the future of the church on earth but refers to a high and secret matter about which the second century of the church knew nothing. That explains why it is never referred to *at all*. It is one of those "teachings of the elders," which, Irenaeus informs us, his generation regarded as "rather mysterious" and could not hope to explain. "In the second century," Harnack discovers, "not a single church father or heretic made any reference to this verse (Matthew 16:18), even in those cases in which one would, in view of its context, expect such a reference. Tertullian and the author of the Clementine homilies are the first to attest it."[224] In this case the Clementine author does not use the word *petra* at all, but instead writes *foundations*.[225] But what, in this earliest reference, could the foundation of the church

---

224. "Im zweiten Jahrhundert hat kein Kirchenvater oder Häretiker auf diesen Vers angespielt, auch dort nicht, wo man nach dem Context eine Anspielung erwartet. Erst Tertullian und der Verfasser der clementinischen Homilien bezeugen ihn." Adolf von Harnack, "Die Acta Archelai und das Diatessaron Tatians," *Texte und Untersuchungen zur Geschichte der altchristlichen Literatur* 1/3 (1883): 150.

225. θεμέλιος. Clement, *Epistola ad Jacobum* 1, in *PG* 2:33.

have been; what was meant by "the rock"? Two of the most distinguished theologians of the fourth century, Hilary and Basil, both say the rock was revelation—the others do not mention it.

Erasmus's marginal note in Hilary's comment on Matthew 16:18, *Ecclesiae fundamentum fides*, is fully borne out by Hilary's own text: "The Son of God the Heavenly Father refers to revelation. O happy foundation for the announcement of the new name of the church!"[226] Elsewhere Hilary writes: "Peter confesses that Christ is the Son of God. This faith is the foundation of the church: through this faith the gates of the lower regions are made weak against her. This faith holds the keys of the kingdom of heaven. This faith will bind in heaven and earth. This faith is the guarantee of revelation from the Father. . . . This is the revelation of the Father; this is the eternal security."[227] Not a word about any geographical conditioning of a grant of power, no dwelling on the name of Peter. "It is this [confession of Peter]," writes Basil, "which is the true rock of piety."[228]

Hermann Strack and Paul Billerbeck, collecting all the New Testament commentaries contained in the Talmud and Midrash, give what scholars consider the best, that is, the most likely rendering of Matthew 16:18 in the original Aramaic, the language that Jesus would have spoken, and translate the passage: "I also tell thee, even thee, Peter [repeated purely for emphasis]: Upon this rock (upon the fact of my

---

226. *Sed Dei filium coelestis patris revelatione conspiciens. . . . O in nuncupatione novi nominis felix Ecclesiae fundamentum.* Hilary, *In Evangelium Matthaei Commentarius* 16.7, in *PL* 9:1009–10.

227. *Haec fides, Ecclesiae fundamentum est: per hanc fidem infirmes adversus eam sunt portae inferorum. Haec fides regni coelestis havet claves. Haec fides quae in terris solverit aut ligaverit, et ligata in coelis sunt et soluta. Haec fides paternae revelationis est munus. . . . Haec revelatio Patris est . . . haec securitas aeternitatis est.* Hilary, *De Trinitate* 6.37, in *PL* 10:187–88.

228. αὕτη γὰρ ἀληθῶς τῆς εὐσεβείας ἡ πέτρα. Basilius Seleuciensis, *Oratio* 25.4, in *PG* 85:297.

Messianic calling and my being the Son of God) I will build my society."[229] "This interpretation is strengthened," Olof Linton tells us, "by the fact that elsewhere in the primitive church it is always Christ and not Peter who is the foundation of the church."[230] "The *Tu es Petrus*," Goguel writes, very much to the point, "does not contain any of the ecclesiastical theories that have been subsequently discovered. It does not justify the authority either of bishops in general or of Rome in particular. It expresses only the fact that the church rests on faith in the resurrection of Jesus and that Peter is the one who, when Christ appeared, had the first revelation of the resurrection, the revelation without which the faith in Jesus would not have survived his death."[231]

In his massive work, *Tu es Petrus*, G. Jacquemet has supplied impressive illustrations of the desperate ends to which defenders of the Roman claim must go to make out a case. Peter's reply and the Lord's reply are, he says, "like a diptych, an intentional parallelism, in which on the one hand Peter confessed the greatness of Christ, while on the other, Jesus

---

229. "Auch ich sage dir, ja dir, Petrus (sage ich es, weil du als erster meine Messiaswürde und meine Gottessohnschaft bekannt hast): Auf diesem Felsen (auf der Tatsache meiner Messiaswürde und meiner Gottessohnschaft) will ich meine Gemeinde bauen." Hermann L. Strack and Paul Billerbeck, *Kommentar zum neuen Testament aus Talmud und Midrash* (Munich: Beck, 1922), 1:732.

230. "Diese Deutung empfiehle sich auch deshalb, weil sonst in der alten Kirche immer Christus und nicht Petrus das Fundament der Kirche ist." Olof Linton, *Das Problem der Urkirche in der neueren Forschung: Eine kritische Darstellung* (Uppsala: Almquist and Wiksells, 1932), 170.

231. "Le *Tu es Petrus* ne contient aucune des théories ecclésiastiques qu'on y a successivement découvertes. Il ne justifie l'autorité ni des évêques en général, ni de celui de Rome en particulier. Il exprime seulement le fait que l'Église repose sur la foi à la résurrection de Jésus et que c'est Pierre qui, dans sa christophanie, a eu le premier la révélation de la résurrection, révélation sans laquelle la foi en Jésus n'aurait pas survécu à la passion." Goguel, *Jésus et les Origines du Christianisme*, 203.

THE OFFICE OF BISHOP IN ROME   227

proclaims the future greatness of Peter."²³² But the essence of diptych and parallelism is in the equality of the members, and there is nothing parallel about the tremendous, immeasurable inequality of glory that must be between these two. If Jacquemet is right and the Lord is really matching glory with glory and power with power, then his glory in heaven can be matched by only one thing—his glory on earth—not Peter's! "It is true," says Jacquemet, "that not a single textual citation of the central part of verse 18 exists before Tertullian. But that is so in the case of a very great number of New Testament verses."²³³ But when the verse in question happens to be put forward as the foundation of the church and the most important verse in all the Bible, that silence becomes most significant. And when that silence covers two hundred years of controversy on the particular subject of authority, and a desperate quest for some central head or authority in the church, it becomes fatal. The silence does not mean that the verse is interpolated, as Harnack argued, but it does mean at the very least that the verse was not regarded in the early church as addressing the key problem of authority.²³⁴

Then Jacquemet comments on the question, "Why does Mark (and hence Luke) omit 'Tu es Petrus?'"²³⁵ Jacquemet's

---

232. "D'un côté, Pierre confesse la grandeur du Christ. De l'autre, Jésus proclame la grandeur future de Pierre. Il y a là, comme dans un diptyque, un parallélisme intentionnel qui ne permet pas d'isoler nos trios versets." G. Jacquemet, *Tu es Petrus* (Paris: Bloud et Gay, 1934), 5.

233. "Certes, il n'existe avant Tertullien (*Pud.* 22) aucune citation textuelle de la partie centrale du verset 18. Mais c'est le cas d'un très grand nombre de versets du Nouveau Testament." Jacquemet, *Tu es Petrus*, 8; Tertullian, *De Pudicitia* 22, in *PG* 2:1080–84.

234. Adolf von Harnack, "Der Spruch über Petrus als den Felsen der Kirche (Matth. 16, 17f)," *Sitzungsberichte der Preussischen Akademie der Wissenschaften, Berlin* (1918): 652–53.

235. "Comment ces deux evangelists, surtout Marc, «l'interprète de Pierre», ont-ils pu ignorer ou négliger et la belle profession de foi faite par l'apôtre: «Tu es le Christ, le Fils du Dieu vivant» et la magnifique promesse du Sauveur: «Tu es Pierre»?" Jacquemet, *Tu es Petrus*, 10.

answer: because Peter "out of humility, would have omitted anything that might be to his praise."[236] But Peter did not write the Gospel; Mark, Peter's greatest admirer, did—and that after his death! There are plenty of praiseworthy things about Peter in the Gospels. If the Lord's commission to Peter is what the Romans say it is, this is no time for a pretty showing of bashfulness. The whole foundation of the church depends on Mark's testimony; to hold back at such a time is nothing short of betrayal of a trust. Does Clement, for all his stammering and blushing as Peter seats him on his throne, fail to declare his own calling in the letters attributed to him? "Mark does not insist on the organization of the church and so says nothing about it," says Jacquemet. "To suppose that Mark must have given in detail the origins of the history of the church . . . is a pretension devoid of all critical sense."[237] But to suppose that Mark would not have given such a detailed account in an official history of Peter is even more difficult. Does not Jacquemet's claim hold equally true of Matthew, who tells almost the same story as Mark and Luke do, and has far less reason for glorifying Peter? That Mark in his short history should introduce and quote the very conversation which culminated in the promise to Peter without so much as hinting at the purpose of the whole conversation is a proposition not only "devoid of all critical sense" but devoid of any sense at all.

Emperors, Popes, Synods, and Rome

The ways in which synods and emperors figure in discussions of authority through the centuries are quite incon-

---

236. "Par humilité, aurait omis tout ce qui était à sa louange." Jacquemet, *Tu es Petrus*, 11.

237. "Marc n'insiste pas sur l'orginisation de l'Église. . . . Estimer que Marc aurait dû detailer les origines historiques de l'Église . . . c'est une prétention dénuée pour le moins de sens critique." Jacquemet, *Tu es Petrus*, 11.

ceivable. Had there been a widespread tradition of a central religious authority anywhere in the church, had there been even a pretense of such authority, Cardinal Bellarmin would not have had to struggle and struggle in vain to show that in theory, at least, it is the pope who summons general synods. The real question, says Hefele, of "who in fact called the general synods or who participated in the calling of the same must be answered thus: the first eight general synods were summoned by the emperors, whereas all later ones were approved and subscribed by the popes; but even in the former instances there appears a certain participation of the popes in the convocation, which in separate cases is sometimes more and others less conspicuous."[238] This Roman Catholic bishop does his best to make a case for papal convocation, but what comfort is there in an "indication" that popes participated more or less, when other great bishops were equally active in the convocations? Or what satisfaction in admitting papal supremacy from the ninth council on? That is a late hour for asserting a rule that is supposed to date directly in immutable organization and full majesty from the days of the apostles.

Hefele then lists the reasons for calling a universal synod: "(1) In case of a dangerous heresy or synod; (2) when two popes stand opposed to each other, and it is doubtful which of them is the correct one; (3) for a common undertaking against the enemies of the Christian name; (4) when the pope stands in suspicion of heresy or other grave offenses;

---

238. "Le point important est du reste de determiner qui peut *en fait* convoquer des conciles *œcuméniques* ou qui peut coopérer à leur convocation? et voici la response: Les huit premiers conciles œcuméniques furent convoqués et promulgués par les *empereurs*, ceux qui suivirent le furent par les *papes*. Ces derniers participèrent cependant dans une certaine mesure à la convocation des premiers conciles œcuméniques et dans certains cas particuliers leur cooperation s'est manifestée d'une manière plus ou moins visible." Hefele, *Histoire des Conciles d'Après les Documents Originaux*, 1:13, emphasis in original.

(5) when the cardinals cannot or will not proceed with a papal election; (6) when it is a question of reforming the church at the head and in its members."[239] In all these situations, as at all councils, the main aim is ever, according to Hefele, "to advance the good of the church through a general consultation with its shepherds."[240] Reflection on each of these points will show that at least five of the six contingencies requiring a general synod would be impossible if there were in the Roman Church a divinely established head and a proper order of succession. Hefele further defines the ecumenical council as a meeting of the bishops of all provinces summoned and bound under the presidency of the pope or his legates[241]— which completely rules out the first eight synods.

One of the earliest synods of Rome mentioned by Joannes Dominicus Mansi is described as "a divine and holy local synod assembled in Rome, by the most blessed Anicetus the pope of that place, and by Polycarp the holy martyr and bishop of Smyrna, and ten other bishops."[242] Even though this passage is a forgery, the identical formula is given in

---

239. "1° s'il s'est produit une hérésie grave ou un schisme; 2° si deux papes étant en presence on ne peut discerner quell est le veritable; 3° s'il s'agit de décréter une enterprise universelle contre les ennemis du nom chrétien; 4° si le pape est soupçonné d'hérésie ou d'autres manquements plus graves; 5° si les cardinaux ne peuvent ou ne veulent procéder à l'élection d'un pape, et enfin 6° s'il s'agit d'une réforme de l'Église dans la personne de son chef ou de ses members." Hefele, *Histoire des Conciles d'Après les Documents Originaux*, 1:13.

240. "La recherché du bien de l'Église par une délibération commune de ses pasteurs." Hefele, *Histoire des Conciles d'Après les Documents Originaux*, 1:9.

241. Hefele, *Histoire des Conciles d'Après les Documents Originaux*, 1:4.

242. Σύνοδος θεία καὶ ἱερὰ τοπικὴ ἐν Ῥώμῃ συναθροισθεῖσα ἀπὸ τοῦ μακαριωτάτου Ἀνικήτου, τοῦ ταύτης πάπα, καὶ Πολυκάρπου ἱερομάρτυρος ἐπισκόπου Σμύρνης; *Synodus divina et sancta provincialis, Romae congregata a beatissimo Aniceto, ejusdem urbis papa, et Polycarpo sancto martyre Smyrnae episcopo, aliisque episcopis decem.* Joannes Dominicus Mansi, *Sacrorum Conciliorum Nova et Amplissima Collectio* (Graz: Akademische Druck- und Verlagsanstalt, 1960), 1:686.

Mansi, with different names and bishops, of course, for the synods of Jerusalem, Caesarea, Lyons, Corinth, etc., so that his description not only gives no precedence to the bishop of Rome, but by specifically describing him as "the bishop of that place" rules out any idea of the high and mighty authority that is now supposed by some to have become his as bishop of the whole church. It is as if one were to introduce the vice president of the United States presiding in the Senate as a notary public. Soon after this we read in Mansi's work a long epistle from the patriarchs of the West to the patriarchs of the East regarding the election of an archbishop for "all of Assyria, Medea, and Persia," yet this document, so vital for the whole church, East and West, contains no mention of Rome.[243]

The absence of any awareness of a head in the church, even as a tradition, comes out in such statements as that of Athanasius, that "even though the fathers of both synods [Nicaea and Antioch] held conflicting opinions regarding the *homoousios*, we must not for that reason split up on one side or the other, but rather try to reconcile them."[244] But whose business should it be to bring such a reconciliation? Where is the head of the church? Speaking of the Middle Ages in general, Frederick Powicke writes: "The Pope himself was not secure, for he was bound by the decisions of the fathers and the great councils. He might err; he might be condemned for heresy. His moral lapses, his administrative errors, it is true, were matters for God alone [Bishop Hefele did not think so], but the most unflinching papalists were agreed that his dogmatic errors were a matter for the Church."[245] If we look back to the

---

243. Mansi, *Sacrorum Conciliorum Nova et Amplissima Collectio*, 1:705–8.

244. οὕτως εἰ ἀμφοτέρων τῶν συνόδων οἱ Πατέρες διαφόρως ἐμνημόνευσαν περὶ τοῦ ὁμοουσίου, οὐ χρὴ πάντες ἡμᾶς διαφέρεσθαι πρὸς αὐτοὺς, ἀλλὰ . . . πάντως εὑρήσομεν ἀμφοτέρων τῶν συνόδων τὴν ὁμόνοιαν. Athanasius, *De Synodis* 45, in PG 26:772.

245. Frederick M. Powicke, *The Christian Life in the Middle Ages and Other Essays* (Oxford: Clarendon, 1935), 28.

most significant surviving account of the organization of the primitive church, the *Didache*, we read that a prophet was to be tested by his life, but not by his doctrines.[246] How the tables are neatly reversed: the man's life is his own business, but his doctrines are subject to review.

Claims of Apostolic Succession

Vogels's list of *Ante-Nicene Texts referring to the Roman Primacy*[247] is feeble and far-fetched in the extreme, but even less convincing is Batiffol's discussion, "Recourse to Rome in the Orient before the Council of Chalcedon."[248] The earliest instance of such recourse is that of Athanasius. Denzinger goes back to the sources to prove that Peter had successors: the bull *Unam Sanctam* of 1302 is given as the main proof; the two other sources date from A.D. 1351 and 1520.[249] The fact that the Roman claims are stated so clearly and boldly in these documents makes it all the more significant that they are the first.

Nothing more completely refutes the claim to the existence in postapostolic times of a central head in the church than those descriptions of church organization and succession in the earliest apologists, which are commonly put forward in support of the claim. First, there is the significant fact that the earliest fathers, when referring to the church as an organization, confine themselves not to speaking about "the church" at all, but always use the plural, "churches." "The apostles," says *1 Clement*, "foresaw the difficulties that would arise regarding the office of bishop everywhere" and so made a special ruling regarding the successions of the

---

246. *Didache* 11.11.
247. Heinrich Vogels, *Textus Antenicaeni ad Primatum Romanum Spectantes*, Florilegium Patristicum tam Veteris quam Medii Aevi Auctores Complectens 9, ed. Bernhard Geyer and Johannes Zellinger (Bonn: Hanstein, 1937).
248. Batiffol, *Cathedra Petri*, 215–48.
249. Denzinger, *Enchiridion Symbolorum*, items 466, 570d, 766.

bishops in the churches which they established.[250] The rule, as Clement's own experience attests, was not very effective, and he himself can only give the rather lame advice that "it is our opinion that those appointed by them [the apostles] or afterwards by other eminent men, with the consent of the whole church . . . and who have for a long time possessed the good opinion of all, cannot justly be dismissed from the ministry."[251]

"As the book of Acts shows," writes Socrates, "the apostles were aware of many differences in their own times already, and since the apostles knew these would be the cause of great disturbance among the gentiles, they all came together and formulated the holy law, which they wrote down in the form of a letter, by which the church of their time was freed from such terrible affliction and troubles. . . . But the teachings of this letter were distorted, and the injunctions of the apostles held as a thing of naught," with the result that Socrates can report from personal observation that it would be hard to find any two churches with the same Easter rites, fasting, ordinances, etc.[252] Surely there was a better way of directing the future of the church—namely, through a continuation of its apostolic head, and we can be perfectly sure that that way would have been followed if the apostles had believed or expected for a moment that the church was designed to remain

---

250. καὶ οἱ ἀπόστολοι . . . ἔγνωσαν . . . ὅτι ἔρις ἔσται ἐπὶ τοῦ ὀνόματος τῆς ἐπισκοπῆς. Clement, *Epistola Primera ad Corinthios* 44.1, in *PG* 1:296–97.

251. τοὺς οὖν κατασταθέντας ὑπ' ἐκείνων ἢ μεταξὺ ὑφ' ἑτέρων ἐλλογίμων ἀνδρῶν, συνευδοκησάσης τῆς πάσης . . . μεμαρτυρημένους τε πολλοῖς χρόνοις ὑπὸ πάντων, τούτους οὐ δικαίως νομίζομεν ἀποβάλλεσθαι τῆς λειτουργίας. Clement, *Epistola Primera ad Corinthios* 44:3, in *PG* 1:297–300.

252. ὡς μαρτυρεῖ ἡ βίβλος τῶν Πράξεων. ἐπεὶ γὰρ ἔγνωσαν οἱ ἀπόστολοι ταραχὴν ἐκ τῆς διαφωνίας τῶν ἐθνῶν κινουμένην τοῖς πιστεύουσι, πάντες ἅμα γενόμενοι θεῖον νόμον ἐθέσπισαν, ἐν τύπῳ ἐπιστολῆς καταγράψαντες· δι' οὗ τῆς βαρυτάτης μὲν περὶ τῶν τοιούτων δουλείας τε καὶ ἐρεσχελίας τοὺς πιστεύοντες ἠλευθέρωσαν. . . . ἀντιστρέψαντες μὲν τὰ τοῦ θεοῦ παραγγέλματα . . . παρ' οὐδὲν δὲ τὴν τῶν ἀποστόλων νομοθεσίαν τιθέμενοι. Socrates Scholasticus, *Historia Ecclesiastica* 5.22, in *PG* 67:641–44.

on earth. Imagine confining all their instructions to a letter. Clement here is as vague and helpless as Socrates.

The Argument of Diffusion

At a time when the church was swarming with heresies so clever and convincing that only an expert could possibly detect them, Irenaeus took upon himself the task of proving to a perplexed world which of many conflicting sects was the right one. "The true gnosis," he says, "which is the teaching of the apostles and the original system common to the church throughout the world and the character of the body of Christ after the successions of the bishops, transmitted to each of them as the church was set up in his particular place, has come down to us." He goes on to say that this treasure takes the form of "the legitimate interpretation of the scriptures," which, he says, is "more precious than the gnosis, more glorious than the gift of prophecy, super eminent above all other gifts of the spirit."[253] Which shows, incidentally, how much more highly the churchmen esteemed a dead prophet than a living one and preferred intellectual exercises to direct revelation. But how does Irenaeus prove the divinity and correctness of the doctrine of his church? "The church," he writes, "although it is scattered abroad throughout all the inhabited world, still since it received its faith teachings from the apostles and from their disciples," teaches the same as we do.[254] "This teaching was accepted by the church, though

---

253. γνῶσις ἀληθής, ἡ τῶν ἀποστόλων διδαχή, καὶ το ἀρχαῖον τῆς ἐκκλησίας σύστημα κατὰ παντὸς τοῦ κόσμου. This is all that exists of the Greek text; the full Latin text follows: *Agnitio vera est apostolorum doctrina et antiquus Ecclesia status, in universo mundo et character corporis Christi secundum successiones episcoporum, quibus illi eam, quae in unoquoque loco est, Ecclesiam tradiderunt: quae pervenit usque ad nos custoditione sine fictione Scripturarum tractatio plenissima . . . quod est pretiosius quam agnitio gloriosius autem quam prophetia, omnibus autem reliquis charismatibus supereminentius.* Irenaeus, *Contra Haereses* 4.33.7, in *PG* 7:1077–78.

254. ἡ μὲν γὰρ ’Εκκλησία, καίπερ καθ’ ὅλης τῆς οἰκουμένης ἕως περάτων τῆς γῆς διεσπαρμένη, παρὰ δὲ τῶν ’αποστόλων, καὶ τῶν ἐκείνων μαθητῶν παραλαβοῦσα τὴν . . . πίστιν. Irenaeus, *Contra Haereses* 1.10.1, in *PG* 7:549.

THE OFFICE OF BISHOP IN ROME

scattered in all parts of the world, and carefully guarded as if dwelling in a single house. And believing uniformly in these matters, as having one soul and one and the same heart, and with perfect harmony it announces these things and teaches them ... as if speaking with a single mouth. And though various languages prevail throughout the world there is but a single and uniform force to this tradition. Neither the Germans, the Iberians, the Celts, the Egyptians, the Libyans, nor those in the middle of the world teach otherwise. But like the sun, God's creature, it is everywhere equal and the same."[255] And again: "But those of the true church, though they are spread around the entire world, all have the same doctrine of the Father, since they have the firm tradition from the apostles, and this gives us all a remarkably uniform faith."[256]

This is Irenaeus's one crushing argument against the heretics, his one conclusive proof. And it derives its entire force from the fact that widely scattered churches preach identical doctrines even when there has been no collusion among them. If there were a central head to bring the churches into harmony, then the argument would be meaningless. Irenaeus insists that close agreement concerning doctrine among the churches can only be explained on one ground: that they all go back to the common apostolic origins. If we want to know what the true old teaching was, he says elsewhere, go to those churches in out-of-the-way

---

255. τοῦτο τὸ κήρυγμα παρειληφυῖα ... ἡ Ἐκκλησία, καίπερ ἐν ὅλῳ τῷ κόσμῳ διεσπαρμένη, ἐπιμελῶς φυλάσσει, ὡς ἕνα οἶκον οἰκοῦσα· καὶ ὁμοίως πιστεύει τούτοις, ὡς μίαν ψυχὴν καὶ τὴν αὐτὴν ἔχουσα καρδίαν, καὶ συμφώνως ταῦτα κηρύσσει, καὶ διδάσκει ... ὡς ἓν στόμα κεκτημένη. καὶ γὰρ αἱ κατὰ τὸν κόσμον διάλεκτοι ἀνόμοιοι, ἀλλ᾽ ἡ δύναμις τῆς παραδόσεως μία καὶ ἡ αὐτή. καὶ οὔτε αἱ ἐν Γερμανίαις ἱδρυμέναι Ἐκκλησία ἄλλως πεπιστεύκασιν, ἢ ἄλλως παραδιδόασιν, οὔτε ἐν ταῖς Ἰβηρίαις, οὔτε ἐν Κελτοῖς, οὔτε κατὰ τὰς ἀνατολάς, οὔτε ἐν Αἰγύπτῳ, οὔτε ἐν Λιβύῃ, οὔτε αἱ κατὰ μέσα τοῦ κόσμου ἱδρυμέναι· ἀλλ᾽ ὥσπερ ὁ ἥλιος, τὸ κτίσμα τοῦ θεοῦ, ἐν ὅλῳ τῷ κόσμῳ εἷς καὶ ὁ αὐτός. Irenaeus, *Contra Haereses* 1.10.2, in *PG* 7:552–53.

256. Irenaeus, *Contra Haereses* 1.10.1–2, in *PG* 7:549–52.

places, at the edges of the world, where the people are illiterate and so have preserved the faith intact in their hearts since the time of the apostles. This is the argument of diffusion, the very opposite of the argument of centralization. If the apostles had established a single official source and control for doctrine, that would, of course, be the thing to which Irenaeus would appeal to argue against the heretics setting up their own centers—it was to Rome, in fact, that much later fathers did appeal. But Irenaeus rests his whole demonstration on the proposition that the remarkable uniformity of doctrine found among churches scattered in all parts of the world is evidence for the apostolic origin of the doctrines in question since such widespread agreement can only be explained by looking back to the days of the apostles.[257] Jerome can still argue against the Jews that "the house of prayer is the church, which is divided in all parts of the world, and not the temple of the Jews, limited as it is to a single narrow spot."[258] Jerome did not know that four hundred years later High Mass would be confined to just one spot in the world and limited to the offices of but a single man—that is the very centralization which he here charges against the Jews.

Three hundred years after Irenaeus, Optatus tangles with a new brand of heresy and uses all the arguments of Irenaeus and more. His favorite argument is that the true church must be found throughout the whole world, while most heretic sects are local phenomena. Over and over he repeats: "Catholic means, *ubiqui diffusa.*"[259] Of course it means nothing of the sort; if he wants to press the meaning of *universal,* it does not mean "every*where*" but "every*body.*" But no one knows better than the raging Optatus that his church does not include everybody—that is why he is so perturbed. So he must insist that it means the church

---

257. Irenaeus, *Contra Haereses* 1.10.2, in *PG* 7:552.
258. *Domusque orationis Ecclesiae est, quae in toto orbe dividitur, et non Templum Judaeorum, quod brevissimis Judaeae terrae arctabantur angustiis.* Jerome, *Commentariorum in Isaiam Prophetam Liber* 15.66, in *PL* 24:542.
259. Source unidentified.

is everywhere and use that as his one unanswerable argument against heretical churches. But why the icy silence regarding Rome? That would be a stronger argument than the test of universal diffusion, but Optatus never uses it. "From every valley the catholic population is gathered," writes Jerome. "There are many congregations, but only one congregation, one church."[260] But while on this theme he never mentions wherein this miraculous unity resides: there is no word of Rome or Peter.

Let us hold a peaceful assembly as in the good old days, says Basil in a heartfelt appeal for leadership. "It was the price of the church in those days that from one end of the empire to the other the brethren of each church could come together with new controls and be fathers and brothers to each other. Today ... letters are sent out in the names of cities, and each society regards its neighbor with suspicion."[261] This clearly shows that the rise of the great city bishoprics was a phenomenon of the fourth century—a characteristic phenomenon of that power-made age—and that it was resented by the better men. "Since all who hoped in Christ make up a single people, and all of Christ's people today make up a single church, though named for different regions, the *patria* and the *oikonomia* of the Lord rejoice and will not believe that any one man can hold supreme authority, but that all things are managed by one church."[262] Basil recalls the doctrine that an angel went

---

260. Source unidentified.
261. τοῦτο γὰρ ἦν ποτε τῆς ἐκκλησίας τὸ καύχημα, ὅτι ἀπὸ τῶν περάτων τῆς οἰκουμένης ἐπὶ τὰ πέρατα μικροῖς συμβόλοις ἐφοδιαζόμενοι οἱ ἐξ ἑκάστης ἐκκλησίας ἀδελφοὶ πάντας πατέρας καὶ ἀδελφοὺς εὕρισκον· ὃ νῦν ... καὶ κατὰ πόλεις περιγεγράμμεθα, καὶ ἕκαστος δι' ὑποψίας ἔχομεν τὸν πλησίον. Basil, *Epistola* 191.1, in *PG* 32:704.
262. ἐπειδὴ δὲ εἷς λαὸς πάντες οἱ εἰς Χριστὸν ἠλπικότες, καὶ μία ἐκκλησία νῦν οἱ Χριστοῦ, κἂν ἐκ διαφόρων τόπων προσαγορεύηται, χαίρει καὶ ἡ πατρὶς καὶ εὐφραίνεται ταῖς τοῦ Κυρίου οἰκονομίαις, καὶ οὐχ ἡγεῖται ἕνα ἄνδρα ἐξημιῶσθαι, ἀλλὰ δι' ἑνὸς ἐκκλησίας ὅλας προσειληφέναι. Basil, *Epistola* 161.1, in *PG* 32:629.

about visiting the churches—"the angel of the churches," an interesting survival of the days of a traveling apostolate.[263]

Irenaeus repeats the doctrine of diffusion: The church received this doctrine and faith and carefully preserved it, though scattered throughout the entire world. Here again the operation of a central controlling head is ruled out, as if living in a single house. Yet the church believes these things as having a single soul and a single heart, preaching them harmoniously and transmitting them as if with a single mouth. Though our languages are different, the power of the tradition is one and the same, whether in Germany, Gaul, Iberia, Egypt, or Libya.[264] In his laborious attempts to bolster this argument with all sorts of rhetoric, Epiphanius displays the weakness of his position, yet never once does he use what would be the crushing argument to all heretic groups were it available: that the apostolic authority is still visibly operative and clearly located. What we have, says he, is a "firm agreement based on the Law, Prophets, gospels, apostles . . ."[265]

---

263. ὁ ἄγγελος ὁ τῆς ἐκκλησίας. Basil, *Epistola* 239.1, in *PG* 32:889.
264. Irenaeus, *Contra Haereses* 1.10.2, in *PG* 7:552–53.
265. Source unidentified.

Editors' Postscript

How Professor Nibley ended these lectures remains unknown. If he finished this course in his typical style, he offered no overall summation. He simply left these pieces of information on the table and let his students make whatever they could or would of them. He always remained open to further examination of old readings and the introduction of new data, and he welcomed criticisms. So, when the final class period came to an end, Nibley probably continued talking as the bell rang and as he walked out of the lecture hall, all the way across campus, and right back into the library.

How Nibley would have concluded these investigations one may infer quite certainly, however, by placing this exposition in the context of Nibley's larger concerns and broader views concerning the changes and losses that occurred during the early Christian centuries. Those views are most specifically presented in two publications, one in 1955 and the other in 1961, statements from which comprise a suitable postscript for these 1954 lectures.

In 1955, when the topic of these lectures was surely still on Nibley's mind, he published a multi-installment series in the *Improvement Era* entitled "The Way of the Church." His overall purpose in that series was to explain why the surviving records of the early Christian fathers do not give straightforward support to the idea of a great apostasy, with the obvious reason being that those who wrote and preserved the patristic writings were not inclined to tell much about any dark elements in their ecclesiastical story and thus those perspectives were either initially kept out of or later filtered out of the record. As part of Nibley's discussion of that problem in early church historiography, he briefly brought up the topic of apostles and bishops, particularly the issue of succession. Almost in passing (as if all of his readers were aware of what he had taught in the classroom the year before), he pointed out the following summation:

> But aren't we forgetting about Christ's "successors"? A "successor" is one who comes after and takes the place of another. To be a successor it is not enough merely to outlive another or come after him; one must hold his identical office and function. Even a regent is not successor to a king—only a king can be that; when a vice president takes over on the death of a president, he does not become his successor until he, too, is president. The scriptures never call the apostles Christ's successors; there is only one successor to the Lord mentioned in the Bible, and that is the Holy Ghost, "whom the Father will send in my name, he shall teach you all things, and bring all things to your remembrance, whatsoever I have said unto you" (John 14:26). Here is a true successor, coming expressly to take the Lord's place: "If I go not away, the Comforter will not come unto you; but if I depart, I will send him unto you" (John 16:7). Sent by the same authority, he will do the very same work, speak the identical words, be a witness for the judgment, and guide the apostles in all things exactly as the Lord had done (John 16:8–15).
>
> As for the disciples, the famous passage in Mark (13:34–37) describes them as servants left behind with authorization to do special jobs: the Lord "left his house, and gave to his servants the authority, to each one his task, and commanded the porter to watch." There is no

mention of supreme authority being given to anyone, but to each the authority for his particular work. The fact that every soldier in the army acts with the authority of the commander-in-chief does not give any one of them the fulness of authority that he possesses.[1]

Nibley's identification of consequences that flowed from the lack of true apostolic successors, so fully covered in these lectures, was not included in "The Way of the Church." Perhaps he minimized his discussion of that dimension because he had already covered it in depth in these lectures and thus felt confident in simply stating his end results. He did, however, reflect a little further on the question of how such an extensive loss could possibly have occurred. First, he pointed to some who were conscious betrayers from the inside: "Others died other ways, but the great danger comes from betrayal—the pagans can neither betray nor corrupt nor pervert the gospel; only members can do that."[2] But on further reflection, he allowed that much of this happened unawares:

> The great apostasy did not happen consciously. The mentally ill ("O foolish Galatians, who hath bewitched you"? [Galatians 3:1]) do not know what is wrong with them or when it happened. What the apostles denounce most strenuously in their letters is the complete complacency and self-satisfaction of the perverters: "Lovers of their own selves, covetous, boasters, proud. . . . Traitors, heady, highminded" (2 Timothy 3:2–4). No lack of assurance here!
>
> Like the slinging of a noose, the end comes silently, quietly, without warning, so that the victim never suspects what is happening, being the while wholly preoccupied with the "cares of this life" (Luke 21:34). It is not a process

---

1. *Mormonism and Early Christianity*, CWHN 4 (Salt Lake City: Deseret Book and FARMS, 1987), 273.
2. *Mormonism and Early Christianity*, 284.

of founding new institutions that the scriptures describe, but one of becoming: "love shall turn to hate," "evil men and seducers shall wax worse and worse" (2 Timothy 3:13), "iniquity shall increase," "the sheep of the fold shall turn into wolves" (*Didache*)—but go right on calling themselves sheep! The false claimants never give up, "Having a form of godliness, but denying the power thereof" (2 Timothy 3:5). The end was never formally declared (heaven forbid!); in the words of Polycarp, "the lights went out."[3]

With Polycarp, Nibley regretted that some of the most important and luminous lights of the gospel and priesthood authority went out in the early years of Christianity, but he was quick to remind readers that the world had been forewarned and that the early Christians should not have expected to be received by the world any more warmly than had been the Savior himself. In response to those who asked, "But even if the apostles were to suffer the same rejection and death as the master, is not the gloom of the 'second act' relieved by the survival of the church? What of the 'little children' whom they taught?" Nibley soberly replied, "Alas! they are given the same promise of extinction; they, too, are required to 'endure to the end' and are given the same comfort and promise—eternal life."[4]

Indeed, throughout these lectures and his other writings on early Christian history, Nibley was sparring intellectually with various antagonists. For example, he was keenly aware of one Catholic writer who had dismissively declared: "The failure of the Mormon spokesmen to explain when, where, and how the present Catholic Church was founded exposes the fatal weakness of their accusation" that a great apostasy had occurred. In response, Nibley was eager to show that "the New Testament is only one of many, many sources that clearly 'explain when, where, and how'

---

3. *Mormonism and Early Christianity*, 287–88.
4. *Mormonism and Early Christianity*, 279.

the Christian church completely changed its nature and the present churches came to be what they are."[5]

Nibley was quick to enlist to his aid unwitting allies from various camps. "Earnest investigators of church history, Catholic and Protestant alike," Nibley happily pointed out, "are discovering as it were for the first time the great gulf that lies between the ancient church and conventional Christianity, and being surprisingly frank in their comments. More and more they are forcing themselves also to face up to the dark interval of the second act," namely the foggy close of the apostolic era.[6] In tune with those scholarly observations, Nibley formulated questions and set an agenda for further Latter-day Saint engagement with this area of research:

> What, then, did happen after the apostles? Do we have reliable reports for the years following? Was it all bad? How did the Christians continue to think of the world and their position in it? Did they expect the lights to go out? Were they surprised when they did? Were they disappointed when the Lord failed to come? Did they believe that what was happening actually was the end? Such questions are the special food of church history in our day. The mere fact that they are being asked now as never before is an invitation to Latter-day Saints to enter the discussion which seems at last to be turning to their own point of view.[7]

Over the ensuing six years, Nibley continued to expand his repertoire of insights and arguments, formulating answers to these questions. Ultimately, in 1961 he published an arresting article, "The Passing of the Primitive Church: Forty Variations on an Unpopular Theme," in the prestigious journal *Church History*. His opening and closing remarks in that

---

5. *Mormonism and Early Christianity*, 284.
6. *Mormonism and Early Christianity*, 297.
7. *Mormonism and Early Christianity*, 298.

article serve as his final published word on the subject of the project that began with these 1954 lectures about the offices of apostle and bishop in the early church. In this final exposition, he introduced what he called the "somber theme" of the passing of the primitive church with these pointed questions and penetrating observations:

> Ever since Eusebius sought with dedicated zeal to prove the survival of the church by blazing a trail back to the apostles, the program of church history has been the same: "To give a clear and comprehensive, scientifically established view of the development of the visible institution of salvation founded by Christ." To describe it—not to question it. By its very definition church history requires unquestioning acceptance of the basic proposition that the church did survive. One may write endlessly about *The Infant Church, l'Eglise naissante, die Pflanzung der Kirche,* etc., but one may not ask why the early Christians themselves described their church not as a lusty infant but as an old and failing woman; one may trace the triumphant spread of *The Unquenchable Light* through storm and shadow, but one may not ask why Jesus himself insisted that the Light was to be taken away. Church history seems to be resolved never to raise the fundamental question of survival as the only way of avoiding a disastrous answer, and the normal reaction to the question—did the church remain on earth?—has not been serious inquiry in a richly documented field, but shocked recoil from the edge of an abyss into which few can look without a shudder.
>
> Yet today that question is being asked again, as it has been in other times of stress and crisis, not with the journalistic flourish of Soltau's *Sind wir noch Christen?* but with the cautious historical appraisal of an H. J. Schoeps, contemplating the age-old tension between eschatology and church with their conflicting ideas about the church's future. Can it be that the repugnance of churchmen to eschatology and their coolness toward the authentic writings of the early Fathers are due in no small part to the dim view which the primitive Christians took of the

prospects of the church? The purpose of this paper is to list briefly the principal arguments supporting the thesis that the church founded by Jesus and the apostles did not survive and was not expected to.[8]

Likewise, the purpose of this series of lectures was to marshal evidence supporting the more focused but similar thesis that the early Christian bishops did not, any sooner, succeed in filling the office that distinctively belonged to the apostles. Thus, Nibley's parting words at the end of "The Passing of the Primitive Church" may readily serve just as well as the final punctuation for this book of lectures: "We have indicated above some of the reasons for suggesting that the church, like its founder, his apostles, and the prophets before them, came into the world, did the works of the Father, *and then went out of the world*, albeit with a promise of return. Some aspects of the problem, at least, deserve closer attention than students have hitherto been willing to give them."[9]

John W. Welch
John F. Hall

---

8. *Mormonism and Early Christianity*, 168–69.
9. *Mormonism and Early Christianity*, 193–94.

Index

Aaronic priesthood, imitation of, 47
absolutions for money, 171
acclamatio, 79, 101
Acesius, Bishop, 143, 144
Adam, Karl, 180
Aix-la-Chapelle, 131
Alexandria, 90, 178
Alföldi, Andreas, 97, 180
Amt and *Geist*, opposition between, 3, 14
Anacletus
    decree of, 90
    letter of, 91
    spurious letters of, 195
ancient church and conventional Christianity, gulf between, 243
angels, visitations of, 24
Antioch, 88, 93, 178
    oldest of the churches, 182
apostasy, great, 240–42
apostle, office of, 7–13
    candidates for, 79
    general jurisdiction of, xiii
apostles
    assemblies of, 136
    authority of, 9, 27
    and bishops, separation of offices of, 29
    commission of, 187
    death of, xv
    divine gifts of, 25
    doctrinal teachings of, handed down, 148
    lack of successors for, 241
    meaning of term, 7, 8, 21
    passing of, 12, 202
    prophetic gift of, 21
    and prophets, importance of, 38, 157
    specially commissioned, xiv
    as special witnesses, 8
    succession of, 33, 232–34
    as traveling general authorities, 11
    unity of opinion among, 74
    work of, 7
apostolate, 3
    Jewish origin of, 43
apostolic authority, 238
    bestowal of, 30
    withdrawal of, 56
apostolic fathers, era of, xv–xvi
archbishop, 89
    spiritual supremacy of, 122
Arian controversy, 107
Arians, elimination of, 179
assemblies, apostolic, 136
Augustine and debtor, 78
authority
    apostolic, 137
    chain of, 106
    of the Christian church, 133
    in the churches, 111
    priesthood, loss of, 242
Auxerre, 128

Badcock, F. J., 95
baptism, 184

Batiffol, Pierre, 4, 12, 17, 18, 23, 41, 55, 134, 181, 195, 196, 232
Baynes, Norman H., 83, 85, 89
Berghampstead, 131
Billerbeck, Paul, 225
bishop
  age of, 64
  characteristics of, 66, 78
  church control over, 126
  as eyes of the Lord, 59
  importance of, based on importance of city, 85–89
  office of, 15–16, 151
    changes in, 61–74
    a city office, 83
    competition for, 207
    elective in nature, 101
    highest in church, 23
    Jewish model for, 55
    in the lower priesthood, 36–41
    nature and function of, 62
    and office of Aaron, 46
    Old Testament patterns of, 47
    origins of, 56–61
    rival candidates for, 56
    vying for, 111
  as a temporal king, 59
bishop lists, in the early Roman Church, xxi, 148, 158–63
bishop of Rome
  elections of, 164–73
  supremacy of, xiii
bishops, 13, 19
  advice of, xxiii, 102
  as aristocrats, 81
  authority of, 81, 113–14
  cities of, xvii–xviii
  commercial affairs of, 71
  duties of, xv, xviii
  equality of, 103–4, 176
  hierarchy of, 177
  installation of, 124
  jealousy and ambition of, 108
  judgment of, 66, 116–22, 200–201
  lack of life tenure for, 50
  length of term of, 21
  letters of, xxiv
  local jurisdiction of, xiii, 25
  ordination of, 49, 200
  plurality of, 63
  popularity of, 78, 80
  primacy of, xviii
  provincial meetings of, 86
  public election of, xviii
  qualifications and training of, 63
  responsibilities of, 65
  rival candidates for, 56
  Roman, 200
  secularization of, xvii
  as shepherds, 74
  spiritual functions of, 115
  as successors to the apostles, 23, 72
  temporal responsibilities of, xvii, 59, 122
  training of, 72–73
  universal meetings of, 135
  versus king, 126
Bligh, John, 94, 144, 184
Boniface, 131
Boniface II, 166
boundaries, ecclesiastical and political, xviii
Brandt, Theodor, 39
bull *Unam Sanctam*, xxiv, 83, 232

Callistus, 164
Calverly, Sir Hugh, 171
cardinal bishops, 173
cardinals, college of, 152, 173–75
Caspar, Erich, 161
catholic, meaning of term, 210
central authority, quest for, 227
centralization, argument of, 236

INDEX 249

children, dedication of, to religious life, 130
Christ, successors of, 240
Christian church, unique function of, 53
Christianity
    hierarchy of, in three degrees, 51
    Jewish sources of, 42–56
Christians versus pagans, 113
church
    authority of, 212–13
    central leadership of, 197–99
    departure and return of, 245
    general officers of, 11–13
    higher offices in, xv, 15
    influence on practices of, 54
    Jewish ideas in, 10
    joining of, 5
    lack of central control in, 100
    lack of leaders in, 209
    as a local community, 2
    organization of, 2, 55
    origin of, 4
    permanence of, 148
    rites and ordinances of, loss of, 57
    Roman leadership of, 191
    as a secular structure, 2
church councils, nature of, 136–44
churches
    disputations among, 56
    lack of unity among, 233
    practicality of, 2
    primacy of, xxii
church law, canons of, 124
churchmen versus nobility, 173
church officers after the resurrection, xiv
church offices, civic pattern of, 89
church organization
    development of, xiii–xiv
    origins of, 60
church property, 127, 129
church slaves, 127, 128, 129, 130
cities
    honor of, 78
    importance of, xviii
    leadership of, 75
    ranking of, xxii–xxiii
    size of, 126, 183
citizen, dignity of, 78
Clement
    ordination of, 158
    qualifications of, 153
    spurious letter of, xx, 152–57
    temporal preparation of, xxi
    writings and doings of, 163
clergy
    confined to one city, 124
    control by, 133
    corruption of, 110
    dispossession of, 112
    ordination of, 122
    responsibilities of, 112
Clermont, 131
communion, 128
congregations, obligations and duties of, 111
Consensus, 2–5
consensus theory, xiv
Constantine
    as bishop of bishops, 196
    as leader of the church, 85
    role of, 204–6
    as self-proclaimed bishop, xix
Constantinople, 95
    as center of Christianity, 97
    as New Rome, 182
controversies in the early church, 195–96
conversion, 144
Corinth as a Roman city, 192–94
Corinthians, affairs of, 189–90
Cornelius, 164
Coudenhove-Kalergi, Richard, 133
Council of Ancyra, 123

Council of Arles, 123, 137, 139
Council of Carthage, 135
Council of Cirta, 122
Council of Constantinople, 88, 89, 93
Council of Elvira, 40, 181
Council of Nicaea, xxii, 86, 124, 137
    account of, 140
    aftermath of, 206
    concluding speech at, 103, 176
    grouping of bishops at, 87
    opening session of, 109
    recognition of Jerusalem at, 88
    replica of senatorial sessions, 141–42
Council of Sardica, 94
Council of Seville, 134
Council of Trent, 195
councils
    hierarchy within, xviii
    imitations of the Roman Senate, 135–36
crimes, 115
Crusade, First, 167–69

Damasus, 164
    and rivalry with Liberius, 80
David, priestly power of, 44
deaconess, 53
    ordination of, 48
deacons, 13, 17, 19, 70
    as bishop's assistants, 62
Dead Sea Scrolls, 44
Deissmann, Adolf, 71
Denzinger, Heinrich, 159, 179, 232
Diaspora, 42
diffusion, argument of, 234–38
Dionysius, bishop of Corinth, 190
divine office, Roman origin of, 74–82
doctrine
    apostolic origins of, 213, 235
    lack of authority on, 221
    questions on, 207
Donatists, massacres of, 120

double apostolate, xxii, 95, 185–88
Duchesne, Louis, 12, 13, 25, 39, 41, 50, 81, 84, 93, 148, 179, 196
Dufourcq, Albert, 93

early church
    fate of, 52
    organization of, 1–6
Easter celebrations, 126
Easter controversy, 28, 199
ecclesiastical histories, xx
ekklesia, 2–3
elders, deeds and sayings of, 57
Emerita, 130
emperor
    as general authority, 105
    power of, 180
    public gifts of, 77
    role of, 118–19
emperors, synods summoned by, 228–29
Encaeniis, 125
Epaon, 126
episcopal authority, 26, 28, 41
    establishment of, 56
episcopal councils, xviii–xix
episcopal election, 208
episcopal equality, 87
episcopal hierarchy, 173–76
episcopal office
    apostolicity of, 198
    historic background of, 55
    Jewish origins of, xvii, 37, 58
episcopal priority, 107
episcopal seat as highest office in the city, 99
episcopal succession, 46
    in Rome, xxi
episcopate as successor to apostles, 14
episcopus, translation of, 201
excommunication, 126, 132

INDEX 251

faith, hope, and charity, 52
faith, uniform, 235
False Isidorian Decretals, 182
Felix, 164
Felix IV, 166
first ecumenical council, 134
fortune-tellers, 131
Froissart, Sir John, 170
fundamentals, disagreement on, 214–16

Gardthausen, Viktor E., 77
gates of hell, 223–24
general authorities
    absence of, 86
    disappearance of, 39
    importance of, 20
    search for, 102–11, 106
    traveling, 81
general conference, no authority to call, 204
gifts, removal of, 52
Goetz, K. G., 59
Goguel, Maurice, 162, 181, 226
gospel knowledge, transmission of, 209
gospel of bigness and power, 144–45
Greek tragedy, 74
Guidbert, 167–68

Harnack, Adolf von, xv, 4, 9, 10, 11, 14, 19, 20, 21, 63, 227
Hatch, Edwin, 2, 19
Hefele, Karl Joseph von, 136, 177, 229
heresies, combating, 219–20
heretics, punishment of, 132
hierarchy
    of church offices, 89
    rules of, 128
Hieraz, Judge, 203
high priest, office of, 46

Hippolytus, 164
Holl, Karl, 3, 7, 9, 10, 197
Holy Ghost, 70, 214
    function of, 20
    as successor, 240
holy places, holders of, 217
Holy See, purpose of, 214

Ignatius, 61
    installed as bishop in Antioch, 186
    rebukes of, to seven churches, 190
imperial favor, 111
independent movements, 112
Iorga, N., 97
Irenaeus, on apostolic authority, 202
isolation, effects of, 206

Jacquemet, G., 226
James, bishop of Jerusalem, 11, 60
    as local and general authority, xvi
    ordination of, 44, 49, 92
    as presiding bishop of the church, 31–36
    as type of all bishops, 88
Jerusalem, 13, 88, 92, 95
    the Holy City, 98
Jesus Christ, the Great High Priest, 48
Jews
    banishment of, 129
    treatment of, 130
John the Beloved, 9
Jülicher, Adolf, 181
Julius of Rome, 177, 205–6

Koch, Hugo, 41, 103, 181
Koester, Wilhelm, 4
Krüger, Gustav, 188

Ladner, Gerhart, 212
Lake, Kirsopp, 6, 157
Lateran IV, 132
Laurentius, 165
leadership
    appeal for, 237
    issues of, 104
Lechner, Joseph, 54
Leclercq, Henri, 4, 149
Lemerle, Paul, 222
Lenkeith, Nancy, 95
Leo, 166
letter of authority, 125
letters of Clement to James, 13
Liberius, 164
Lietzmann, Hans, 5, 6, 9, 42
Lightfoot, J. B., 1, 8
Linton, Olof, 2, 226
Lord, successor of, 147
lower priesthood
    authority of, 41
    functions of, 61

Macarius, 119
Macon, 128
Madrian, 166
majority opinion as God's
    opinion, 104
Manson, T. W., 6
Martin, Victor, 181
Mass, ritual and liturgy of, 54
Matalius, 166
Matthew 16:18, use of, to claim
    Roman preeminence, xxiv,
    222–28
Meyer, Eduard, 9, 58
Middle Ages, 60
    religious life in, 54
Migne, J.-P., 67
Milan, 93
    power of, 97
millennium, 216
Milman, 110

Mommsen, Theodor, 75
monastery, desertion of, 129
monks and marriage, 127
Morris, John, 106
mother church, 83, 203
moving to another city, 125

Narbonne, 128
Neocaesarea, 124
New Testament, interpretation
    of, 211
Nicomedia, bishop of, 93
Novatus, 164

ordination, Jewish pattern of, 45
Orleans, 126

Paderborn, 131
pagan rites, 131
papal chancellery, 79
papal succession, xxi, 173
    lack of, 169
papal supremacy, xxiv
Paraclete, 209
Paris, 127, 129
parousia, 6
patriarchs, 91, 121
Paul of Samosata, 113
peace of God, 131
people of God, 42
Peter
    as a general authority, 158
    keys of, 31
    in Rome, 31, 162–63
    succession of, xix–xxi, 64, 83,
        147–52, 187
Peter, James, and John, 36
    as presidency of the church, 34
Pighi, Giovanni Battista, 7, 159
Polycarp of Smyrna, 190
    death of, 198
pope
    election of, 174–75
    insecurity of, 231

INDEX 253

power, 118
   civil and ecclesiastical, 120–21
   competing claims of, 96–99
   fight for, 99–102
   issue of, 108
   transmission of, 150
Powicke, Frederick, 231
presbyter, office of, 40
presbyters, 19
   as successors to apostles, 14, 17
presidential hypothesis, xiv, 2
presiding bishop
   disappearance of office of, 35, 41
   office of, xvi
priesthood
   functions of, 17
   in public life, 75
   two kinds of, xiv–xv
   types of, 18
priesthood of Aaron, 36
priests, 13, 70
   as bishop's assistants, 62
primates, 91
primitive church, passing of, 243–45
Prince of the Captivity, 61
prophets, 121
   solvers of church's questions, 220
prosperity, 111
province, rule of, 125
punishment, 115
Pythian oracle, 101

Reims, 129
Renan, Ernest, 1
revelation, 135, 234
   as the rock, 225
Reville, Jean, 26, 56
revivalist groups, imitation of early church by, 38
rioting, 101
ritual, conformity to, 57

Roman bishop, veto power of, 177–78
Roman church, lack of leading role of, 194–222
Rome, 131
   Alban migration to, 76
   apostolic calling of, 94
   aristocratic rule of, 76–77
   bishopric of, xx, 13
   claims of, 181, 184–85
   episcopal authority at, xix
   episcopal succession in, 164
   as first city of the world, 85
   geographical advantages of, 180
   intervention of, 189
   as mother city of the church, 84
   politics of, 75
   position of, 178
   supremacy of, xxiii, 189–94
   as ruler of the church, 99
Rossi, Giovanni Battista de, 60
royal spies, 58

sacrament, administering, 124
Sardika, 126
Scheel, Otto, 3
Schermann, Theodor, 5, 29
Schmidt, Carl, 157, 160
Schütz, Roland, 3
Schwartz, Eduard, 39, 42, 182
scriptures
   interpretation of, 234
   and schools of philosophy, 72
   as substitute for revelation, 217
   value of, 212
sects, conflicting, 234
seventy, 124
Sidonius, 78
slaves, church, 127, 128, 129, 130
Sohm, Rudolf, 2, 3, 4, 5, 10, 13, 14, 20
soothsayers, 131

Soter, bishop of Rome, 190
Souchon, Martin, 173
Spenser, Henry, 171
spiritual gifts, 42
St. Gelasius, claim of, 182
St. Peter's dome, scripture on, 223
Stauffer, Ethelbert, 45
Strack, Hermann, 225
succession, 209, 240
    by default, xxii
    horizontal, 152
    rule of, 165
Symeon (Simeon), election of, 45
Symmachus, 165
Symmachus (2), 166
synagogue as model for local church, 42
Synod of Carthage, 139
Synod of Frankfort, 139
Synod of Orléans, 139
synods, xviii–xix, 134, 228–32
    convened by popes and emperors, xxiii–xxiv, 228–29
    fourth century, 218
    passing laws by, 177
    power of, 125

teacher, office of, 13, 57
Teicher, J. L., 44
Theodoric, 165
Theodosius the Great, 166
thieves, 131
"thou art Peter," 223
Toledo, 128, 129, 130
Tours, 127
traditores, 122
Trinity, nature of, 108
true church, 218
Tullus, 76
Twelve, 9, 43
    historicity of, 3

unity in the church, 142
universal synod, reasons for calling, 229–30
Urban II, 167–68
Ursinus, 164
Usener, Hermann, 79

Van Cauwelaert, R., 191
Vatican excavations, 222
Vatican Library, microfilming of records from, 149
Vigilius, 166
Vogels, Heinrich, 194, 232
Vogelstein, Hermann, 10
von Campenhausen, Hans, 220

wandering heretics, 130
Weiss, Johannes, 4
Wissowa, Georg, 75
worldly clothing, 131

Zeiller, Jacques, 189